D0906214

PLAYING WITH THE BIG BOYS

Playing with the Big Boys

Basketball, American Imperialism, and Subaltern Discourse in the Philippines

LOU ANTOLIHAO

UNIVERSITY OF NEBRASKA PRESS
Lincoln and London

Chapter 2 originally appeared as "From
Baseball Colony to Basketball Republic:
Post-Colonial Transition and the Making
of a National Sport in the Philippines," by
Lou Antolihao, in *Sport in Society* 15,
no. 10 (2012): 1396–1412. Reprinted by
permission of the publisher, Taylor and
Francis Ltd., tandf.co.uk/journals.

An earlier version of chapter 4
appeared as "Rooting for the Underdog:
Spectatorship and Subalternity in
Philippine Basketball," by Lou Antolihao,
in *Philippine Studies: Historical and
Ethnographic Viewpoints* 58, no. 4 (2010):
449–80, published by Ateneo de Manila
University.

Library of Congress Control Number:
2014959534

Set in Minion by Westchester Publishing Services.

For Luis

CONTENTS

List of Illustrations   ix

List of Tables   xi

Acknowledgments   xiii

List of Abbreviations   xvii

Introduction   1

1. Spheroid of Influence: Sports, Colonization, Modernity   33

2. From Baseball Colony to Basketball Republic:
Postcolonial Transition and National Sporting Culture   64

3. The Hollywoodization of Hoops: Basketball, Mass
Media, Popular Culture   93

4. Rooting for the Underdog: Sports, Spectatorship,
Subalternity   121

5. Basketball without Borders: Globalization and National
Sports in Postcolonial Context   149

Conclusion   177

Notes   191

Bibliography   211

Index   227

ILLUSTRATIONS

Following page 120

1. The Internal Revenue Team, 1916

2. Champion Philippine Team, 1915

3. The Philippines versus Uruguay at the 1936 Olympics

4. Philippine National Basketball Team in Rio de Janeiro, 1954

5. The Derby Ace Llamados versus the Meralco Bolts

6. Ateneo de Manila University versus Far Eastern University

7. Filipino defenders and Kevin Durant, 2012 Ultimate All-Star Weekend

8. Members of the Smart Gilas, the Philippines' national team

TABLES

1. Most popular sports in the Philippines   12

2. Average height in the Philippines and
selected countries   14

3. Winners of the National Basketball Championship,
1911–23   74

4. Winners of the National Basketball Open
Championship, 1924–35   76

5. Winners of the Asian Baseball and Basketball
Championships, 1950s–60s   91

6. Basketball results in the Asian Games   166

ACKNOWLEDGMENTS

Far from the speedy run-and-gun style that Philippine basketball has come to be known for, the making of this book had been a painstaking trudge to the final buzzer. Nonetheless the grit-and-grind process was made endurable by the generosity of various institutions and individuals who contributed to the completion of this project. At different stages—in conceptualizing the research, in gathering data, writing the book, and in the publication process—I was a recipient of various forms of assistance, intellectual stimulation, and warm encouragement from colleagues, teachers, friends, and family members to whom I am very grateful.

My interest in academic life grew from my first job as a research assistant at the Institute of Philippine Culture. Our project on community-based forest management allowed me to travel around the Philippines, explore beautiful sights, and listen to the stories of the people I met. During long hikes into some of the country's largest forests, I started to map a career path in academic research and teaching which, despite the inhospitable terrain, I still continue to follow. I am grateful to Angela Desiree Aguirre for prying me out of Davao with a vague promise that I would get the chance to work somewhere in Mindanao. Germelino Bautista, our director, supported me even after I left our project by providing part-time research jobs, which helped me survive the early part of my graduate studies at Ateneo de Manila University.

The National University of Singapore (NUS) afforded me a supportive academic environment and an ideal place to nurture the early stages of this project. The university's Graduate Research Support Scheme provided funds that allowed me to do research for a year in the United States and in the Philippines. Anne Raffin, my PhD advisor, patiently coached me on the finer points of historical-sociological analysis and went through the first drafts of this book. Reynaldo Ileto, Daniel Goh, Misha Petrovic, Maitrii Aung-Thwin, and Deenesh Sohoni formed a dissertation committee of insightful and supportive readers. The wisdom and guidance of my teachers and mentors Heng Ai Yun, Maribeth Erb, Bryan Turner, Habibul Khondker, Chua Beng Huat, Eric Thompson, Reynaldo Ileto, Goh Beng Lan, and Vattana Phoelsena have had a welcome influence on my thinking.

The friendship of Roland Tolentino, Julius Bautista, Merce Planta, Nikki Briones, Trina Tinio, Jun Cayron, Nathan Cruz, Andie Soco, Niño Leviste, Rommel Curaming, Rica Sauler, Magdalene Kong, Devi Ramasamy, Kaoko Takahashi, Genevieve Duggan, Yang Chengseng, Zhou Wei, Nick Sim, Seuty Sabur, Sarbeswar Sahoo, Saiful Islam, and Taberez Neyazi provided ample breaks as graduate studies wound through the ups and downs of coursework, research, and writing.

I deeply appreciate the assistance given to me by the staffs of several libraries and archives. In particular, I warmly thank Dagmar Getz of the Kautz Family YMCA Archives and Maricel Raynera of the University of the Philippines' (UP) Vargas Museum as well as the staffs of the U.S. National Archives; U.S. Library of Congress; Bancroft Library, University of California, Berkeley; Bentley Library, University of Michigan, Ann Arbor; UP Main Library; UP College of Human Kinetics Library; Philippine Sports Commission Library; Philippine National Library; and CSEAS Library, Kyoto University. My informants in Metro Manila and Davao City were very generous with their time. Their insights helped make the book's arguments more grounded and well-balanced.

Cesar, Wednes, and the rest of the Bugas family provided a restful yet lively place to recharge in New Jersey after weeks of neck-straining work in the archives and libraries of Washington DC. Jojo Ramos and his family provided a literal oasis in Las Vegas as I moved my research from Minnesota to California. Across the Pacific, Poli Ty, Rudsend Paragas, Melchor Castañeda, and the late Al Alegre, and the seminarians at the Eymard Formation Center provided not only a place to stay but allowed me to be part of their community as I conducted my research in Metro Manila in 2007–8. In Davao my extended family, relatives, and friends were always ready to throw a party for me whenever I was in town. My parents kept my books as well as the other "trash" that I accumulated during my years of study and research.

In a number of seminars and conferences as well as in informal discussions and correspondence, Richard Ruth, Ho Kong Chong, Chou Younghan, Maitrii Aung-Thwin, Julius Bautista, Aaron Miller, Luo Qing, Miguel de Moragas, Susan Brownell, David Rowe, Claudia Mullen, Daniel Woodman, Holland Wilde, Steven Brier, Michael Burawoy, Albert Alejo, Jae Estuar, Emma Porio, Ricardo Abad, Filomeno Aguilar Jr., and Raul Pertierra provided research materials, comments, and suggestions that strengthened the manuscript.

A JSPS Postdoctoral Fellowship at the Center for Southeast Asian Studies (CSEAS) at Kyoto University allowed me to revise my doctoral dissertation and turn it into a book manuscript. I am thankful to my host professor, Hiromu Shimizu, for his understanding and support, which allowed me to work on the book alongside my main research project. While at CSEAS, I benefited from the assistance of Wakana Nakamura, Motoko Kondo, and Michiyo Ide, who did all the administrative and logistical tasks so I could concentrate on my work. I also learned from my discussions with and enjoyed the company of Taberez Neyazi, Asuna Yoshizawa, David Malitz, Bhaskar Gautam, Adrian Albano, Cayetano Paderanga, Simon Creak, Loh Kah Seng, Noboru Ishikawa,

Carol Hau, and the members of the Kyoto Association of Pinoy Scholars (KAPS).

At the University of Nebraska Press, Robert Taylor showed genuine interest in my manuscript and guided it through the different stages of publication. Courtney Ochsner, Debbie Masi, and Brett Keener expertly helped me through the production process. I am also grateful to the anonymous reviewers whose insightful comments and invaluable suggestions helped craft the final version of this work.

Chapter 2 was originally published in *Sport in Society*. Likewise, an earlier version of chapter 4 appeared in *Philippine Studies*. I appreciate the contributions of the editors and anonymous readers at those publications for their thoughtful comments and suggestions. I am also thankful to the respective publishers for granting permission to reprint versions of the articles here.

Finally I deeply appreciate the support and sacrifices that my wife and my son have given for this project. Both endured my absences, whether I was on a sixteen-month-long postdoctoral fellowship, on short conference trips, or even when I was "away" facing the computer to work on this book. Nona proofread my drafts and even became a San Antonio Spurs fan after spending countless hours with me talking about basketball. Luis, who was born two days after the first draft of this book was completed, did not seem to care when, at times, I read my reference material to him instead of *Goodnight Moon, Soccer Star*, or any of his favorite bedtime stories. This book is dedicated to him.

ABBREVIATIONS

ABL	Asean Basketball League
BOE	Bureau of Education
FECG	Far Eastern Championship Games
FIBA	Fédération Internationale de Basketball
GANEFO	Games of the New Emerging Forces
IBL	Indonesian Basketball League
IOC	International Olympic Committee
MBBL	Manila Bay Baseball League
MICAA	Manila Industrial and Commercial Athletic Association
MNBL	Malaysian National Basketball League
MNC	Multinational Company/Corporation
MYSD	Ministry of Youth and Sports Development
NBA	National Basketball Association (U.S.)
NCAA	National Collegiate Athletic Association
PAAF	Philippine Amateur Athletic Federation
PBA	Philippine Basketball Association
SEA	Southeast Asian
SEABA	Southeast Asian Basketball Association
UAAP	University Athletic Association of the Philippines
YMCA	Young Men's Christian Association

PLAYING WITH THE BIG BOYS

Introduction

Tatangkad din ako! (I will grow taller!) was the trademark catch-phrase in a series of television advertisements promoting Growee, a popular children's multivitamin in the Philippines. As the product's name suggests, the ads enticed consumers by touting the brand's unique formula, which the company promised would enhance the physical growth of young kids. For the TV commercial's debut in 2006, basketball was the subject of the ad's upbeat video montage. Designed as an MTV-style hip-hop music video, the television spot showed five youngsters sporting NBA jerseys and other basketball-inspired fashion accessories doing a song-and-dance performance. The kids were shown performing different basketball tricks and even exhibiting a rare skill among Filipino basketball players: dunking the ball. By creatively stitching together different elements of contemporary youth culture (MTV, hip-hop, and basketball), the commercial became one of the most popular in the country; the ad's jingle evolved into a trendy children's song and in a short time the advertising slogan itself became an everyday adage.

The evolution of *Tatangkad din ako!* from a marketing catch-phrase to a familiar saying reflects some of the most interesting aspects of Philippine society. For one, it highlights the Filipinos' obsession with "getting tall," as shown by the popularity of growth-enhancement formulas that, aside from their use in supplements, are also added to milk, sandwich spreads, sausages, and other food products. Having above-average height is valued in most societies for its various practical and perceived advantages; however, the Growee commercial reveals that Filipinos' preoccupation with growing tall is intimately associated with their other obsession: the sport of basketball.

Furthermore, *Tatangkad din ako!* illustrates the relationship between sports and subalternity that serves as the central theme of this book. The entangled history of these two phenomena goes back over a hundred years, when the advent of modernity significantly altered the dynamics of colonialism. Beginning in the mid-nineteenth century, Western empires discovered the efficacy of spreading modern sports as a means to "bind" their colonial subjects "more firmly, and more happily to their rule."[1] They helped introduce new beliefs, practices, social behaviors, and moral standards and encouraged a conformity that helped the colonizers maintain control over their colonies.[2] Sports took on the role that the earlier introduction of Western religions, languages, and other cultural practices occupied in building a channel of communication between the colonizers and their colonies. For instance, the sports of cricket in India and *pelota* in many South American countries are just some of the legacies of the British and Spanish empires; these sports remained popular in the empires' former colonial territories even long after independence.

The United States, which emerged as the new colonial power after the 1898 Spanish-American War, recognized the pedagogical significance of sports and employed it in its undertaking to "Americanize" the Filipinos. In his seminal work *The Athletic Crusade*, Gerald Gems noted how the United States introduced physical education and sports to fulfill the "'white man's burden'; [the] moral imperative to bring civilization, technology, and a particular brand of the Christian religion (Protestantism) to those deemed to be lower on the Social Darwinism ladder."[3] Early in the colonial period there were a number of notable pieces written on the success of sports in achieving these goals.[4] The most notable of these was authored by U.S. general Franklin Bell who, as provost marshal of Manila, noted that sports, particularly baseball, "had done more to civilize Filipinos than anything else."[5] As a result sports were increasingly encouraged, particularly through the public school system that was established by the colonial government.

As sport continued to attract a strong following among the local population, it eventually evolved into an important venue for the fragmented Filipino society to come together and forge closer ties. Victory in international competitions, particularly in basketball, was celebrated as a source of national pride and promoted as a platform to gain international recognition. Most notably the Philippine basketball team's successful participation at the 1936 Berlin Olympics became a rallying point in the "coming of age" of the emerging nation. The Philippine team's fifth-place finish became a subject of controversy because their 4-1 win-loss record was better than those of fourth-place Poland (1-2), third-place Mexico (3-2) and even second-place Canada (3-1). The Philippines even defeated the Mexican team in their encounter, coming from behind to win by a 32–30 score. It was later discovered that a loophole in the bracketing system resulted in the questionable ranking. Since it was the first time that basketball was played at the Olympics the problem was largely brushed aside, although the loophole was later corrected for subsequent Olympic Games.[6] Nevertheless, the controversy heightened the significance of the event from a hitherto unremarkable fifth-place finish to a nationalist narrative depicting a subaltern victory that was stolen by Western "conspirators." This timely event happened during a crucial period two years after the ratification of the Philippine Independence Act,[7] when the country acquired self-governing power as a commonwealth state.

Eighteen years later a third-place finish at the FIBA (*Fédération Internationale de Basketball*) World Basketball Championship[8] in 1954 cemented basketball's position as the Philippines' most popular pastime. Some people capitalized on popular nationalist sentiments by using the Philippine team's victory to show that, despite their physical disadvantage, small Filipino players could make their mark in the game of giants. Moreover as the Philippines emerged as an independent country after the Second World War, one observer noted how the sport remained one of the "key components of an evolving national culture, one no longer imposed by the United States but searching for an identity that might unify the multitude of island peoples."[9] No longer a foreign game, basketball became an important channel for gaining international recognition and a timely symbol of the new nation-state.

After reaching a high point with the 1954 FIBA World Championship, Philippine basketball continued its run for another two decades. Notably it bagged the top honors four times in eight Asian Basketball Championships between 1960 and 1975, missing the top-three ranking only once. The Philippines also won four consecutive Asian Games basketball championships from 1951 to 1962. At the Olympics the country was not able to get into the medal column, but it continued to qualify for the Games until 1972 and for the FIBA World Championship until 1978.[10]

Since the 1970s, however, the performance of the Philippine Men's National Basketball Team has declined and the squad has failed to regain its status as one of the world's top basketball-playing nations. The country has not qualified for the Olympics after 1972 and since 1986, only qualified for the recent 2014 FIBA World Cup (formerly the World Championships). The Filipinos' gutsy play during the 2014 FIBA World Cup in Spain enabled them to hold stronger teams to a 5-point winning average and despite a 1-4 win/loss record, caught the adulation of many Filipino basketball fans around the world. Given their woeful record, however, many are still skeptical about the long-term prospect of the national team, especially given the fact that its best player (Andray Blatche) is a borderline NBA player who was only conferred Filipino citizenship about three months before the FIBA World Cup. Days later news about Blatche's ineligibility to play for the 2014 Asian Games due to falling short of the three-year residency rule for naturalized citizens, dampened the high spirit of Filipino fans who were hopeful to regain the Asian Games basketball crown the team last won in 1962. Without Blatche, the Philippines, yet again, suffered a major setback by finishing seventh—the country's worst finish ever in the history of the Asian Games basketball.

Over the past four decades, fans have expressed their frustration over the national team's inability to win the regional tournament's basketball championship, which the Philippines dominated in its early years. Initially, the professionalization of the country's premier basketball league in 1975 barred the top Filipino players from participating in many international meets due to a rule that excluded professionals from FIBA-sanctioned competitions.[11] In more recent years, the significant improvement of other teams, particularly China, has made the regional tournaments more competitive. On top of these factors, however, many have been quick to point to the possible correlation between the Philippines' basketball debacles and the larger economic and political crisis that has hampered the nation's growth since the ascension of the U.S.-backed Marcos authoritarian regime in the 1960s. There is a general perception that the rampant corruption and overall political instability during that period penetrated almost every aspect of Philippine society, an issue that continues to plague the country today.

This situation is exacerbated by the number of politicians serving in leadership roles in the country's national basketball federation. Their patronage was obtained to facilitate access to funding and other means of government support. However, these officials often ended up squabbling among each other in their efforts to capitalize on the widespread influence of basketball to shore up their political influence. At the turn of the millennium, the lengthy leadership crisis in the Basketball Association of the Philippines (BAP) resulted in its suspension by FIBA in 2001 and 2005. These suspensions prevented the Philippines from participating in international competitions and from implementing a much-needed development program for its national team. The leadership squabble, which was largely attributed to the larger crisis in the Philippine political system, was largely abhorred by the ordinary Filipino basketball fans who saw their beloved game deteriorate from a source of inspiration and pride to a perennial cause of disappointment and shame.

Can the Subaltern Play?

Sporting cultures highlight some of the distinctive marks of nations. They are often seen as symbols that reveal important aspects of a country's history, traditions, and values. Despite their apparent familiarity, understanding the workings and meanings of some of the most prominent sporting cultures around the world has proven to be a challenging task. Perhaps no other country receives more questions about the origin and rationality of its national sports than the Philippines.[12] The immense popularity of basketball in this Southeast Asian archipelago is often an object of curiosity that invites questions—like the makeshift hoops that unexpectedly appear in many of Manila's side streets. People especially wonder how a sport that is dominated by six-footers attracts a strong following in a country where the average height is less than five and a half feet.

Playing with the Big Boys tries to answer this question as well as a few other more probing inquiries on the origin, development, and contemporary significance of basketball in the Philippines. This historical-sociological odyssey is guided by the following objectives: 1) to give a historical account of the sport's introduction and popularity; 2) to illustrate the patterns of its spread and significance; 3) to examine its social relevance in the different periods of the country's history; and 4) explore how it can contribute to the discourses on imperialism, state formation, popular culture, subalternity, and globalization.

Postcolonialism provides a more pertinent framework for understanding Philippine basketball. The inherent interest of postcolonial theory in confronting the residual effects of colonialism makes the U.S.-introduced sport an ideal subject of analysis. Beyond this apparent compatibility, however, the rootedness of postcolonial theory in understanding long-term historical processes also fits with the goal of accounting for the different forces that shaped the evolution of Philippine basketball. John Bale and Mike Cronin, in setting the scope of their work *Sport and Postcolonialism*, noted that even if postcolonialism literally means "after colonialism, most works espousing a postcolonial approach deal with the period of colonization and imperialism."[13] Thus the term is used here to refer to an expansive chronological corridor that spans the different eras in the history of Philippine basketball (i.e., colonial, Commonwealth, post-independence, Cold War, global).

Within this conceptual framework, the book argues that the entangled strands of narratives and discourses on the logic and legacies of Filipino basketball can be unraveled through what I refer to as the subaltern predicament of "playing with the big boys." Historically this notion illustrates the dilemma that local athletes faced in competing against taller American players during the latter's occupation of the Philippines. This predicament eventually became a prevalent theme that was used to articulate and, more often, to animate the experiences that Filipino basketball teams faced in their many arduous forays into international competition. Symbolically, "playing with the big boys" demonstrates the desire for growth, the struggle for recognition, the excitement of competing, the joy of victory, and the pain of losing. These are the dilemmas that the Philippines, as a subaltern society, has to contend with in its relationship with hegemonic countries, particularly the United States—the country's early-twentieth-century colonial master and the current global superpower.

As such the word "subaltern" refers to Philippine basketball in general, as well as to the game's various characterizations as a representation of the nation or society, or in reference to the Philippines' marginal location in the global "hoopsphere."[14] The concept originates from Ranajit Guha's work on the historiography of colonial India.[15] By expanding on the Marxist definition used by Guha, James Mills in his introduction to "Subaltern Sports" referred to the term subaltern as "the dominated party in any power relationship [while] the study of subalternity is of relationships characterized by 'dominance without hegemony.'" Thus "the importance of the concept of subalternity," he further noted,

> lies in its recognition of the "autonomous domain" of the subaltern agent or agents. While dominated, the subaltern is not entirely obliterated and retains values, ideas and modes of action that are not prescribed by the dominant and which can draw upon beliefs and experiences exclusive to the individual or group. In other words the subaltern always has the potential to oppose or resist the dominant as he or she may draw upon alternative values and ideas and can refer back to different experiences and behavioral expectations.[16]

Despite its fundamental adherence to the original Thirteen Rules developed by Dr. James Naismith, the game's inventor, Philippine basketball has evolved throughout the years to assume its own unique form and culture. In 1975, American historian Michael Cullinane wrote a seminal article entitled "Basketball and Culture: A Problem in Private Transitory Ownership?" exploring how American and Filipino players interpreted a particular basketball rule—the offensive charge—in different ways. According to Cullinane, the practice of "taking a charge"—when a defensive player positions himself between a dribbler and the goal in anticipation of a physical contact that would prevent the dribbler from scoring—is for Americans a violation against the offensive player called a "charging foul." On the contrary, the Filipinos would call the violation on the defensive player, referred to as a "blocking foul." The American interpretation of the rule, Cullinane notes, is in accordance with the conventional rules of the game, something the American basketball player has learned "since his early training in fundamentals." In comparison Cullinane attributes the Filipinos' interpretation of the rule as something that is "culturally rooted" in the social norms governing the occupation of public space.[17] Cullinane's description of the practice of calling a blocking or charging foul is no longer evident in contemporary basketball games in the Philippines. Perhaps the globalization of the game in recent decades has resulted in homogenization of rules, and to a certain extent, playing styles. However, it shows the use of the rational-cultural, modern-backward, west-east dichotomies that are prevalent in understanding the different aspects of postcolonial cultures and societies.

More recently the culture of basketball in the Philippines have received more attention, especially in popular literature. Among this increasing body of work is Rafe Bartholomew's *Pacific Rims*, the first book-length work on Philippine basketball. Just like Cullinane's earlier work, the American author again highlights Philippine basketball's uniqueness by uncovering the reasons behind the "Philippines' unlikely love affair with basketball." His ethnographic adventure led him to discover the game's various oddities: the wearing of flip-flops in pickup games, the amusing names of Philippine Basketball Association teams (e.g., Beermen, Milkmen), and even an interesting tournament between midgets and transvestites.[18] Bartholomew presents Philippine basketball and the Filipinos in general as the "bizarre Other," specifically one who fumbles in its attempt to mimic and replicate a particular U.S. sport, which happens to be one of America's most visible symbols as a global hegemon. Despite its Orientalist overtones, the book is quite engaging, especially to scholars who are interested in postcolonial and subaltern theories, because it highlights the "autonomous domain" of the subaltern. Particularly, the book presents mimicry not only as a resourceful means of accommodating new sets of knowledge but also as a creative approach for allaying the threat posed by a domineering force. Nonetheless, the recurrent use of American basketball standards and rationalities as a reference point in understanding the social significance of Philippine basketball prevents the discussion from raising a unique and more expansive analysis beyond the limits of an East–West dichotomy.

Going beyond the use of American basketball standards and rationalities as a reference point, this book follows a post-binary framework in order to present a broader picture of the social significance of basketball in the Philippines. Exploring other factors beyond the readily evident American influence also provides a channel for avoiding the postcolonial fixation on unraveling the colonizer-colony conundrum. The sport historian Douglas Booth defines this analytical structure as the "attempts to break down the tendency in Western thought to dichotomize natural and social phenomena, and to describe and define them in terms of oppositional characteristics and neutrally opposed terms."[19] The post-binary approach provides a way out of the theoretical quagmire that often results from the futile fixation on undoing or redoing the legacies of colonialism. In sport studies this approach explores the spaces between oppositional poles, particularly in the empire-subaltern dichotomy, to analyze the development of sporting cultures in postcolonial societies.[20] This specific study seeks to contribute to the current literature on post-binary theory by introducing a multidimensional framework for exploring the colonial trajectories beyond the empire-subaltern binary. Particularly, the book tries to come up with a comparative investigation of the development of basketball in the Philippines within the Asian context. This is done by highlighting its links to the larger processes that have influenced the growth of modern sports in twentieth-century Asia, particularly in the neighboring countries of China and Japan.

The discussion attempts to link the history of U.S. colonial rule in the Philippines to the larger process of regional geopolitics, particularly the rise of modern nation-states in early-twentieth-century Asia. The imposition of American (and other Western countries') political, economic, and cultural influence in the region was also spurred by the effort of Asian countries to make use of new products, technologies, and ideas to strengthen their standing against their neighbors. The study argues that aside from the influence of the United States, the Filipinos' engagements with Chinese and Japanese basketball teams and their rivalries as emerging Asian nations in the early twentieth century also contributed to the growth of basketball in the Philippines. As such, *Playing with the Big Boys* suggests a multidimensional framework of postcolonial analysis. Instead of narrowing its focus to the space between oppositional entities (East-West, metropole-colony, foreign-native) in creating hybrid cultural forms (e.g., Filipino-American basketball culture), it tries to explore a range of comparisons to explain the persistence of certain colonial practices and traditions in many postcolonial societies.

Hoops Hysteria: Basketball as a Hegemonic Sport Culture

In their research on the convergence of culture and power, Andrei Markovits and Steven Hellerman's concept of "hegemonic sports culture" offers a pertinent framework for understanding the importance of basketball in Philippine society.[21] Their emphasis on "emotional attachment"[22] in evaluating the importance of a particular sport in a society articulates the "hoops hysteria" that generally characterizes the fervent and pervasive interest in basketball throughout the country.

Recent studies provide glimpses into the extent of basketball's mass appeal. For instance, shortly before the 2005 Southeast Asian (SEA) Games in Manila, survey respondents were asked to list the sporting events that they expect the Philippines to win. Interestingly, basketball topped the survey, emerging as the first choice for 44 percent of the respondents even though the sport was not even on the list of disciplines scheduled for the regional event.[23] In addition, basketball, along with boxing, ranked first in a survey of "sports Filipinos are good at." Basketball and boxing each garnered 55 percent of respondents' votes, followed by billiards and bowling with 37 and 15 percent, respectively. The other sports mentioned received a single-digit percentage of the total votes.[24]

Much earlier, a study (see Table 1) named basketball as the favorite sport to play as well as the favorite sport to watch among male respondents. It is the second-favorite sport to play among females, although it remains their favorite sport to watch.

Table 1. Most popular sports in the Philippines

	FAVORITE SPORTS TO PLAY		FAVORITE SPORTS TO WATCH		EDUCATION DEPT. RANKING	
	MALE	FEMALE	MALE	FEMALE	MALE	FEMALE
Basketball	58%	9%	83%	64%	1	2
Volleyball	22	27	18	22	3	1
Baseball/ Softball	11	8	6	8		5
Swimming	6	3	2	3		
Table Tennis	5	2	1	1		
Bowling	4	2	1	2	5	4
Tennis	4	2	5	7		6
Boxing	3	0	21	5		
Billiards	3	0	3	0		
Football/ Soccer	0	0	6	2	4	
Track & Field	0	0	2	1	2	3

Sources: Beran, "Physical Education and Sport"; Sandoval and Abad, "Sports and the Filipino."

Moreover, a ranking made by teachers, students, and sport specialists from different regions of the Philippines produced similar results, with basketball emerging in first place. It is the number one game for males and the second-most popular sport among females after volleyball.

Of course this current popularity of basketball in the Philippines does not stand unchallenged. The uproar over the recent performance of the national team at the Southeast Asian Basketball Association (SEABA) Champions Cup in Jakarta in April 2008 shows the Filipinos' general displeasure with the present state of basketball in the country. Many were disappointed that the Philippines could only finish second to the host country, Indonesia—"the very Asian squad we used to whip before," a Manila newspaper columnist noted. He added, "Something's seriously wrong here. Over the years, the quality of Philippine basketball has continuously failed us."[25] From its "shocking dethronement" at the 1966 Asian Games,[26] to the country's banishment from the 2006 World Championship in Doha because of a FIBA suspension,[27] to the seventh-place finish at the recent 2014 Asian Games in South Korea, the country's inability to capture a major basketball championship in the past forty years has been a long-standing source of frustration for Filipino basketball fans. Moreover, this lack of success has also become the basis for incessant criticism of the overemphasis on basketball by some groups, a focus that many think unduly marginalizes other sports. In highlighting the importance of height in basketball, critics argue that the country is wasting time and resources in the sport and should instead focus more attention on other sports where Filipinos have greater chances of winning.

Despite this well-founded criticism, statistics illustrate that basketball continues to be the number one sport in the Philippines. However, one does not have to resort to figures to measure the popularity of basketball among Filipinos. It is one of the most ubiquitous sports in the country; from air-conditioned arenas in Metro Manila and other major cities to makeshift hoops in small villages across the countryside, basketball is played and watched by people from different walks of life. In addition, various institutions such as schools, churches, companies, and other organizations hold regular basketball tournaments to mark the much-awaited summer breaks and to celebrate religious festivals, Christmas holidays, and other occasions.

Playing with the Big Boys

Arguably no other country's choice of national sport has been called more into question than that of the Philippines. People especially wonder how a game that is largely known for having exceptionally tall players could attract a strong following in a country where the typical physical height is fairly average. The

Table 2. Average height in the Philippines and selected countries

COUNTRY	AGE RANGE	AVERAGE HEIGHT	
		MALE	FEMALE
Philippines	20–39	163.5 cm (5'4.4")	151.8 cm (4'11.8")
United States	20+	175.8 cm (5'9.3")	162.0 cm (5'3.8")
Spain	21	178.0 cm (5'10")	165.0 cm (5'4.7)
China	17	168.2 cm (5'6.2")	157.8 cm (5'2.2")
Japan	20–24	172.0 cm (5'7.5")	158.7 cm (5'2.5")
Indonesia	19–23	162.4 cm (5'3.9")	151.3 cm (4'11.5")
Malaysia	20+	164.7 cm (5'4.8")	153.3 cm (5'0.4")

Sources: FMI, "Youth Profile"; FNRI, *6th National Nutrition Survey*; Garcia and Quintana-Domeque, "Evolution of Adult Height"; Lim, et.al., "Distribution of Body Weight"; MEXT, *Official Statistics 2004*; Ogden, et.al., "Mean Body Weight"; Yang, et al., *Study on Weight and Height*.

Philippines literally fall short if the average height of its population is compared with that of the United States and Spain (see Table 2), the top two countries in international basketball competitions and, interestingly enough, the country's former colonial masters. The United States bagged the Olympic gold medal in basketball during the recent 2012 Olympics in London. The U.S. team dominated all competitions except the championship game, where the Spanish team fought well before eventually losing, 107–100. Even among its perennial rivals in Asian basketball competitions, Filipinos are on average shorter than the Chinese, Japanese, and South Koreans. However, the Filipino height is comparable to Southeast Asian neighbors such as Indonesia and Malaysia, which may have contributed to the country's better track records at the SEA Games and other subregional competitions.

Understanding why basketball is popular in the Philippines despite the general lack of height among Filipino players is a bewildering exercise even for those who are more than passing observers of Philippine basketball. Basically, height provides a greater advantage in basketball than in any other sport because scoring involves putting a ball in a goal suspended ten feet above the floor. However, basketball is such a complex sport that having tall players, despite the advantage that it can give, is not an assurance of victory. Particularly, speeding up the pace of the game often exposes the limitations of tall players who generally run and move slower compared to shorter players. In fact "small ball" is a popular basketball technique even in the National Basketball Association (NBA), where coaches field smaller players to ensure fast, high-scoring games that mitigate the advantage held by tall players. Moreover, these "small ball" teams often become more popular among fans since a fast-paced, high-scoring game is considered more entertaining to watch.

For Philippine basketball teams, however, "small ball" is not just a technique; it is something that defines their game and their identity. For example, the 1936 Olympic basketball team, more popularly known as the "Islanders," is often cited for using this style of play. "They were small," a writer observed, "but they made up in speed . . . [for] what they lacked in height." And with the team's notable showing, he concluded that "in the end the Filipinos proved that the Orientals could also vie with their Western counterpart in this young sport which later proved to be the special preserve of tall men."[28] At the subsequent 1948 Olympics in London the Philippine basketball team was "conspicuously small in stature," so much so that they were referred to as the "little brown players from the Far East." However, it was again reported that what they lacked in height they made up for with their speed as well as their "agility, cleverness, and dog-like tenacity."[29]

Filipinos' use of speed to compensate for their lack of height was supposed to be temporary. The Filipinos were thought to be showing signs of physical (and economic) growth when the Philippine Independence Act was ratified in 1934. Adherents of social Darwinism believed at that time that "height and weight are determined by nutrition, not genetics," although recent scientific findings argue that both factors matter.[30] This evolutionary premise posited that developed nations' increased capacity to produce or import food resulted in better nutrition. This achievement in turn promoted taller, bigger, and stronger physical structures among a nation's peoples. For instance, it was discovered that "immediately after World War II, the average height of Japanese men and women quickly shot up several inches when they were introduced to the Western diet."[31] In the same way the Filipinos were hoping that with their country's impending development, they would also improve their physical stature.

Top Filipino sport leaders also ascribed to this idea, giving them an optimistic outlook about the prospect of sports in the Philippines, especially basketball. During the annual meeting of the Philippine Amateur Athletic Federation (PAAF) in 1952, president Jorge Vargas and some executive committee members pointed out how "the improvement of Philippine living condition as well as the acceleration of athletic activities among the people" had enabled the average Filipino to increase his or her height.[32] The chair of the Basketball Committee, Dionisio Calvo, was even more audacious in highlighting the Filipinos' "imminent growth." When asked about the status of a petition to create a limited international division in which only players below the height of six foot two inches could participate, he explained that the petition was not approved by FIBA because some countries, led by the United States, considered it discriminatory. He added that, "the new plan will not help the Filipinos anyway," maintaining that

> during the last few years, a number of tall players have showed up in our local courts, and there is no telling just how tall Filipinos will become within the next three or four years. As for as we are concerned now, a division at a height limit of 6'2", will inevitably exclude or eliminate from our team a number of good tall players who are well above the 6'2" limit.[33]

Putting aside the debate on imposing a height limit, these Filipino sport leaders had good reason to be optimistic about the prospect of Philippine basketball during that time.[34] Aside from being a fixture in top international basketball competitions, the Philippines had also by this time established its dominance in regional competitions after not facing any serious competition from other Asian countries. Beginning with the first Asian Games in New Delhi in 1951, where the national basketball team "won with apparent ease,"[35] the country would capture the first four Asian Games championships. In 1954 the Philippines won its highest finish in international basketball competition, and the best performance to date by any Asian country, at the World Basketball Championship in Rio de Janeiro, Brazil. During that event the national team placed third overall and one of its players, Carlos Loyzaga, was chosen as part of the Mythical Team, representing the top players in the tournament. The Philippines remains the only Asian country to ever win a medal at the World Basketball Championship, the world's most prestigious basketball tournament and the sport's equivalent to football's World Cup. Events like the 1954 World Basketball Championship helped sustain the sport's prominence in the Philippines by making heroes and celebrities of such players as Ambrosio Padilla and Carlos Loyzaga, whose talents and feats were admired and inspired many basketball fans. Just like the nation that it represents, a national sport is celebrated through the commemoration of heroes and events that help preserve its relevance and legitimacy.[36] These icons prove that *Tatangkad din ako!*, far from being an irrational and absurd obsession, is rhetorically sound and historically grounded as a symbol of Philippine basketball's fortitude and optimism.

However, in spite of this argument's pertinent rationalities, it is not enough to totally attribute the origins of the popularity of basketball in the Philippines to a number of founding fathers and some watershed events. Heroes are in some ways mere inventions and landmark events often lose their meaning over time. The more important keys to understanding the basketball phenomenon in the Philippines lie not in the ideals but in the experience. The sport's deeper meaning rests not on heroes and events alone but how they are produced and reproduced as part of the everyday lives of ordinary basketball players and followers. *Playing with the Big Boys*, therefore, is not merely concerned with "growth," but rather puts emphasis on the process of "growing."

The Promise of Growth: Basketball, Modernity, Subalternity

Ironically, apart from being an expression of the nation's self-confidence and optimism, *Tatangkad din ako!* is also an oblique demonstration of one's adherence to "the promise of the foreign." This concept, which is elaborated in Vicente Rafael's book of the same title, provides an insightful analysis of the growth of nationalism during the late period of the Spanish colonial regime in the Philippines (1820s–90s). Rafael pointed out how the advances in transportation, communication, and technology "brought the promise of the colony's transformation." According to Rafael, the export of "goods and people while importing capital, books, newspapers, political movements, secret societies, and ideologies . . . circulated the expectation of a society other than what it had been, becoming, that is modern in its proximity to events in the metropole and the rest of the 'civilized' world."[37]

This "promise of the foreign" became more enticing when the Philippines came under the control of the United States after the Spanish-American War (1898) and the subsequent Philippine-American War (1899–1902). Armed with a liberal and democratic ideology, more advanced technology, and superior economic resources, the United States took the effort of "modernizing" the Philippines to a higher level. Through a comprehensive development plan, various infrastructure projects were implemented and programs in education, health, and other social services were initiated. Along with the transformations that resulted from these initiatives, American cultural beliefs and practices made inroads into society, largely remaining long after the soldiers, missionaries, and other colonial workers left. One of the new "technical" developments that would generate greater cultural impact was the introduction of modern sports, including the newly invented game of basketball.

Since the beginning of the Spanish-American War, sport had played an important role in the American military structure. A new generation of officers had instituted sporting participation as a vital part of the organization, extolling its effectiveness in fighting vices, boosting morale, and instilling "soldierly values" of duty, courage, and patriotism.[38] Administrators soon realized the means used to control soldiers could also be effective in managing the colony. In time, American colonial officials started using sports to establish standards of behaviors, relations, and conformity. As a result, athletics and sports also became an important pedagogical tool, a means of cultivating values and practices that the colonizers deemed acceptable in the "civilized world" and a way of imparting the "modern ways" to the "savage" natives.[39] During the early twentieth century, U.S. print media ran headlines such as "baseball replaced headhunting" and reported on the holding of tug-of-war contests in lieu of tribal wars; these and other similar reports were used to portray the progress of the Americans' effort to "uplift" the conditions in the Philippines.[40] Basketball apparently rose in popularity as a varsity sport because of its capacity for infusing discipline, leadership, and cooperation. Compared to baseball, for instance, the hoops game has more team-oriented offensive and defensive schemes, which necessitates continuous effort among the players to communicate and cooperate.

Apart from its pedagogical significance, "the promise of the foreign" represents the rhetorical and communicative underpinnings of colonial projects such as literature, an idea that is central to Rafael's work on the rise of Philippine nationalism. His examination of the importance of language in the "formative period" that spanned the colonial era and the subsequent rise of an independent nation-state shows how one's ability to "translate" can open up the possibilities of emancipation. Particularly, Rafael tries to illustrate how the early Filipino nationalists' knowledge of Castilian enabled them to speak with one another and allowed them to communicate and seek recognition from Spanish officials in Spain.[41] "We can think of Filipino nationalism," Rafael suggests, "as a practice of translation, here understood first as the coming into contact with the foreign and subsequently its reformation into an element of oneself."[42]

This representation of the colonial-national nexus is especially valuable to this study since it highlights the contradictory origin of the subaltern subject, a predicament that besets the history of Philippine basketball. Akin to the *illustrado's* acquisition of Castilian, learning how to play basketball allowed the Filipinos to interact with the metropole and even with other basketball players from beyond the nation's borders, which helped the emerging Philippine nation-state gain international recognition. In this respect, basketball is in itself a form of language, and playing the game became a process of communication that enabled the Filipinos to incorporate aspects of *Americano* into their own identity. This transformation permitted them to embody the "promise of the foreign, or more precisely, of becoming foreign associated with the experience of modernity."[43]

In a wider context, Rafael's ideas mirror an earlier proposition laid down by Arjun Appadurai in his work on the decolonization of cricket in India.[44] Comparable to Rafael's establishment of the link between the Filipinos' acquisition of the colonial language and the rise of Philippine nationalism, Appadurai argues that cricket "became indigenized through a set of complex and contradictory processes that parallel the emergence of an Indian 'nation' from the British Empire."[45] Just like Rafael, Appadurai recognizes the important role of language and mass media in understanding the popularity of cricket in India. Akin to the former's concept of translation, the latter describes a "process of vernacularization" that "provides a verbal repertoire that allows a large numbers of Indians to experience cricket as a linguistically familiar form, thus liberating cricket from that very Englishness that first gave it its moral authority and intrigue."[46] Generally, "translation" or "vernacularization" enabled local players to express foreign terms in their own words, integrating rationalities shaped by their own social and cultural contexts.

The game, as a channel and a product of vernacularization, stands like a bridge that connects the native to the foreign. This bridge affords the native players a certain degree of mobility that enables them to cross into, get a glimpse of, and briefly immerse themselves in the strangeness and mysteries of the world of the "Other." In examining the social role of cockfighting during the Spanish era, Filomeno Aguilar Jr. noted a similar local strategy where the "*indios* [native Filipinos] moved back and forth between the overlapping worlds constituted by the indigenous and the colonial in a gamble that they would not be caught in either one."[47] As the Philippines' most popular "sport" at that time, cockfighting roughly represented what cricket did in colonial India: a means of interaction with the world of the colonizers. Cricket's popularity in India, according to Appadurai, hinged on its ability to allow people—from players to organizers, from the ordinary fans to high-ranking government officials—the opportunity to experience, experiment, and play with the "means of modernity."[48]

This idea of "playing with modernity" can be used to understand the importance of basketball in the early twentieth-century Philippines. Like the emergence of cricket as a national sport in India, basketball came to prominence in a period when the general political and social conditions allowed the larger population to have a heightened sense of agency and more opportunities for social mobility. With its origin as an American sport and as a popular collegiate game, basketball became closely associated with higher education, the urban centers (where institutions of higher learning are located), and with the bourgeoisie. In comparison the most popular sport at that time, baseball—the timeless symbol of "pastoral America"[49]—was more widely played in rural areas, in public elementary or secondary schools, or among working-class urban dwellers.

In fact the two decades before the Second World War saw the "battle of the ballgames" between baseball and basketball to become the most popular sport in the Philippines (see chapter 2). While boisterous cheers greeted every basketball game in colleges and universities in Manila and other major cities, baseball held its ground in the provinces and in the long-entrenched Manila Bay Baseball League (MBBL), where teams consisted of players from neighboring sugar plantations and manufacturing companies. Primarily due to its association with modernity, basketball's popularity eventually spread from the emerging urban-based, educated class to almost every corner of the country. It did not take long for basketball to supplant baseball as the number one sport in the Philippines.

In India, although there had been no dominant modern sport prior to cricket's introduction, that game had to compete with hockey (India's official national sport) and football before it eventually emerged as the country's premier sport. Cricket initially came to prominence, according to Appadurai, after it became the "unofficial instrument of state cultural policy" during the British colonial regime.[50] However, just like basketball in the Philippines, cricket only attracted widespread interest during the early twentieth century. Amid a relatively liberal social environment, the sport provided players and other actors from the larger sector of the local population greater opportunities for political participation and social recognition.

More generally the game provided the viewing public a "sense of cultural literacy in a world sport (associated with the notion of Western technological superiority) and the more diffuse pleasures of association with glamour, cosmopolitanism, and national competitiveness."[51] This "cultural literacy" as a form of enlightenment is the result of the subaltern acquiring the capacity to "translate," to use Rafael's words; that enables him or her to understand and experience limited aspects of the world of the foreign.

Moreover, cultural literacy entails the development of a common consciousness. Following Rafael's example, a shared knowledge of the language of Castilian, for instance, enabled the *illustrados*—the nineteenth-century Filipino nationalist group—to establish a sense of community and common identity even though its members came from different linguistic origins. During the American colonial regime, sports, along with education and other "development innovations" that were implemented in even the most far-flung provinces, eventually contributed to the integration of the vast archipelago into a nation. Arguably the emerging game of basketball, which at that time quickly gained a strong following around the country, became a timely symbol of national unity.

In India the pleasure of "playing with modernity" that is embodied by cricket has created "a confluence of lived interests, where the producers and consumers of [the sport] can share the excitement of Indianness without its many divisive scars."[52] Like Indian cricket, basketball not only afforded the Filipinos the chance to play with modernity but it also expanded this opportunity to transcend various class, ethnic, religious, linguistic, and geographical divisions that kept the nation under a constant threat of disintegration. The shared experience of playing and following basketball games, and especially the collective outpouring of emotion in celebrating victories and mourning defeats in international competitions, contributed to the development of a national consciousness. In this way "playing with modernity" is synonymous with "the promise of the foreign" since they both pertain not only to the opportunity for individual citizens to experience and experiment with modernity but also for the nation itself "to play with progress" and to experiment with and experience (albeit in fleeting ways) the economic advancement and political stability that describes the overall conditions enjoyed by its colonial master or any other modern society.

At the theoretical level, Rafael's and Appadurai's ideas correspond with the body of postcolonial literature developed by Homi K. Bhabha. His concepts of "mimicry" and "hybridity," specifically, provide a unique perspective for analyzing the dynamics of sports in postcolonial societies. In general, "mimicry" can be useful in explaining the receptivity of the Filipinos to the colonial effort to instill American ideologies, knowledge, and values in the

Philippines. "The Filipinos are great imitators," wrote Elwood Brown in his annual report as the YMCA Physical Director in Manila. "When they see the constabulary soldiers playing . . . and engaging in all sorts of races, it is entirely possible that they will in turn take the games up and substitute them as rapidly as possible for their foolish *sipa* and cockfighting."[53]

In the contemporary context, the notion of mimicry can be applied to the case of basketball in the Philippines at two levels. First, at the institutional level, mimicry refers to how the professional basketball leagues in the Philippines try to imitate the league format and promotional techniques of the United States' NBA. Second, at the individual level, this concept explains why a Filipino basketball player attempts to copy the "moves" of popular NBA stars like Michael Jordan, Kobe Bryant, or LeBron James, as those players' styles have become largely accepted as models of excellence.

Eventually mimicry results in hybridity. The ability to translate and the opportunity to play with modernity enable the subaltern to create new spaces that allow appropriation and subversion of the colonial power. Thus hybridity "reverses the effects of the colonialist disavowal, so that other 'denied' knowledge enter upon the dominant discourse and estrange the basis of its authority."[54] Basketball, for instance, became a key component "of an evolving national culture, one no longer imposed by the U.S. but searching for a [unifying sets of practices and ideals]."[55] Thus the immediate integration of basketball as part of the Filipinos' everyday life and cultural consciousness during the American colonial era illustrates the incorporation of a "new knowledge" that enabled them to use the sport as a venue to construct and express their own identity.

The Game Plan

This project started as an attempt to answer to a simple question: *Why is basketball popular in the Philippines?* The original plan was to conduct an ethnographic investigation to understand the contemporary significance of basketball as a cultural phenomenon. However, initial research has revealed the scarcity of academic works on Philippine basketball, including on its history, which makes the study more ideal for a trailblazing historical examination than a deep-probing ethnographic inquiry. Moreover, the dearth of literature on Philippine basketball has given the study a seemingly boundless opportunity to explore a broad range of issues (e.g., colonialism, nationalism, imperialism, popular culture, and globalization) and cover a relatively long period of time (1900s–2000s). This expansive thematic and chronological scope has made a multidisciplinary approach a necessity rather than a conscious effort to fit what currently seems to be a fashionable scholarly fad.

The multidisciplinary nature of the book is noticeably expressed in the fundamental role that historical analysis plays in understanding issues that appear to be exclusively rooted in the current structure of Philippine society. Although the main objective is to understand the social significance of basketball as an important aspect of contemporary Filipino culture, looking into the past has proven to be a valuable tool for getting a firmer grasp of what is at hand. The first three chapters in particular rely on data taken from colonial literature held in archives and libraries on both sides of the Pacific Ocean. In the Philippines, the American Historical Collection of the Ateneo de Manila University's Rizal Library; the University of the Philippines' Vargas Museum, Main Library, and College of Human Kinetics Library; the library of the Philippine Sports Commission; and the Philippine National Library were valuable sources of information on local sports as well as on the American colonial period in the Philippines. In addition the Social Weather Stations in Quezon City provided current data on Philippine sports.

In the United States, the National Archives and Records Administration in College Park, Maryland, and the Library of Congress in Washington DC, were inexhaustible sources of colonial reports, personal documents of colonial administrators, early physical education books published for the Philippines, and other valuable historical materials. Likewise, the Bancroft Library at the University of California, Berkeley and the Bentley Historical Library at the University of Michigan in Ann Arbor contain sizeable collections on the colonial programs involving sports and other related topics.[56] Finally, the University of Minnesota's Kautz Family YMCA Archives yielded important materials on the early-twentieth-century expansion of the YMCA in the Philippines, as well as in China and Japan.

The broad scope of archival sources covered in the study reflects the exploratory nature of the data collection process. The dearth of literature on sports in the Philippines and on basketball in particular necessitated the time-consuming effort of visiting distant archives that, in a few cases, only produced a handful of useful materials. However, the limited data on basketball, as expected, gradually decreased as the time covered in the study moved closer to the contemporary period. From the post-independence era, for instance, numerous magazines, journals, and newspapers carried feature stories, intensive documentation, and regular columns on the different events and personalities surrounding Philippine basketball, and these resources are readily available.

Apart from the information culled from periodicals and secondary literature, chapters 4 and 5, which cover the more recent period (1970s–2000s), also rely on a limited number of interviews and observations of basketball activities at the grassroots level. To provide some contrast in the narrative, the interviews were conducted among a number of individuals from Metro Manila and a rural village on the outskirts of Davao City, on the southern island of Mindanao. Interviews were conducted over two time periods: in June and July 2006 and from July 2007 to January 2008. The interviewees were chosen based on their knowledge of the national and international stages as well as for their involvement in local basketball leagues and informal pickup games.

The initial plan to interview prominent basketball personalities such as professional athletes, sport administrators, and renowned journalists did not materialize. Attempts to contact a newspaper writer and a television anchor were left unanswered. Meanwhile, during my research, the leadership in the country's premier league was in disarray, and attempting to get a hold of its interim commissioner was like chasing a slippery ball. At that juncture, crossing out the plan to interview "basketball celebrities" was altogether not a very difficult decision to make, especially amid the already hectic schedule of visiting the various libraries and archives in Metro Manila. Fortunately, despite the difficulty of meeting or setting up personal correspondence with them, these personalities are relatively accessible through books, magazine feature stories, and newspaper articles where their lives and viewpoints are laid out in words and pictures. Looking back, it was a blessing in disguise since the absence of these prominent figures allowed the study to adhere to its goal of representing the subaltern.

This book's contribution to scholarship hinges on its exploration of the regional context in the processes of colonialism, modernization, and globalization. This is particularly true in the references to China and Japan, both as on-court rivals that shaped the growth of Filipino basketball and as points of comparison to contrast the development of sporting culture in each of these nations with that of the Philippines. However, the data for both Japan and China is limited to that found in archival materials that have been gathered in the Philippines and in the United States, and to a number of academic and popular literatures written in English. Newspapers and other documents written in Chinese and Japanese languages would have been accessible through the author's visits to Beijing in 2007. Similar data sources were available in libraries in Manila and Singapore but the author lacks knowledge of both languages. However, a postdoctoral fellowship spent at Kyoto University from November 2011 to March 2013 allowed access to more research materials as well as first-hand exposure to the sporting cultures in Japan.

The challenge is synthesizing the enormous amount of data that results from the analysis of a range of issues over a relatively long time period (1900s to 2000s) into a book-length monograph. To address this problem, the discussions that compose this dissertation are presented as a series of independent *thematic* chapters rather than a unbroken narrative that chronicles the evolution of Philippine basketball from its beginning as a colonial imposition up to its current state as a popular pastime. Presenting the argument in this way enables the coverage of important issues over a long time period without spreading the discussion too thin. Nevertheless, despite its seemingly fragmented structure, the book attempts to present a coherent and unified story by focusing on a fundamental *problématique* and by closely following a recurring and all-pervading conceptual theme. Although each chapter devotes specific attention to different aspects and issues regarding basketball in twentieth-century Philippines, these series of propositions are linked together by their common objective of addressing our primary question: *Why is basketball popular in the Philippines?* In addition, the subaltern concept of "playing with the big boys" serves as the focal point that binds the different chapters together to form a comprehensive argument.

Like a tightly contested basketball game that is composed of four regular quarters and an extra five-minute overtime period, this book includes five chapters that cover the entire twentieth century, with the final chapter spilling into the early years of the new millennium. Chapter 1 ("Spheroid of Influence") attempts to reconstruct the genesis of basketball in the Philippines by identifying its role in the overall process of colonization. In general, the discussion shows how the multifaceted structure of American colonial rule shaped the early history of sports in the Philippines. Apart from the bureaucracy, players from various religious, business, and other private-interest groups also played important roles. For instance, the government's Bureau of Education embodied the philosophy of "bodybuilding as nation-building" while the Protestant YMCA pursued its goal of instilling "muscular Christianity"; both played crucial roles in introducing sports and physical education and fostering their importance among the "weak" Filipinos. Apart from promoting good health, it was also through athletics that good citizens and good Christians were molded through a meritocratic and rational system that imparted such "modern" values as self-discipline, hard work, and fair play. Hence modern sports became a growth chart used in measuring the local people's "fitness" for self-government.

The ability of the local population to easily adopt modern sports was interpreted by the Americans as an indication of the success of their "civilizing mission." For the Filipinos, however, their good performance in the different athletics fields was seen as a sign of their own physical and intellectual advancement, which came as a result of their long exposure to Western education and metropolitan sensibilities as a former colony of Spain. Ironically, sports eventually became an important venue where the locals found the opportunity to contend with their colonial masters.

Chapter 2 ("From Baseball Colony to Basketball Republic") traces the development of a national sporting culture in the Philippines. It begins in the early American colonial era (1900s) and runs up to the first decade of the post-independence period (1946–56). The discussion tries to address our main question, *Why is basketball popular in the Philippines?*, by examining the reasons behind the failure of other sporting fields, specifically baseball, to sustain the popularity that they enjoyed during the early twentieth century. The chapter argues that the close association of baseball with the Americans as an "occupation force," in contrast to basketball's general image as a representation of the "benevolent America," has resulted in the declining interest in the former and the rise of the latter.

This period also marks the era when Filipinos, fueled by a couple victories in international competitions, started to appropriate basketball as their own. Consequently, "Filipino basketball" slowly replaced baseball, "America's favorite pastime," as the most popular sports in the Philippines. This crucial change coincidentally unfolded as the country was seeing an intensification in the local clamor for independence. In particular, the national basketball team's notable showings during the 1936 Olympics in Berlin and the 1954 World Basketball Championship in Rio de Janeiro made the game a venue for showcasing the Philippines' ability to be at par with other countries, including the United States.

Chapter 3 ("The Hollywoodization of Hoops") examines the influence of American popular culture in Asia during the late Cold War era (1975–91) in the context of Philippine basketball. The rise of visual mass media and the promotion of American "cultural commodities" in the Asian region was part of the "containment" policy used to counter the growing influence of communism. In the Philippines, the strategic "Americanization of Asia" resulted in the transformation of the local professional basketball league from a widely followed sporting attraction into a highly popular entertainment spectacle. Referring to the process as the "Hollywoodization of hoops," the chapter shows how the country's premier basketball league evolved into a multifaceted enterprise that encompassed the realms of sports, television, film, and music. The chapter explains how the Philippine Basketball Association (PBA) attained soaring popularity and the country's celebrity-studded entertainment industry was able to sustain basketball's prominence in spite of the country's mediocre performance in international competitions.

Chapter 4 ("Rooting for the Underdog") provides a view of the historical and social significance of basketball in the Philippines from the perspective of the sports fans during the last decade of the twentieth century. This period is largely considered the country's golden age of mass-entertainment basketball. The chapter argues that the popularity of basketball in the Philippines partly hinges on the sport's evolution into a subaltern spectacle wherein the struggles of ordinary Filipinos are symbolically played out. Thus by rooting for the underdog, local basketball followers are clearly not only cheering for their favorite team but also rooting for themselves, and for the many other real underdogs outside the playing court.

The chapter focuses on the case of Barangay Ginebra, more popularly known in the PBA as the "team of the masses" for its strong fan appeal, especially among the ordinary Filipino basketball followers. The discussion is split into three parts: The first section links basketball with the practice of cockfighting, a form of entertainment and gambling that was prevalent during the Spanish colonial period. The "fowl game" is often referred to as the most popular public spectacle in the country before basketball was introduced at the turn of the twentieth century. The next two sections center on a textual analysis of a couple of novelty songs that portray the sentiments of an avid basketball follower. The object of the fan's affection is, of course, Barangay Ginebra. The songs, "Kapag Natatalo ang Ginebra" ("When Ginebra Loses") and "Kapag Nananalo ang Ginebra" ("When Ginebra Wins"), were released during the team's celebrated championship run in 1997, and they became the "national anthems" of the team's millions of fans. Although the songs are riddled with hyperbolic imagery and lyrics, they nonetheless reflect the devotion and passion that many Filipinos have for their favorite pastime.

Chapter 5 ("Basketball without Borders") examines the impact of globalization on Philippine basketball, especially during the decade around the turn of the new millennium (1998–2008). It describes how the greater integration of the world economic system resulted in the following developments: 1) the increased movement of players from one country to another; 2) the rapid expansion of the American "basketball entertainment industry"; 3) the rise of local collegiate and other professional leagues; 4) the significant improvement of players and teams from many countries, especially in Asia. This turn of events significantly altered the national basketball scene, posing serious threats to the long-standing position of the PBA as the center of basketball in the country.

This chapter suggests that globalization is essentially a legacy of what in an earlier chapter was referred to as the "Americanization" process. In turn, the origin of globalization is traced back to the earlier overseas expansion of American economic, political, and cultural influences at the turn of the twentieth century. Exploring the fundamental link between these two paradigms provides a sense of continuity in the analysis of the contemporary significance of basketball in the Philippines. However, the case of Philippine basketball has also highlighted the difference between the concepts of Americanization and globalization. A unilateral movement of knowledge from the metropole to the colony largely characterizes the former, while the latter has shown to be a more multidimensional arena in which the United States merely serves as one of the players. Although America still dominates basketball, both in the competitive and business arenas, other basketball-playing countries such as Greece, Spain, and Argentina have started to make their mark in the past decade. Philippine basketball, on the other hand, has long been fixated with retaining its top ranking in Asia; any anticolonial themes, which are prevalent in other sports traditions in the region (e.g., Indian cricket, Japanese baseball) have long been abandoned, if not totally forgotten.

1 Spheroid of Influence

Sports, Colonization, Modernity

> What need have these men to attack? Why are men disturbed
> in this spectacle? Why are they totally committed to it? Why
> this useless combat? What is sport?
> —Roland Barthes

The word "exercise," which in contemporary usage is associated
with physical fitness and sports training, has a primordial link to
earlier forms of territorial and political conflict. Having emerged
in medieval Europe, the word has its origins in the Latin term
exercitium, which is derived from *exercitare*, to train; a frequenta-
tive of *exercēre*, to train, to occupy; from *ex* + *arcēre* to enclose,
to hold off.[1] Physical strength was not only essential for survival in
that era but was also important to groups and societies seeking to
protect their resource bases or expand their territories. Early civilizations from China to Persia recognized the importance of
physical fitness to the optimal performance of combatants and so
they developed various training regimens and martial arts forms.[2]
In particular, leaders of premodern kingdoms and empires are
often attributed with legendary physical abilities. In precolonial
Southeast Asia, the demonstration of special physical prowess
often served as the basis of a personality cult, which leaders
employed to rally supporters and strike alliances with other groups
for the maintenance and expansion of their territories and political

influence.[3] Physical exercise played an important role in subsequent historical eras until it reached a much wider influence after the Industrial Revolution, when it took on a new meaning as a form of leisure activity. Despite this shift, ancient concepts of "exercise" and "prowess" are still expressed through the global politics of sports. From the 1904 St. Louis Olympics to the upcoming 2016 Games in Rio de Janeiro, sporting achievements are rhetorically used to convey civilizational or racial supremacy, cultural preeminence, and economic progress.

This chapter deals with the geopolitics of exercise and the exercise of geopolitics, and the blurring of the distinction between the two in the context of colonial sports. It attempts to retrace the genesis of the "national basketball culture" in the Philippines during the early period of the American colonial regime. In particular the chapter argues that the social engineering project of the American regime in the early twentieth century served as the catalyst for the emergence of basketball as the Philippines' most popular sport. These social engineering programs were part of the Americans' "effort to mold, and often to restructure" their new colony according to U.S. colonial designs.[4] This concept was couched in the glossy rhetoric of modernization, used by the United States as a pretext for altering the social and cultural landscape in the Philippines. Sports was one of the colonial initiatives that was immediately associated with modernity. It appealed especially to the young Filipinos who, with greater access to formal education, were finding more time and opportunities to indulge in new pastimes. More than the other American sports, basketball in particular was identified with liberal religious denominations, higher educational institutions, and some of the esteemed values of urbanism.

The rise of nationalism in eighteenth-century Europe paved the way for the development of modern fitness systems. Apart from its importance in preparing citizens for defending national territories, the health benefits of physical exercise were also increasingly recognized. This awareness resulted in the development of gymnastics and its inclusion in the curriculums of educational institutions in Germany, Denmark, Sweden, Great Britain and other countries.[5] The word "exercise" started to take on a new meaning during that period as the Industrial Revolution saw the rise of modern sports out of traditional games and a more rigid work-leisure dichotomy afforded ordinary people ample time for recreation. Thereafter the development of exercise into popular pastimes gradually shifted the association of the word from its traditional martial function to a more ludic rationale.[6] This crucial change did not sever the ties between the concepts of exercise and expansionism, however. On the contrary, the diffusion of modern sports throughout the different parts of the world has been shaped by larger international power relations.

Outside Europe, physical education and modern sports were largely introduced by Western colonial powers, many of whom had well-established footholds in almost every part of the world by the mid-nineteenth century. These new sporting practices joined the more entrenched "metropolitan cultural traditions," such as religion and language, in fostering a colonial culture. As such, modern sport provided a more accessible channel, serving not only as a bridge spanning the physical and cultural distance between colonizer and the colonized but also as an instrument for strengthening the control of the former over the latter. In his analysis of the basis of British colonial power in sub-Saharan Africa, Andrew Apter noted how "[the] thin white line of imperial power in the colonies rested not on British force and fortitude alone, but on the foundations of colonial culture."[7] This cultural linkage facilitated the administration of far-flung colonies, which enabled many imperial powers to retain and even increase their influence without needing much help from their armies.

In the Philippines, the history of its national pastime has been largely shaped by the country's relationship with the United States, its former colonial master. From basketball's introduction as an exercise regimen and a leisure activity in Manila's Young Men's Christian Association (YMCA) in the early twentieth century, the sport evolved into an imperative cultural force that played a crucial role in consolidating American control over the archipelago. With its strong appeal as a popular intercollegiate game, basketball was seen as a good diversion to keep young people from participating in subversive activities. More importantly, the new sporting discipline, along with other forms of modern athletics, was also used as a pedagogical tool to impart modern values to the "savage natives" who needed physical as well as moral exercise to prepare themselves for self-government. Moreover, the promotion of sports was also utilized by the Americans as a channel to advance their political interest in the Asian region.

"Fitness" for Self-Government: Racial Politics, Physical Training, and Colonial Rule

When pushed to explain the U.S. government's retention of the Philippines as a colony, President William McKinley argued that the decision was made after American officials determined that the Filipinos were still "unfit for self-government."[8] In retrospect he might not have only been referring to the local population's lack of knowledge and experience in democratic governance, but could also have been calling attention to some perceived "physical deficiencies" that the Filipinos needed to correct in order to effectively defend and run their nation. In particular, Americans believed "the susceptibility to illness, the high death rate, and the comparatively small amount of industry" to be some of the factors inhibiting Filipino self-government.[9] At a glance the first two problems could be solved by developing an efficient health system while the last one could be addressed by fostering a motivating work culture. To all problems, however, the United States readily employed an all-embracing solution: physical exercise and competitive sports.

During the height of colonial conquest, U.S. soldiers became the first to introduce baseball and other American games in many parts of the Philippines. After the Philippine-American War, the soldiers' presence even in remote provinces was tapped to promote modern sports in a much wider scope. Particularly, the Santa Lucia Barracks, headquarters of the colonial Bureau of Constabulary in the Philippine capital of Manila, was considered a strategic location for spreading modern sports. It was there that the YMCA trained soldiers "on the various points necessary while they are in Manila so that when they go back to their provincial posts they will have little difficulty in getting athletics under way."[10] Filipino writer Nick Joaquin even described the Santa Lucia Barracks as "the cradle of the basketball in the Philippines," since apart from many Filipinos learning the sport in the U.S. military gymnasium, the first Filipino basketball leagues were also based there.[11] In fact, athletics also played an important role in "pacifying" some of the remaining territories that were yet to be fully integrated into the nation-state. In the mountainous Cordillera region, for instance, sports competitions were utilized to defuse the tension between indigenous groups who were known for periodically waging tribal wars or embarking on the more notorious headhunting expeditions between neighboring communities.

Around the same time, the establishment of the Bureau of Public Instruction in 1901 also afforded the newly established colonial government with "armies" that would carry on the task of bringing the colonial government closer to the people. The public school teachers, under the newly reorganized Bureau of Education (BOE), were specifically targeted for this purpose because, according to one American official, it was "the only unit of the government that touches intimately and without friction with the whole people of the Philippine Islands."[12] Physical education and modern sports were included in the school curriculum and the rising popularity of athletic activities was largely attributed to the schoolteachers.

Moreover, the introduction of sports and athletics constituted an important element of the effort to implement a comprehensive program of health and sanitation.[13] In a decade marked by famines and epidemics, the role of physical education and modern sports "in the process of making the body sound and vigorous, capable of resisting disease and of doing hard work without unnatural fatigue" was one of the main motivating factors for its active promotion. By 1911, Frederick England, the BOE's Playground Director, estimated that about 95 percent of the country's 700,000 pupils were engaged in physical education.[14] This figure did not include the increasing number of sports enthusiasts outside the schools and institutions of higher education. In highlighting the importance of health science in the U.S. colonial administration, the medical historian Warwick Anderson noted how, "[By] 1902, the well-ordered laboratory, more than the army camp, appeared to represent the exemplary site for modern Filipino bodies and culture."[15] In a few years, however, the laboratory would eventually yield to the gymnasium.

Beyond its pragmatic value in promoting a healthy well-being, exercise was also recognized for its efficacy in instilling some of the civic values essential to a modern democratic society. "The self-restraint, the obedience to rules, the respect for other fellow's rights that the athlete learns in the vigorous practice of give and take," Elwood Brown, the YMCA Physical Director noted, were just some of the attributes that the Filipinos needed to strengthen along with their "weak" muscles.[16] To serve this goal, a sports-for-all program was promoted, particularly among those who were working in the colonial bureaucracy. This initiative proved to be especially useful in providing a much-needed diversion for government employees who were required to make the annual pilgrimage to the colonial hill station of Baguio City,[17] where the entire government moved each summer so the Americans could escape the punishing tropical heat. Brown, who was loaned by the YMCA to the colonial government to promote physical education and sports programs in 1911, quoted a correspondence with the American director of the Bureau of Public Works. He reported that Filipinos

> showed their displeasures at being sent to Baguio, away from their families and into the cold region by defacing the buildings, destroying important papers, damaging the plumbing, cutting

the bed nets, etc. This year not one malicious mischief was reported, due to the athletic program which absorbed their attention completely.[18]

Aside from providing for the recreational needs of government employees, the fitness program in Baguio was also strategically introduced so its participants could bring their knowledge and even newfound passion for sports to their respective provinces after the summer season. The use of the summer sessions in Baguio City to promote sports among the members of the colonial bureaucracy was similar to the system in the constabulary headquarters where soldiers were trained to propagate athletics in their assigned posts.

From Savages to Sportsmen: Race, Athletics, Americanization

In the course of the implementation of the social engineering agenda, special attention was given to young Filipinos, particularly in choosing the participants in the Americans' sports development programs. According to a BOE superintendent, this was due to the belief that one "cannot make Americans of the adult Filipinos."[19] Nonetheless, the child-adult distinction apparently did not matter much since the Filipinos as a whole were viewed to be physically and culturally immature. A YMCA official, for instance, assumed that "the Filipino as a race are in the childhood of their development, and exhibit all the peculiarities, faults, and virtues of a rapidly developing adolescent boy."[20] In this social Darwinist model, the perceived inferiority of the Filipino physique illustrated the hierarchy of difference between the backward colony and the modern metropole, a contrast that was vital in underscoring the racial foundation of American colonial power.

The 1909 exercise handbook *Physical Training for Filipinos* highlighted this difference, pointing out how the "the physical development of an Eastern tropical people differs widely than that of a Western people in the temperate zone," and thereby suggested that "a course in physical training for Philippine schools should be designed to meet existing conditions, and should be especially adapted to correct the physical deficiencies of the Filipinos."[21] This line was not only an affirmation of the superiority of the white Anglo-Saxon race but also reflected the racialized rationalities of American expansionism that included the more controversial notions of Manifest Destiny and "the white man's burden."[22]

Generally, the distinctive bodily attributes of the local inhabitants became an integral aspect of what Paul Kramer would call "the racial politics of empire." This concept essentially described how the Americans arranged "the way in which hierarchies of difference were generated and mobilized in order to legitimate and to organize invasion, conquest, and colonial administration."[23] Like the country's unexplored mineral reserves and undeveloped agricultural lands, the Filipino physique, as a perceived marker of racial inferiority, became a target of colonial intervention that was intended to maximize its productivity and enhance its contribution to the process of nation-building.

More than skin color, the most accentuated feature of the physical difference between the Americans and the Filipinos was height. From the battleground to the basketball court, in real as well as in symbolic terms, physical size was one of the measures used to distinguish the dominant from the dominated. This general observation follows Gerald Gems's assertion that "the concept of whiteness adhered not only to skin color but to intellectual and physical capacities as well."[24] More than a mere physical distinction, height demonstrated in a more vivid, quantifiable scale the difference between Americans and Filipinos. Anthropometric data and photographs were popularly used as part of the larger colonial discourse that presented local indigenous peoples as "savages" and "wild men." The U.S. colonial regime used this strategy to depict the Filipinos "as genetically inferior and unable to govern themselves without proper American guidance."[25] Subsequently, this imperial rhetoric proliferated through official government documents and different literary forms, and was promoted through the display of the different indigenous groups in major exhibitions, both locally and abroad.

From Tribal War to Tug-of-War

The American period (1901–46) was noted for U.S. efforts to incorporate two geographic areas that the previous Spanish colonial regime (1565–1898) had failed to conquer and integrate into mainstream Filipino society. Loosely categorized as the territories of the non-Christian tribes, these regions were eventually put under two administrative units: the Mountain Province in the northern island of Luzon and the Moro Province in the southern part of the archipelago. The relative isolation of these two areas from the rest of the population enabled their people to maintain traditional practices that clashed with prevailing social principles in the United States as well as with the majority of Filipinos. The practice of slavery in Moro Province and headhunting in the Mountain Province, for instance, were often used by the American colonial regime to demonstrate the necessity to "civilize" the non-Christian groups, as well as the rest of the population whose level of development was merely a few steps ahead of the former.

One of the most notable works that tried to account for the Filipino "savagery" was colonial Interior Secretary Dean C. Worcester's "Field Sports among the Wild Men of Northern Luzon," which appeared in the March 1911 issue of *National Geographic*.[26] The piece described one of Worcester's many field inspection trips to communities in the Cordillera Range in the northern Philippines. The piece describes the role that modern sports played in "taming the natives" of what was considered as a largely isolated and unincorporated region. In his article, Worcester pointed out the success of the local American officials in preventing the occurrence of tribal wars and stabilizing the volatile area. Particularly, Worcester highlighted how "the effort to suppress [headhunting] has been unexpectedly successful and [it] is rapidly becoming a thing of the past."[27] Nevertheless, he noted how "superabundant animal spirits will inevitably find an outlet, and in this case we have tried, with a good deal of success, to direct them into less turbulent channels by teaching them American athletic games."[28] Along with the construction of roads, providing access to social services, and setting up local administrative order, the promotion of sport and athletic competitions was generally recognized as a successful diversion, particularly as a less violent means of settling conflicts between the communities in the Mountain Province.

At the other end of the archipelago, the excitement and the positive values that modern sports imparted led the Moros[29] to allegedly lay down their bolos (bladed weapons) in favor of the baseball bat.[30] After years of steadfast resistance against the expansion of Spanish colonial rule, the Filipino Muslims continued their resistance and fought fiercely to deter the advance of American power into their long-held domains. While the Philippine-American War officially ended after three years in 1902, the war against the Muslim Filipino fighters persisted until 1913. However, despite this unfavorable social condition, modern sports seemed to make more progress than any efforts to completely put the Moro areas under colonial control. A San Francisco newspaper, for instance, reported a story about an American teacher named Michael O'Holligan who successfully organized a baseball team out of his students in an elementary school in the town of Jolo. At one point O'Holligan arranged for a tournament against a team from Zamboanga, the provincial capital. After a decisive win, the Jolo players went home and were greeted with cheers and a big feast. At the end of the celebration, O'Holligan was made an honorary "Datu" (chieftain) by the Sultan of Sulu.[31]

A year after the last major armed confrontation in 1913, the jurisdiction of Moro Province was transferred to a newly instituted civilian administration known as the Department of Mindanao and Sulu. The new government's emphasis on education had Governor Frank Carpenter preoccupied with fielding teachers, just as his predecessors were busy sending off soldiers to the different districts of the vast territory.[32] Like in other parts of the country, physical training was introduced as one of the basic subjects in elementary schools. The tremendous support that this initiative received was reflected in Carpenter's letter to Vernon Whitney, the District Governor of Sulu, endorsing the importance of athletics not only in imparting civic values but also as a form of social diversion for the people who were still coming to terms with American rule. He wrote:

> I wish that you would give your best thought to the consideration and outlining of a scheme for athletics of a type customary or acceptable to the young men of your district, by which it may be possible to give them an outlet for their surplus physical energy and make it more easy for them to refrain from activities of lawless character. It is not a new idea that opportunity for display of physical prowess is a prime factor, perhaps the controlling motive, for much of the lawlessness, and particularly crimes of violence, which are committed by uncivilized people. You yourself have been prominent and successful in athletics in years gone by, and I have no doubt you have already been thinking along this line.[33]

Teachers, soldiers, and other colonial personnel like Whitney were educated under the prevailing philosophy of *sit mens sana in corpore sano* (a healthy mind in a healthy body), an idea that greatly influenced the U.S. educational system in the early twentieth century. They were instructed to pass on the same appreciation for sports and athletics to their Filipino students. Beyond the specific objective of promoting physical fitness, the colonial administrations in the non-Christian territories were occupied with the larger goal of stabilizing the peace-and-order situation among longtime rival communities. Efforts to replace village and kin loyalties with the more ideal identification with the nation started with the regular holding of sport competitions between villages and municipalities, as illustrated in the story of O'Holligan's baseball team.

The promise, and eventually the achievements, of this initiative were noted by American officials such as Dean Worcester and

David Barrows, who all recognized the role of sports in promoting national unity. One U.S. political analyst reported how sports were "largely responsible for the breaking down of many of the barriers that have long stood in the way of unity and harmony between the different tribes, and in this respect . . . bid fair to play an important role in the nationalization of the Filipino people."[34] Thus the colonial project to promote "bodybuilding" among the members of the non-Christian communities was also deemed as an essential foundation in the larger undertaking of "nation-building."

Body Politic: Sport, Masculinity, Citizenship

While sport was noted for its contribution in stabilizing the peace-and-order condition in the Mountain and Moro Provinces, it also proved to be an effective mechanism for social diversion, particularly in helping "ameliorate any liberation sentiments" among the Christianized Filipinos whose members figured prominently in the Philippine-American War (1898–1902) and in the ensuing independence movement.[35] Sports events, particularly the major interscholastic tournaments, provided venues for interaction and means for the promotion of national unity among a populace beset by various geographical and cultural divisions. Apart from their utility as an instrument for colonial control and social integration, physical education and Western games were also more constructively viewed as an important tool in preparing people for a greater role in a popular democratic government.

When American personnel embarked on their effort to modernize their new colonial possession, one of their most contentious pronouncements about the local population was the perceived lack of industry among the Filipinos.[36] Perhaps this observation stemmed from most farmers' practice of taking long lunch breaks to avoid the punishing midday heat and to compensate for waking up before sunrise to get a head start before the tropical temperature became unbearable. This custom suited the Spanish practice of taking *siesta* or afternoon nap, which was also popular among urban dwellers. In addition, the Filipinos were also noted for their penchant for celebration, with *fiestas* (feast days) and other festivities sometimes keeping an individual from work for days.[37] On the other hand, indolence could also be something James Scott would refer to as an "everyday form of resistance,"[38] particularly against the practice of forced labor employed during the Spanish period. Nevertheless, the Americans who saw the considerable amount of time wasted on "sleeping and carousing" dismissively abhorred this "laziness" as generally counterproductive, one of the "traditional" practices that hindered the development of the Philippines.

The elite that was supposed to lead the country to economic progress was notorious for spending large amounts of time in leisure and socializing. Their *señoritos* and *señoritas* (sons and daughters) were generally considered to be "spoiled brats" who were largely shielded from chores and other responsibilities by the household's legions of servants. Hence, when J. M. Groves, the YMCA Secretary-General of the Philippines in the early 1900s, wrote about the fulfillment of promoting physical fitness among the Filipinos, he also envisioned "the privilege of upbuilding a whole race, teaching them to play the games for which they are hungry, and substituting for the false ideal of a gentleman as a perfumed dandy, afraid of soiling his fingers, an ideal grafted on an Oriental stock."[39] A similar trend also happened in China, where those who had shown interest toward sports were "largely recruits from the families of the literary class, whose 'burning of the midnight oil' for many centuries has rendered them, as a class, anemic and wanting in physical stamina."[40] In both places the American YMCA led the way in promoting sports and athletics, using these socially appealing practices as a means of addressing the cultural problem of native indolence as well as the so-called deteriorating masculinity of the educated youth.

Along with the institution of a comprehensive mass education system, the effort to promote sports and athletics was initiated to mold "modern citizens" out of the "partly civilized" Christian

Filipinos. Although the new colonial regime believed that "as a race . . . [most of the local population] has been elevated above the level of other Oriental and tropical races . . . by three centuries of contact with European (Spanish) civilization,"[41] this level of development still fell short of American ideals. On the contrary, the deeply rooted Spanish influence on the country was generally viewed by most American colonial officials as an obstacle to Philippine progress due to the enduring impact of what they considered the Iberian empire's traditional and backward institutions. At best, the majority of the country's population was considered medieval, particularly when measured against the evolutionary timeline of the American nation-state.[42] Thus while the mountain tribes of Luzon and the Moros remained stranded among the far-flung outcrops of savagery, the Christian Filipinos were largely viewed as a nation aimlessly drifting in a turbulent channel that separated the primitive from the modern.

To set the Filipinos in the right direction, the American colonial regime introduced sports and athletics not only for the physical development of the local population, but also for their political growth. These activities were used to impart civic values such as competition, fair play, confidence, teamwork, and discipline that were deemed essential in building a modern nation. Sports and athletics diffused ideas of citizenship responsibility and social equality in a country where feudal systems had thrived for centuries. In 1914, O. Garfield Jones, a former official in the Philippine Bureau of Education, wrote an interesting assessment of the impact of sports and athletics in the country, highlighting their success in teaching the Filipinos how to be good citizens. He pointed out how "the future of democracy in the Philippine Islands does not depend upon the cleverness of the aristocratic class of Filipinos so much as upon the kind of everyday training in individual self-control that the mass of the people receive."[43]

Jones's statement is a repudiation of the feudal patron-client system that had defined the prevalent form of political relations in the country before the Americans arrived in the archipelago at the dawn of the twentieth century. One of the arguments used to justify the U.S. colonization of the archipelago was the belief that "the withdrawal of America in the Philippines would result in government by a small oligarchy."[44] The monopoly of power by a land-owning elite that held a large part of the population in perpetual bondage reminded the colonial rulers of the oppressive agriculture-based economy of the Southern states that came to end with the U.S. Civil War.

Under this hierarchical system, Jones described the common Filipino as someone "who could hardly have been called an individual at all; he was only one section of a group of relatives, 'parientes,' who worked, ate, slept, and amused himself much as a child of twelve or fourteen years would depending on a rich uncle or cousin to look after his political affairs and loan him rice in time of need."[45]

This patron-client relationship developed over time through "gifts and grants that create debt and obligations." The debt was often not entirely settled, thus resulting in a relationship of "habitual payments so that another round of patronage (or, conversely, clientage) can be enacted in the future."[46] The debt could never be completely repaid with any monetary or material compensation since it came as an *utang na loob* (moral indebtedness). People who turned their back on their *utang na loob* were deemed *walang hiya* (shameless) and would often lose credibility and the respect of others.[47] Generally, the American colonial regime abhorred this form of unequal social relation; they considered it one of the feudal remnants of the Spanish *encomienda* (labor trusteeship) system, the antithesis to the populist democratic government that they sought to establish in their colony.[48] Jones, like other U.S. officials, distinguished American colonial rule from that of the Spaniards by highlighting their advancement vis-à-vis the latter's technological and political backwardness. He observed about how

The present political heritage of the Filipinos came from the corrupt system of Spanish colonial politics; but the Philippine political traditions of the future are going to be shaped by the habits and deals of the present generation of Filipino boys and girls who are being molded in a system of public school athletics that is superior to any state-wide system of public school athletics in America.[49]

Sports, with its emphasis on participation and teamwork as a means of promoting the ideals of citizenship, emphasized the idea that being part of a nation entails the fulfillment of certain duties and responsibilities. From a passive subject that often looked up to his or her landlord for decision-making, the people were developed to exercise their free will and to be responsible through their participation in athletics and popular games. This consistently fits with the colonial discourse of the "unfitness of the Filipinos for self-government," emphasizing individual autonomy as an essential prerequisite to the larger goal of national independence.

The root of the patron-client relations in the Philippines, according to Jones, lay in the highly paternalistic structure of the Filipino extended family or clan system. The clan was presented as a microcosm of society where the head of the family basically ruled as a dictator and as a benevolent protector. Aside from monopolizing decision-making, the father (or grandfather) was also largely viewed as the provider, and on whose shoulders rested the responsibility to protect the family from danger and aggression. This setup often resulted in the marginalization of the other members of the family. Jones noted that

> Since it was only the heads of families who had to bear the brunt of competition and responsibility in the past it is not surprising that the common Filipinos should become too excited over inter-municipal baseball games. But it is only by such contest that association is not based on community interest. It is only thus that leaders can be made to yield quickly to individualism. And it is only thus that leaders can be quickly taught to choose men because of their efficiency rather than because of their kinship.[50]

Although sport itself has its paternalistic tendencies, with the roles of coaches and patrons indispensable aspects of athletic competitions, athletes nonetheless play based on their physical capacities and individual skills. Basketball and other modern sports have not only been used to promote people empowerment and participation but are also aimed at imparting the ways of democratic governance to a country's future leaders. The initial test that separates modern leaders from the traditional comes during election time; an electoral race could be likened to an athletic competition where a candidate's "fitness" for a particular government position is determined by the number of votes that he or she receives from the constituent population. Just as in an athletic event, an electoral contest should be conducted by the rule of fair play, which competing parties need to respect.

Moreover, the rule of fair play should remain as the guiding principle of democratic leaders even after getting elected. In a way, as the responsibility of running administrative organizations falls on their shoulders, they move from being competitors (in an election) to being coaches. "Just how important the sense of fair play is to good government is hard to say," Jones mulled, "but certain it is that fair play and favoritism are contradictory terms, and favoritism is the fountainhead of both graft and inefficiency."[51] Involvement in sports allows individuals to expand their affiliation and affinity from their kin or close peers to a larger team or league whose membership extends beyond the limits of the players' immediate community. In the same way, leaders are called on to transcend their personal social networks to operate according to a more abstract form of association that embodies the nation.

Nation-building compares to a sports team where individual players who do not necessarily know each other try to build an "imagined community," to use Benedict Anderson's phrase, and contribute according to their unique skills in order to achieve a common objective. Varsity players, for instance, are chosen not according to kinship ties or other personal connections but through a meritocratic evaluation of athletic skills and other related criteria. Democratic leadership requires a sense of impartiality that will allow an elected official to avoid nepotism, one of the distinctive marks of the "traditional politics" of the Philippines that the Americans were trying to erase. Witnessing some political progress in the country toward this ideal, Jones highlighted how

> self-governing ability in athletics has now been established, because the reactionary influence of priests and old-line politicians has been nil on the baseball field. Naturally, such progress has not been achieved in those fields where the older generation has retained control, but with the development of individual self-control, a vigorous sense of fair play, and respect for duly-constituted authority among the rising generation of Filipinos, and with the recrystallization of Philippine society upon a municipal as opposed to the relationship basis, the groundwork for real political progress is being laid in the Philippine Islands as nowhere else in the world.[52]

Furthermore, apart from adhering to the rules of fair competition, a modern politician should also be a good loser. A good leader should be prepared to accept the mandate of the people and respect the outcome of an election. This ideal situation seemed impossible to achieve in the early twentieth century in the Philippines, as local elections during the American colonial regime often were marred by mass protests and conflicts between opposing parties.[53] This "political setback" seemed to confirm Fred Atkinson's (the first American education director) belief that it was impossible to teach the old Filipinos the new tricks that embody a modern society.[54] "In short, good losers are those who have learned the better lesson in their boyhood games, and without such training anyone is apt to be a spoiled child," Jones stated. "The older generation of Filipinos will probably never learn to lose a ball game or a political contest; the younger generation not only will, but in many cases have learned it."[55]

Jones's argument juxtaposed the political legacies of Spanish rule to the early "accomplishments" of the United States' "benevolent assimilation" project as the new colonizer of the Philippines. By demonizing Spain and by belittling the achievements and capabilities of the Filipino leaders, the American colonial discourse used the rising influence of sports to demonstrate the advancement of their "civilization." This claim to cultural primacy was then used to justify their occupation of the Philippines as a necessary "mission" to uplift the social condition in the colony. Physical education and other disciplinary measures became important channels through which the American colonial government sought to mold their "little brown brothers" in the Americans' image.[56] These "modern" practices became aspects of American values and culture that Filipino subjects needed to incorporate in order to prove their fitness for self-government to their colonial overseers.

Ballers in Bloomers: Sport, Gender, Participation

As part of the larger representation of Filipinos as a "weak race," the United States used a feminized representation of the Philippines to portray an image of innocence and vulnerability. It should be noted that the potential threat from British, French, and German colonial forces during the Spanish-American War was one of the reasons used to justify the United States' subsequent occupation of the Philippines. The use of the female body in propagating a picture of vulnerability to renewed foreign aggression was common to the pages of many newspapers and magazines in the United States during that period.[57] More than mere imperial propaganda, this representation of susceptibility was also used to underscore the role of women in molding a new generation of independent and industrious citizens.

While still decades away from gaining full political status, Filipino women benefited from a more liberal colonial system that afforded them greater access to education and other opportunities to participate in society. Sports and athletics were introduced to Filipino women through schools, primarily to keep them alert during class and to promote their overall well-being. One

American teacher assigned to the province of Zambales in 1913, for instance, introduced basketball in response to the "almost daily complaints and excuses for absences caused by headaches and other ailments." She was pleased with the result of her initiative, noting how

> the girls took a great interest in the game from the first and soon became very enthusiastic, insisting upon practicing every evening until a late hour. The headache excuses for absences became fewer and the girls became more active both in school and society work. This continued throughout the school year 1911–12 and today, in a class of more than forty, the girls of this same team are the healthiest in schools; their grades are higher both in industrial and academic subjects, while in all tests requiring self-control, skill of ability, they greatly outclass the non-athletic girls.[58]

Interestingly, basketball was first introduced to the public school system as a women's sport in 1910. This undertaking was based on the popular programs of some women's educational institutions in the United States, where basketball had shown a marked increase in popularity during the early twentieth century. Consequently girls' basketball was officially included in the inter-scholastic meets in the Philippines from 1911 to 1913. It was one of the featured events in the Carnival Athletic Meet, where it immediately became one of the crowd favorites.[59] The popularity of women's basketball was noted in one small town, where there was a total of twenty-five girls' basketball teams.[60] The sight of women participating in sports, especially on actively competing teams, was a rarity at that time.

It was a period when the norm was for young girls to incorporate the values and social bearing of Maria Clara,[61] the socially constructed "ideal" Filipino woman distinguished by her prim and proper ways. After taking notice of the increasing involvement of women in sports in the country, an American journalist wrote with enthusiasm at how

The prejudice against allowing women to take part in athletics in the Philippines has been entirely wiped out, and today we find the girls in school playing such games as are played by young ladies in the United States. Ten years ago the ladies who played or attempted to play tennis or basketball would be ridiculed by her people. Today they are admired, and those who were strongest in their criticism are now loudest in their praise.[62]

Moreover, women's participation in basketball was seen to have greater implications beyond athletics. Colonial public education official O. Garfield Jones wrote how athletics "not only develop healthful, vigorous, self-reliant mothers for the future, but they also develop within these mothers of the future a case of fair play that is lacking among non-athletic peoples."[63] Here, good motherhood was presented not merely as a familial responsibility, but also as a duty and an obligation of a citizen—a good example that fittingly embodies the concept of *bodybuilding for nation-building*. Jones went on: "This sense of fair play will not only make better citizens out of these girls, should they be given the right to take part in the government, but also it will enable them to hand down this sense of fair play to their children more successfully than the less athletic mothers of Europe and America can do it."[64] Women were not only citizens, they were valued for their roles and responsibilities in molding their children into good citizens. Thus the social engineering goal of creating new, enlightened leaders and involved citizens was being passed on from the colonial administrators to the local population, particularly through the newly bestowed role of the Filipino mothers as "nurturers of civilization."[65]

The increasing popularity of girls' basketball, however, had alarmed some groups, particularly those in the conservative Catholic Church hierarchies who saw the rigorous sport as an inappropriate practice for young Filipino women. One of the subjects of contention was the use of bloomers (long baggy pants) in basketball competitions, a cause of concern among those who believed that women should not wear manly outfits.[66] As a compromise, the Bureau of Education advised public school officials that "athletic suits for girls include skirts over bloomers." With that directive, the agency "believed that both girls and parents will be better pleased with this combination than with bloomers alone."[67] Nonetheless, the change in regulation came a little too late: at that time women's basketball was already limited to local and provincial interscholastic meets and had earlier been eliminated from the national championship tournaments, apparently due to the prevailing public opinion against its appropriateness as a women's sport.[68] The game was deemed too strenuous and rough by a largely conservative population of the belief that women should exercise physical restraint and refinement.

Eventually indoor baseball (softball) gained popularity and crowded out basketball as the preferred game for girls. Volleyball also attracted increasing interest among women and in time would supersede indoor baseball as the most popular women's sport in the country.[69] Over the course of two decades (during which the use of athletics skirts over bloomers was abandoned), basketball had lost its popularity as an interscholastic women's sport.[70] Criticism of women's basketball and suggestions of volleyball as an alternative also happened in Republican China. The following excerpt from a 1922 article in *Ladies Journal* captured the overall viewpoint of volleyball's proponents. It noted that "ballgames suitable for women are quite rare," adding how

> basketball is too intense, as sometimes people may fall down. Thus volleyball is the only game really suitable for women. There is no physical contact (chongtu) to speak of with the opponent, and since every person covers her own zone there is not too much running involved. (Women) using both hands to hit the ball is a graceful sight to behold.[71]

Although the highly popular women's basketball tournaments in interscholastic athletics did not last, the sport continued to be a major crowd-drawer, even when the competitions involved men. Eventually the much-anticipated basketball matches moved to Manila's major colleges and universities where they became the main attraction in intercollegiate tournaments, a position that the game continues to enjoy. One of the reasons behind basketball's popularity as a sporting spectacle can be traced to its brief prominence as a women's sport: women who were familiar with the game became avid followers later on, giving basketball a wider fan base.

From Evangelization to Exercise Instruction

After more than a decade of promoting athletics and sports in the Philippines, David Barrows, the first director of the U.S. colonial government's Bureau of Public Instruction, praised their impact on the local population in his 1914 book. He wrote: "The physique of the Filipino is also being modified for the better. The race is physically small, but agile, athletic, and comely. The schools have introduced everywhere the games of ball and athletic sports of America to the notable *moral* [italics mine] benefit of the population."[72]

Quite interestingly, Barrows's assessment is different from the others previously discussed as it highlights the less-touted "moral" impact of athletics during the American colonial regime in the Philippines. More recently, Gerald Gems, in his seminal work *The Athletic Crusade*, wrote about how physical education and sports were generally introduced in the Philippines by the American colonizers to fulfill the "moral imperative to bring civilization, technology, and a particular brand of the Christian religion [Protestantism] to those deemed to be lower on the Social Darwinism ladder."[73] Indeed, sports and colonialism were not only politically linked—they were also bound by their embedded moral impetus.

The establishment of a YMCA branch in Manila in particular brought a new breed of Protestant missionaries who adopted athletics and sports as a means of molding the moral, social, and physical characteristics of young men and women.[74] The organization started sending preachers to the Philippines as well as to other parts of Asia in the late nineteenth century. As evangelizers, however, they were more successful in spreading the gospel of modern sports than in propagating Christianity. Two YMCA missionaries, Charles Glunx and Frank Jackson, arrived with the U.S. troops sent to occupy the Philippines in August 1898 after the end of the Spanish-American War. They were initially given the task of keeping the occupation force occupied and were charged with setting up literary and debating clubs, baseball matches, and other activities to keep the American soldiers from vices and other "temptations." After the end of the subsequent Philippine-American War in 1902 and the establishment of a civilian colonial government, the YMCA started to expand its services to the city's civilian white population.[75] In fact, most YMCA international branches were initially organized to respond to the notable increase of young European and North American expatriates in various urban centers across the world. In the port city of Manila, the YMCA was initially administered solely to the American and European military personnel, professionals, and businessmen.

By the mid-1910s, however, the number of American military and administrative personnel had significantly dwindled because of the "Filipinization" of the colonial bureaucracy. By 1914 a YMCA official lamented how "*despididas* (farewell parties) are the most frequently announced functions"[76] throughout most of the year. This turn of events nonetheless allowed the association to branch out and start catering to the local population. The opening of the Filipino Branch on January 1, 1915, was heralded as a milestone for the YMCA that "marked the entrance of another race—the Malay—into this world brotherhood."[77] After a year the new branch was seen to be doing exceptionally well, particularly its Physical Department, which the Philippine YMCA Secretary-General E. Stanton Turner specially mentioned as the branch's "most popular department."[78]

It has been widely regarded that the Spanish conquest of the Philippines was achieved through "the sword and the cross," highlighting the equal importance of military force and the cultural influence of the Catholic religion in the process of colonization. In the case of the Americans, it can be argued that their colonial power rested on the efficacy of "the rifle and the baseball bat." Essentially, physical education and sports were used not only to mold the body, but the spirit as well. They eventually grew into influential cultural forces that shaped the way education, health, and leisure were perceived and practiced.

In fact, the introduction of sports, particularly as part of a public education program, was one of the examples used by the United States to distinguish itself from Spain. Specifically, the doctrine of "muscular Christianity" was utilized by American Protestants to highlight their liberal and progressive religious ideals vis-à-vis the "conservative and backward" legacies of Catholic Spain. For instance, Pedro Villanueva, a Filipino YMCA staff member, criticized the limited appreciation for physical exercise before the American period, pointing out how Filipino children "were made to see the folly of spending so much energy running around the house in some form of tag game. This was particularly true during the Spanish [period]," when "in many instances children in church schools during that time were punished with 'no play' ban."[79] In contrast the YMCA presented a Christian movement that stressed the need for energetic activism, fusing religious piety with physical health.[80]

Hence when the Catholic hierarchy in Manila started planning a facility similar to the YMCA (a complex of dormitories, swimming pools, and athletic facilities now called the Pope Pius XII Catholic Center) as a response to what they saw as the alarming increase of the Protestant organization, the plan was immediately downplayed by YMCA officials. Secretary-General Turner commented: "[It] is my candid opinion that they will be unsuccessful in their campaign if they attempt to raise money for this building among the Filipinos. The priesthood has been too greedy, too immoral, and too medieval in thought to be able to raise 200,000 [Philippine pesos]."[81] Although Protestantism eventually failed to topple the deeply rooted influence of the Roman Catholic

Church in the Philippines, the YMCA nevertheless played an important role in the formation of a sporting and athletic culture in the country during the first half of the twentieth century. Physical Director J. Truitt Maxwell in his 1925 annual report to the association's headquarters wrote about how "the idea of physical education has taken root in the Islands much faster than the YMCA as a whole has grown."[82]

Even before the Filipino Branch was established in 1915, the YMCA, through its partnerships with the Bureau of Education and other colonial administrative units, was already working to develop sports and athletics in the country. Notably, Elwood S. Brown, the first Physical Director of the Philippine YMCA who arrived in Manila in 1910, had worked so extensively in training local instructors, producing manuals, and in setting up the Philippine Amateur Athletic Association that he is widely considered "The Father of Modern Sports" in the Philippines. He pioneered the promotion of the widespread practice of sport through his "play-for-all" program, which promoted physical education in public schools around the country.[83] From 1911 to 1917, Brown was also the Director of Athletics for the annual Manila Carnival, where athletic contests were one of the highlights; he also played a prominent role in the expansion of the carnival's athletic contests into a regional tournament involving other Asian countries. In 1913 he was instrumental in bringing participants from China and Japan for the inaugural Far Eastern Championship Games (FECG) in Manila. The FECG proved to be crucial in the American colonial regime's efforts to promote its achievements in the Philippines to the other countries in the region and across the world.

Moreover, YMCA missionaries who came with the U.S. troops as military chaplains earnestly promoted the new game of basketball, a sport their organization invented in 1891. Elwood Brown himself was a basketball coach for the YMCA's Chicago Branch before moving to the Philippines, where he was tasked with mentoring the Manila YMCA basketball team. The team won the National Basketball Championships seven times between 1911 and

1921. From the YMCA, basketball spread its popularity to the colleges around Manila, and eventually to the rest of the country.

Play and Display: Sports Events as Colonial Spectacles

In a modest ceremony, American Governor-General of the Philippines William Cameron Forbes stood on a makeshift stage in Manila's Carnival Grounds to officially open the First Far Eastern Championship Games on February 1, 1913. Dubbed the "Olympics of the Orient," the event was a pioneering regional multisport competition. Around 130 athletes from China, Japan, and the Philippines participated in ten days of sporting tournaments that were witnessed by more than 150,000 spectators.[84] The organization of the FECG, according to Gerald Gems, "had two aims: to bring Asia into the modern world as defined by Anglos, and to assimilate Filipino tribes in a focused nationalism against foreign opponents."[85] Between these two goals, however, was the grander aim of the international promotion of the American colonial regime in the Philippines through the athletic achievements of the Filipinos.

Aside from being the highest official of the host country, Governor-General Forbes—an avid polo player and sports patron—was also the president of the Philippine Amateur Athletic Federation (PAAF), the main organizer of the FECG. His opening speech highlighted the importance of the occasion as the harbinger of the development of sports in the region. One line captured the main point of his message: "I hope that all your contests will be carried on in the spirit of fair play, which in years may govern your conduct in business and other vocations of grown-ups."[86] Although he was underscoring the importance of athletics in imparting "modern values" to the throngs of young delegates (mostly students), his remark could also be taken as condescending advice to the three "young" nations that the athletes were representing.

The first decades of the twentieth century were a period of "rebirths" that saw waves of economic, political, and cultural changes sweeping through much of the region. In 1911 China evolved from a long-established empire into a fledging republic, while in Japan the end of the Meiji era in 1912 ushered in the "Taisho Democracy" that brought sweeping transformations to Japanese society. The Philippines itself was getting ready for the "Filipinization" of the government bureaucracy that started roughly a year after the event.[87] Hence, Forbes's message on the instructive significance of sports fits the kind of advice deemed appropriate for the emerging nation-states, who at that time were still getting acquainted with the workings of a democratic government.

Indeed, athletics played an important role in the process of nation-building in both Republican China and Taisho Japan; it has been noted that "sport did not only provide the Republican Chinese opportunities to incorporate 'Western' and 'modern' practices but it also provided an alternative practice and discourse against the oppressive ruling regime and tradition."[88] This mirrored the case in the American-ruled Philippines, where sport was also used to distinguish the U.S. regime from the earlier Spanish colonial administration that was largely presented as corrupt and backward. Building on the foundation that had been started by the YMCA when the organization arrived in China toward the end of the nineteenth century, "the Republican government continued to use sports in its efforts to create a modern nation-state."[89] In that same period, similar processes also happened in Taisho Japan, where "the Ministry of Education was wholeheartedly supportive of the diffusion of modern sports in the schools."[90] The parallelism between the principles of "muscular Christianity" and the time-honored ethos of the *bushido* (self-discipline) allowed for the assimilation of American sports (such as baseball) as something modern yet traditional.

Moreover, the message of Governor-General Forbes could also refer to his opinion on the importance of building favorable relationships among the participating countries. The 1913 FECG was most likely the first occasion where delegates from a number of Asian countries came together. Thus Forbes's advice to play the games in the "spirit of fair play" underscored the importance of the sporting event as a foundation for establishing goodwill and a venue for constructing positive relationships among Asian nations. A local newspaper noted how

> The Far Eastern Olympiad is quite the most significant event that has touched Oriental peoples in united action. They have never met before for united action on any other basis than athletics. The Olympiad is democracy in itself . . . The Far Eastern Olympiad is the outward manifestation of the spirit of younger generation. The "effete, effulgent Eat" of the poets is passing away and the rise of the common man and the solidarity of nations is coming apace.[91]

Furthermore, the first international sports tournament in the region was primarily organized to put the spotlight on the United States. The event evolved from the athletic competitions in the Manila Carnival, a major exposition organized to showcase America's achievements in the Philippines. Writing on the 1904 Olympics, which was held alongside the St. Louis Exposition, Nancy Parezo noted how the world's fairs "served as tools for the imperialist countries that staged them to justify and essentially celebrate the subjugation and dispossession of indigenous peoples worldwide."[92] Following this philosophy, both the Manila Carnival and the Far Eastern Games served as venues for the emerging world power to tout the progress of its new colony and promote its image as a "benevolent colonizer."

With its exceptionalist rationality, Julian Go noted how the U.S. rule in the Philippines was not presented as "exploitative or tyrannical . . . but was benign, a civilizing mission rather than one of the missions of conquest that ostensibly characterize the 'world history' of imperialism."[93] For instance, just a few weeks after the Philippines emerged as the overall champion of the First Far Eastern Games, a Northern California newspaper published a piece extolling the role of the U.S. in training the successful Filipino athletes: "[Up] to the time of American occupation the Filipino had done absolutely nothing in athletics. The race, in an athletic standpoint, was in very poor condition. They were, perhaps, the weakest of all Orientals. Today, they are at the head."[94] By flying the Stars and Stripes alongside their own flag, the Filipinos were essentially playing to demonstrate American superiority to the other countries in the region. Thus the FECG was meant to emphasize this "American benevolence" and the colonizers' success in uplifting the economic condition in the Philippines. This pomposity was especially directed toward the "traditional" colonial powers such as France, the Netherlands, and Great Britain, whose colonies in the region had remained poor and backward. In fact, despite U.S. efforts to gain their cooperation, many neighboring countries under European control were unable to participate in the regional sports event until Netherlands East Indies (Indonesia) sent a small delegation to the final FECG in 1934.

Finally, international sports competitions, especially the FECG, allowed the United States to refocus the basis of Filipino nationalism away from anticolonial sentiments to regional rivalries.[95] The United States was able to assume a respected position as mentor/ coach and deflect Filipino antagonism away from itself and toward neighboring countries. This position enabled the United States to participate in regional politics without necessarily getting involved in the actual tussle. Overall the initiative reflects the principles of American "tutelage" of the Filipinos, which the United States utilized to argue for the legitimacy of its occupation of the country. Thus sports coaching became part of the larger "coaching" in the rudiments of nation-building meant to prepare the Filipinos for self-government.

The Philippines won the overall championship in the first FECG. Although the size of its delegation as the host country became the deciding factor in its victory, U.S. officials expressed much appreciation and pride for the athletic achievements of their protégés. The Filipinos were not to be left behind in the celebration, and the colony immediately appropriated the commendable performance of its athletes as a national victory. Shortly after the game, an

American magazine noted how the success of the first FECG contributed to the development of "national self-consciousness among the Filipinos. Their baseball teams have competed with the Japanese teams for several years, and in February of last year a picked team of Filipinos won the first Oriental Olympics, defeating strong teams of baseball and track athletes from both Japan and China."[96] The Filipino victory emphasized the crucial role of regional competition in the construction of national identity. The display of each country's flag, athletic uniforms, and other symbols reinforced people's sense of belonging to a particular nation.

Finally, the first FECG was also significant as a watershed in the development of Philippine basketball. The national team's success in the basketball tournament stimulated the initial interest of the Filipinos in the game. Afterward, the Philippines dominated the basketball tournaments at the FECG, where it won nine out of ten championships until the FECG's last staging, also in Manila, in 1934.

2 From Baseball Colony to Basketball Republic

Postcolonial Transition and National Sporting Culture

> The games people play are as valid a barometer of any culture
> as politics, religion, economics, or history. Inversely, then, so
> too, are the games people refuse to play.
> —Joseph A. Reaves

Following Reaves, this chapter presents a comparative sociohistorical analysis juxtaposing basketball with baseball, which represents the game that Filipinos "refuse to play." The discussion highlights the sports' historical trajectories in the formation of a national sporting culture in the Philippines, following a time line roughly spanning the early American and early post-independent periods (1900–1960). Punctuated by the two World Wars and other key events, this time span also marked a significant period in Philippine sports history. The tumultuous era witnessed a largely overlooked course of events that saw the decline of baseball as the country's favorite pastime and the rise of basketball in its place. The displacement of the diamond by the hardwood, in spite of the former's entrenchment as the Philippines' pioneering sporting pastime, illustrates how a society's sports space "is not 'filled' simply on a first-come, first-served basis."[1] It highlights the contested positions of the world's most popular sporting pastimes, exposing how they are shaped by historical events as well as by various actors who are motivated by their own sets of interests.

What are the factors that catapulted baseball to prominence in the early years of American colonial rule and what are the reasons behind its ensuing decline? What influenced the phenomenal rise of basketball and how did it surpass the widespread popularity of baseball? These are just some of the questions that this chapter tries to answer by taking a closer look into the complex relationship between imperialist sporting traditions and national sports culture, and the different points of convergence and disjuncture in the two sports' entangled histories. The discussion attempts to address our main question of *Why is basketball popular in the Philippines?* by examining the reasons why other sports, specifically baseball, failed to sustain widespread influence during the early twentieth century.

The emergence of a national sporting culture, according to Markovitz and Hellerman, starts with a contest to fill in a society's "sport space." They contend that this extended process "denotes a qualitative dimension of cultural construction and group contestation that reflect power relationships in society at large, and in sport in particular."[2] Within the scope of state-building, athletic fields can become key instruments in fostering a shared interest among people from different backgrounds, serving as a mode of collective self-expression and standing as symbols of a common identity. However, in many cases the state only provides the initial impetus, after which sporting cultures evolve almost independently through the participation, patronage, and innovation of various formal and informal organizations. A few even emerge entirely from the people themselves, taking root as important everyday practices before assuming a more modern form through the rationalization of rules, commercialization, and professionalization. Despite their different origins, however, competitive sports always need to compete with each other for the public attention and support that determine their position in a society's sporting hierarchy.

In postcolonial societies, the rise and decline of modern sports (most of which were introduced by ruling imperial powers) points both to the process of assimilation and of rejection, or to certain strategies between these polar extremes that the colony employs to construct its own unique cultural features. Often, modern sports play an important role in the process of disavowing the imperial "Other," despite the games' oftentimes imperialist origins. For instance, the rise in popularity of baseball in Cuba in the late nineteenth century came as a form of opposition to Spanish colonialism. Cuban students and expatriates who had lived in the United States introduced the American game to their home country. It eventually replaced bullfighting, a popular public spectacle brought in by their Iberian colonizer, as the nation's favorite pastime.[3] In the Philippines (a former Spanish colony like Cuba), the U.S. colonial regime promoted baseball to attract public interest and to curb the deeply entrenched influence of Spanish culture in its new colony. The members of American-organized Protestant churches in particular decried the widespread popularity of cockfighting as an immoral and socially degrading spectacle. However, unlike in Cuba where baseball was largely successful in countering the influence of bullfighting, the sport made little progress in completely eradicating the influence of cockfighting among the Filipinos. The practice continued well into the twenty-first century, although on a much smaller scale and under strict control.

There are three factors that shaped this divergent outcome. First, the Cubans themselves were actively promoting baseball while the Filipinos merely followed the lead from a few Americans who pursued the game's advancement in the Philippines. Second, bullfighting was closely identified with Spain while Filipino cockfighting was largely a "native" practice with pre-Spanish origins, and it was also popular in neighboring Southeast Asian countries. Lastly, the amount of resources needed for the staging of bullfights largely necessitated the patronage of the state or the elite while cockfighting, apart from its regular appearance in fiestas and other prominent occasions, also existed in unsanctioned and community-organized events.

Despite these differences, baseball emerged as a popular sporting pastime in both countries in the early twentieth century. The opportunity for natives to become participants and performers rather than mere spectators allowed the sport to grow and penetrate the everyday cultural realms of Cuba and the Philippines. Apart from baseball, these two countries also share the same colonial history, with both falling under U.S. rule after the Spanish-American War in 1898. From this period, however, the histories of the two countries diverge. Cuba was granted independence in 1902, becoming the last Spanish colony in the Americas to gain full sovereignty. Meanwhile the Filipinos' achievement in establishing the first republic in Asia was short-lived, as the United States took control of the country and ruled it until 1946. Likewise the post-independence relations of Cuba and the Philippines with the United States also followed differing paths. Cuba evolved into a socialist state after the Second World War, becoming one of the Soviet Union's closest supporters during the Cold War. On the other hand, the Philippines forged a strong alliance with the United States, turning the archipelago into the most "Americanized" country in Asia.

The histories of baseball in Cuba and the Philippines took some ironic and unexpected turns. The game remained popular as the former's national sport despite the unfavorable relationship that developed between the socialist nation and the United States. On the other side of the world, baseball gradually waned in the Philippines until it was eventually surpassed by basketball. Was the rejection of American baseball in post-independence Philippines ultimately an expression of nationalist sentiment similar to the rejection of Spanish bullfighting in late nineteenth-century Cuba? Not quite, especially since the sport that the Filipinos chose to displace baseball with was invented in the United States, and is every inch an American sport as well. In his effort to make sense of the "faded glory" of Philippine baseball, Joseph Reaves noted:

In fact, the dynamics of Filipino society and culture throughout the decades since the war indicates a continued strong affinity to things American. The enormous popularity of basketball, an indisputably American game, is one of the many signs that a "motive of imitation" continues. And that, in turn, eliminates any likelihood baseball's steady decline spawned from an "impulse of rejection."[4]

The Rise and Fall of Baseball

After gaining a foothold in Manila and the surrounding provinces through a series of decisive victories in the early period of the Philippine-American War, U.S. forces swiftly moved outside the capital to establish control over the rest of the islands. In Cebu City the American soldiers startled the local population by turning a hallowed convent into a horse stable for the Army's cavalry regiment in 1899. The convent's spacious front lawn, the Recollect Plaza, was renamed Plaza Washington and was utilized for military exercises and baseball games.[5] The occupation of the friars' residence and its sprawling plaza had arguably a more profound significance than the American takeover of nearby Casa Real (Government House) because during the friar-dominated Spanish regime those who lived in the convent held relatively greater cultural influence than the colonial administrators who worked at the government building. Moreover, the "desecration" of the convent's grounds represented the triumph of the new forms of public spectacles (military exercises and baseball games) over the primacy of the Catholic religious activities of the Spanish era, symbolizing the transfer of power from the Spaniards to the Americans. This episode would presage a similar event in China almost ten years later when the area around the Temple of Heaven in Beijing was utilized as a venue for the Second National Games, where the "untraditional use of this area as a sports field—reminding observers of the new primacy of Western culture all around the world"[6] was noted. In the case of Cebu City's Plaza Washington,[7] its use for military exercises and baseball games was a symbolic display of the United States' supremacy over its new colonial possession.

Eventually, baseball attracted a sort of "religious following" that challenged the power of the Church as the main proponent of most local public congregations. This turn of events was seen as a major achievement by the early American administrators who largely regarded the influential Catholic religion a representation of both the cultural status quo and of the "traditional structures" that the new colonial regime was trying to topple. The impact of this social transition was observed when Sunday rituals were increasingly hampered by a decrease in attendance due to the weekend doubleheader games that drew thousands of people to the ballparks.[8] Early-twentieth-century observers of American colonialism in the Philippines such as O. Garfield Jones, William Freer, and David Barrows considered the rapid diffusion of baseball across the archipelago as a demonstration of the success of American conquest and colonial administration, as well as an indication of the United States' deepening cultural influence in the Philippines.

As early as 1901, the country's first baseball league was organized even as the Philippine-American War still raged in different parts of the country (including the capital city's immediate surroundings). Known as the Manila Baseball League, the amateur circuit comprised U.S. soldiers and other colonial personnel. For over a decade, the league remained almost exclusively American and it was not until 1912 when the first all-Filipino team was included.[9] The participation of the local population, however, was more evident outside Manila where baseball competitions became popular spectacles even in far-flung provinces.

In 1906 an American teacher who was assigned to a remote town in northern Luzon reported how "of late years baseball is played, and one of the most encouraging sign of progress in the Islands is the readiness with which the young boys take to this game." In Baguio City he observed how children developed a "baseball language" by interspersing English into their local dialect.[10] Two years priors to the teacher's observations, the first interscholastic athletic organization in the Philippines had been set up on the Bicol peninsula, located on the southern tip of the main island of Luzon. Known as the Southern Luzon Athletic Association, it was organized in 1904 primarily to run baseball competitions between the region's provinces. A few years later in 1908, the Philippine Interscholastic Meet was instituted as part of the First Manila Carnival and baseball became one of the featured attractions and easily the most popular among the spectators.[11] Thus in the mere decade between the arrival of American troops in 1898 and the first national interscholastic championship competition in 1908, baseball evolved from a little-known colonial game to a premier national sporting spectacle.

Among the early notable local teams was the San Mateo High School squad, which represented the province of Rizal at the Carnival Athletic Meet in 1912.[12] Although they eventually lost to a powerhouse team from Manila High School, the team earned the admiration of local fans with their skill and determination. In fact they had started garnering public attention even before the Carnival Athletic Meet when the secondary school squad beat a team of American soldiers in a five-game series at their base in Fort McKinley the year prior. The team's success mirrored the victory in 1896 of the Tokyo First Higher School (Tokyo Ichiko) against a team of American sailors and expatriates from Yokohama.[13] The latter event became a celebrated episode in the history of Japanese baseball, a symbol of emancipation against the increasing influence of the United States in late nineteenth-century Japan. The victory of Tokyo Ichiko against the Americans is regarded as the origin of the game's rise to prominence as Japan's national pastime. In the same way, the Bengalis (Indians) had their moment of jubilation in 1911 when a group of "barefooted players" defeated a team of British soldiers in a game of football in Calcutta. Like the Tokyo Ichiko victory, this almost-mythic event is credited as the foundation for the enduring popularity of football in West Bengal despite the overwhelming influence of cricket in the rest of India.[14] Unlike the Tokyo Ichiko team or the Calcutta squad's celebrated triumphs, however, the remarkable feat of the San Mateo High School team was not given any nationalistic value as a symbol of emancipation, nor did it serve as an inspiration for the long-term viability of baseball as the most popular sport in the Philippines.

Nevertheless after a little more than a decade of U.S. rule, America's favorite pastime had become the Philippines' favored recreational activity. Baseball served as the main event at the inaugural Far Eastern Games in 1913, with each game drawing an average crowd of about five thousand people to Manila's Carnival Grounds.[15] A California journalist tried to capture the widespread popularity of baseball in the country: "Over all the archipelago, from the village in the mountains to the fishermen's barrio on the coast, baseball diamonds have been laid out and baseball is being played."[16] In time, Filipino baseball teams began venturing overseas and local clubs started competing against teams from the United States and elsewhere. By the 1910s professional players from the U.S. Major Leagues had on several occasions visited the country for matchups against Filipino teams; in turn, an all-Filipino team embarked on an extended trip in 1913 for a series of games in Japan and the United States. In 1926, a professional tournament was created in the country after the Philippine Baseball League relinquished its amateur status. In addition, several amateur leagues, such as the Industrial League, the Independent League, and the Manila Bay Baseball League, were also organized.[17]

The biggest event in Philippine baseball history occurred when George Herman "Babe" Ruth, arguably the greatest baseball player of all time, came to Manila in 1934.[18] Ruth arrived with a group of other top professional baseball players from the United States, including Jimmie Foxx, Lefty Gomez, and Lou Gehrig, to play a couple of exhibition games against a selection of local teams. The big leaguers won all their games against the starstruck Filipino players. This visit by some of the biggest stars of Major League Baseball became one of the most cherished events in the history of baseball in the Philippines.

Although the big leaguers' visit proved to be a huge success, the tremendous hype that surrounded the event contradicted the alarming state of baseball at that time. By the mid-1930s the deterioration of the quality of the game in local competitions and the decreasing interest of the fans were already noted, especially at the grassroots level. The decline was generally blamed on the lack of competent coaches resulting from the exodus of American teachers.[19] The presence of American teachers and coaches in the country had resulted in colonial dependency rather than serving as a foundation for the establishment of a viable national baseball program. In February 1940, a report in the country's top sporting magazine, *The Filipino Athlete*, noted how an American high school principal's observation about the decline of baseball was confirmed by a report from the Bureau of Education. It revealed that the sport was no longer promoted among elementary students in most provinces in southern Luzon, a trend that the principal had first observed in Laguna, the province where he was assigned.[20] Shortly after World War II, a commentator noted how baseball was "not only on the wane but is gradually passing out of existence and very few seem to care if the sport should disappear. The school children are turning to basketball and very few are enthusiastic about baseball."[21] Three years after that observation, basketball had so overtaken baseball that a 1950 article on the history of the Philippine National Collegiate Athletic Association (NCAA) described how the transition was reflected in the rampant practice of ticket scalping:

> Old timers now could call to mind the days when fans could buy more NCAA tickets than they used to way back in the 1920s. Nozaleda Park which was to seat 5,000 was never jampacked as it was when the sluggers come to town. But as baseball gradually gave way to basketball, the trend-wise scalper moved his shop from the ball park to the hardcourt, was happy to make 10 centavos on a 20 centavo ticket, made a killing when he converted it to a peso bill.[22]

It seemed that basketball was not the only sport that had overtaken baseball: football was also making some progress in the postwar era. A football writer claimed that "after basketball, no other major sports here [Manila] have recovered from the doldrums as fast as football."[23] In 1951, the visits of several football teams from England, Spain, Sweden, Denmark, Singapore, China, and Hong Kong gave a major boost to local football by providing what another writer would refer to as "a kind of internationalism that will enable it to stamp up anywhere in the world."[24]

Apart from baseball's weakened link to its grassroots base, the dominance of the Japanese teams in Asian baseball competitions also deprived local followers of the victories essential in attracting more interest in the game. Without any notable accomplishment in international baseball competition, the game did not get the chance to bring honor to the country. In comparison, the phenomenal growth of basketball between the country's credible showing at the 1936 Olympics and its third-place finish at the 1954 World Basketball Championship was widely celebrated as a symbol of the country's emergence in the international sports scene. These revered events delivered the final shot that ultimately ended the heyday of baseball in the Philippines.

The Battle of the Ballgames

The first hint of the impending "battle of the ballgames" in the Philippines came one fateful day in February 1910 when Governor-General William Cameron Forbes unexpectedly awarded basketball uniforms to the division champions in that year's interscholastic baseball tournament. Over the previous five years, the highest-ranked American colonial official had made it a tradition to hand out baseball equipment to the successful schools.[25] From then on, basketball took a more prominent position, challenging baseball as the most popular sport in the country. American soldiers shared the credit with the YMCA for "planting the first seeds of the game" in the Philippines in 1905.[26] However, it was through the nurturance of the missionaries that the efforts to develop

Table 3. Winners of the National Basketball Championship, 1911–23

YEAR	AMERICAN DIVISION	FILIPINO DIVISION
1911	American YMCA	NA
1912	American YMCA	NA
1913	Amercian YMCA	NA
1914	American YMCA	NA
1915	American YMCA	NA
1916	American YMCA	Internal Revenue
1917	U.S. Army	University of the Philippines
1918	American YMCA	Internal Revenue
1919	None	None
1920	15th Infantry	Reach Co.
1921	USS Huron	Reach Co.
1922	Columbia Club	Spartan Co.
1923	Submarine Flotilla	City YMCA

Sources: The Filipino Athlete, "Basketball in the Philippines"; research data.

basketball in the country came to fruition. Elwood Brown, the YMCA Physical Education Director, formally introduced a number of sport programs, first to the members of the American-European YMCA Branch, then to public school students through his affiliation with the Bureau of Education. Prior to his assignment to the Philippines, he had been a basketball coach for one year at the University of Illinois.[27] He was the coach of the American YMCA team that won the National Basketball Championship in the Philippines for six straight years from 1911 to 1916.

The National Basketball Championship started in 1911, ten years after a similar league for baseball was organized in Manila. The tournament mainly consisted of teams supported by the same organizations that sponsored the decade-old baseball association. Thus from 1911 to 1916 only American teams representing

Columbia Club, American YMCA, Fort William McKinley, and the occasional visiting U.S. Navy team competed in these championships. It was only in 1916 that a separate Filipino division was established. The two divisions were later combined to form the National Open Championship in 1923 after the number of American teams dwindled with the Filipinization of the colonial bureaucracy.[28]

At the grassroots level, basketball had caught the interest of many students, including women who had no previous exposure to any sport. In 1910, the game was officially included in the physical education curriculum of public schools as a women's physical education course. Because of its novelty, women's basketball became one of the greatest crowd-drawers during the Manila Carnival's National Athletic Championship from 1911 to 1913. The game suffered a small setback when some conservatives criticized the sport for its highly strenuous nature, which they largely saw as inappropriate for women. Conversely, others labeled basketball a "sissy game" because of its popularity as a women's sport, which for a significant amount of time deflected any further interest from male players.[29] In the sport's early years, basketball's ranking among the top sports in the country fluctuated between second and third place as it competed with the continuing mass appeal of baseball and the rise of volleyball among students and urban workers.

It was only in 1924—when it was included as part of the newly organized NCAA—that basketball received a new lease on life. The sport immediately caught the attention of tertiary-level students and became the biggest crowd-drawer during the increasingly popular multisport intercollegiate tournaments. The renewed interest in basketball spread quickly from the country's top colleges and universities to the rest of the population. Consequently the game was recommended for inclusion as an official event in national interscholastic tournaments in 1935 due to its increasing popularity at the elementary and secondary levels, as well as in many interprovincial competitions.[30] Shortly thereafter the sport

Table 4. Winners of the National Basketball Open Championship, 1924–35

YEAR	TEAM
1924	Manila Sporting Goods
1925	Manila Sporting Goods
1926	University of the Philippines
1927	University of the Philippines
1928	University of the Philippines
1929	University of the Philippines
1930	Manila Interscholastic Athletic Association
1931	National Collegiate Athletic Association
1932	Meralco Athletic Club
1933	No Award
1934	60th Coast Artillery (U.S. Army)
1935	University of Santo Tomas

Sources: *The Filipino Athlete*, "Basketball in the Philippines"; research data.

was featured in a November 1935 article in *The Filipino Athlete*, one of the earliest recorded references to basketball as the most popular sport in the country. The highlight of the piece reads:

> Perhaps no other game is as widely played today in the Philippines as basketball. No school is so small or obscure that it does not have a team that aspires to local championship at least. In every nook or corner of the archipelago there are ardent basketball fans and wherever there is a vacant lot anywhere, barefooted kids indulge in the sport with the zeal and enthusiasm of true amateurs. In the Philippines, basketball is the sport "par excellence."[31]

This pronouncement mirrored the depiction of the pervasive influence of baseball in the Philippines made thirty years earlier by American writers such as Dean Worcester, William Freer, and

David Barrows.[32] Interestingly, the rise of basketball paralleled the period when nationalist sentiment rose in the lead-up to the establishment of the Philippine Commonwealth in 1934.

The Invader vs. the Innovator

A year after the rise of basketball to the top echelon of Philippine sports was first reported, the Philippine basketball team turned in a remarkable performance at the 1936 Olympic Games in Berlin. This much-acclaimed event further boosted the position of basketball in the country's sporting hierarchy. As the celebrations waned, proponents of the displaced and rapidly declining sport of baseball pondered the misfortune that had befallen their beloved game. Of the various factors that were seen to have contributed to its decline, the decrease in the number of American military personnel was one of the most interesting. A piece in a notable sports magazine articulated this observation:

> The progress that baseball has made in the Islands during the past years is due largely to the extensive competition which was made possible by the organization of strong army post teams that are located in various parts of the country. This was an advantage which, for many years, the Philippine baseball teams had over those in China and Japan and which was greatly responsible for the supremacy of our teams in Oriental Games. Unfortunately for baseball, the U.S. Army forces were withdrawn from many parts of the country, and what Army troops there are that remain hardly play baseball. Thus we have lost one of the greatest factors that had been responsible for the development of America's national sport in the Islands.[33]

Earlier, the prominent role of American military personnel in the national baseball scene had resulted in Filipinos associating the sport with the United States, the "occupying power." Adding to this reputation was the fact that many baseball fields were also marching grounds for the soldiers who landed in the country during the Philippine-American War. Likewise, many of the pioneering teachers who introduced the game through the public school system were former soldiers who had either shifted to a less perilous profession or decided to stay in America's new frontier after the Philippine-American War ended.

Furthermore, baseball's continued dependency on American military personnel also revealed its failure to completely acquire distinct local characteristics and integrate into the national cultural milieu. The Filipinization of baseball never really took hold, and it largely remained an American sport that simply happened to be popular in the Philippines because of a continued strong U.S. presence. Thus the numerous baseball fields, just like the number of sprawling U.S. bases and other military installations around the country, stood as monuments to the American hegemonic presence. In contrast, despite its origin as an American sport and the continued influence of the United States in its development, basketball had been successfully integrated and reinvented as distinctively Filipino. Both the 1936 and 1954 national basketball teams, for instance, were noted for their unique playing style characterized by their use of "speed, agility, and defensive tenacity."[34]

Rural Baseball vs. Urban Basketball

In his highly acclaimed book on the social role of sports in the United States, Michael Mandelbaum described the rules, the techniques, and the overall playing pattern of baseball as reflective of its rural, agricultural, and traditional origins.[35] After it evolved from an old English game, baseball became the first "American sport" and the first modern sport to attract a widespread following in the United States.[36] As a product of its time, baseball embodied the largely agrarian, pastoral, and ever-expanding nineteenth-century U.S. society. When this expansion reached the Philippines in 1898, baseball was at the forefront, reflecting a popular American saying that "wherever the flag goes, baseball follows." Expectedly, baseball's flag fluttered more splendidly in the expansive countryside where U.S. soldiers claimed forests and farmlands to make way for their sprawling encampments. One of these military cantonments was Fort McKinley on the outskirts of Manila. There many local players, such as the legendary San Mateo High School baseball squad of Luis Santiago, learned and mastered the game of baseball.

The sport also spread to the provinces through the public school system that the Americans had established across the archipelago. The new school buildings and their playgrounds were welcome additions not only to villages where basic educational institutions were nonexistent but also to towns whose existing Catholic parochial schools mainly catered to children from elite families. It was on these playgrounds that Filipino students learned baseball terms even before they were able to master the English alphabet.[37] Moreover, provincial interscholastic baseball tournaments also fed into village and provincial rivalries, consequently attracting enormous followings among the local populations. It was because of this strong influence in the countryside that interest in baseball was sustained after it had almost completely disappeared from the sports scene of postwar Manila. This largely explains why news of the controversial victory of a Zamboanga team in the Little League World Series in 1992 came as a complete surprise to many Filipinos.[38] The issue showed that only a small number of people were aware that baseball still thrived in a few places around the country.

Plantation teams such as the Canlubang Sugar Estate and the Pampanga Sugar Mill dominated the country's premier baseball leagues. In particular, the Canlubang squad (nicknamed the Sugar Barons), which could boast of the only regulation baseball field other than that at Manila's Rizal Memorial Stadium, was a topnotch team that won several championships in the Manila Bay Baseball League (MBBL).[39] The long prominence of this organization in the national baseball scene reflected the association of the game with the agrarian way of life. This perception mirrored the general view in the United States, where baseball had nostalgic value as a reminder of a pastoral past long since overshadowed by an urban-centered way of life. The Canlubang Sugar Barons eventually folded when the MBBL was shut down in 1979; even the

Canlubang Sugar Estate, the bastion of baseball in the Philippines, disappeared as it gave way to industrialization and other development projects. On its site now stand the first and biggest industrial park in the Philippines, one of the country's largest golf courses, and several residential subdivisions and a commercial complex.

As the popularity of baseball faded with the passing of the agrarian era, basketball continued to rise as industrialization took a greater role in Philippine economy and society. In contrast to baseball, which he described as a traditional, pastoral game, Mandelbaum presented basketball as "the post-industrial game" that reflects the character and the dynamics of twenty-first-century society.[40] Unlike in the United States, in the Philippines the scope of basketball's popularity also covered the "industrial period," a prominence Mandelbaum attributed to the lack of Filipino interest in American football. The latter sport, associated with the industrial era in the United States, never had any significant influence in the country; besides, it was only quite recently that industrialization started to have a widespread impact in the Philippines. Thus the baseball-basketball transition basically represented the passing from agrarian to industrial, from a rural-oriented to an urban-centered society.

This distinction could easily be discerned by looking at the teams that composed the country's top leagues in each specific period. The baseball era was the heyday of plantation and local industrial teams like the Canlubang Sugar Barons, whereas the basketball period saw the rise of clubs that were sponsored by big corporations, one of the salient features of postindustrial societies. Although the popularity of basketball eventually spread to the countryside, its strong public appeal came as a result of the influence of modern mass media, particularly in the form of radio and television.

Apart from the abstract basis of the rural baseball–urban basketball dichotomy, the more tangible factor of space use also helped determine the fates of these two sports. The rapid urbanization of Manila and its immediate environs hampered the development of baseball because of that sport's need for a large playing field.[41] The average baseball field measures between 90 and 125 meters from home plate to the fence, while a standard basketball court has only 28 meters between the opposing goals. Thus the space-hogging sport of baseball simply did not suit the increasingly crowded spaces of Metro Manila and other urban centers. Although the resulting congestion from the urbanization of the country's major cities provided a throng of enthusiastic new baseball players, finding a place to play became increasingly difficult, if not completely impossible. Home runs and foul balls often flew beyond the playing field and it became a challenge to build a ballpark or a makeshift diamond in the urban centers without necessarily endangering glass windows and unsuspecting passersby.

Rising real estate values and the intense land-use competition in cities put baseball at a serious disadvantage. This unfavorable situation worsened when other sports, such as basketball, could also provide approximately the same form of leisure while requiring much less space. A 1935 report from the Department of Public Instruction noted that, "In the schools and colleges, particularly the larger ones, athletic games which can be played in small-sized playgrounds were popular."[42] Congestion and overpopulation had especially compounded the problem of space in Metro Manila. As the ballparks and other "empty lots" gave way to housing tenements, slum communities, and other urban structures, baseball's place as one of the premier sports in the country weakened. For instance, in the scramble for space to rebuild war-ravaged Manila after the Second World War, the Osmeña Park in downtown was razed to make way for the construction of the city's Central Market. Interviewed thirty years after the demolition of the historic playground, Conrado Serrano, one of its forgotten stars, grieved over what he considered a great loss to Philippine baseball. According to him, the park was the "spawning ground of most of the country's best and brightest baseball stars at that time . . . [where the] 'Potato League,' a baseball competition among grade school teams in the city's various districts, took place." He remembered playing for his school's varsity team at Osmeña Park in 1934, and "told of how 'the old Park' hummed almost the whole year with baseball activity, improving grade school students from all over the city."[43]

But more than the fact that Philippine junior baseball's home is no more, Serrano said that what saddened him about the old stadium's passing was that not too long after, local baseball also went into a sharp decline from which it never recovered. Indirectly, Serrano blamed the present state of baseball on what the tearing down of Osmeña Park symbolized. It was, he said, "more than a structure that was dismantled but a system which in the golden years of Philippine baseball had enabled the sport to build a wellspring of talent from which replacements of aging stars could be drawn."[44]

The space factor indeed played a big role in the decline of baseball in the Philippines. However, the problem was not simply about the "availability" of space but also its "allocation." The case of the Osmeña Park had shown that for urban planners and city officials, the importance of a new market far outweighed the significance of the area as a ballpark. In the same way that one of its most famous ballparks is remembered as the present site of the Central Market, the glory days of baseball are also often recalled in reference to basketball as the current sporting pastime of the country. In this way the present space occupant can also serve as a memorial to the one replaced. "I guess," Serrano lamented, "you can say that what stood there wasn't a market but a baseball field, baseball held a place in our sports strata now occupied by basketball."[45]

Interscholastic Baseball vs. Collegiate Basketball

The close association of basketball with urban centers was already established even during the sport's infancy in the early twentieth century. During this period, basketball started to attract public attention as the favorite event in Manila's top intercollegiate tournaments. Meanwhile, baseball, despite its widespread popularity and the presence of top amateur leagues in the Philippine capital, was more prominently identified with elementary and secondary interscholastic tournaments, through which the game gained a widespread following. Generally collegiate basketball was urban-based, with the members of some of its top leagues, such as the UAAP and the NCAA, hailing from tertiary educational institutions located in Metro Manila, whereas the elementary and secondary schools that participated in interscholastic baseball competitions were mostly from the provinces.

Apart from being an important attribute of the rural-urban dichotomy, the identification of the two major sports with particular levels of the Philippine educational system was also one of the crucial factors that contributed to the baseball-basketball transition. The latter's popularity among urban-based students and graduates of higher education institutions allowed it to appropriate the distinction of being a "modern sport." This image attracted the interest of the country's growing number of professionals and the expanding bourgeoisie, which was closely connected to the colleges and universities, either as alumni or as parents of students. This association with higher education, especially with the highly regarded private schools, also boded well for those who promoted basketball to the rest of the population. The sport caught the attention of aspiring students from the provinces who looked to the country's top universities as channels to achieving their dreams. This aspiration for higher education grew as the public education system established by the American colonial regime opened up greater opportunities for its realization.

Conversely the underdevelopment of varsity baseball at the postsecondary level deprived the professional Manila Bay Baseball League of a deep talent pool essential for its long-term viability. High school baseball players were often too young and inexperienced to make the direct jump to the professional league, where some athletes were in their forties. A 1940 magazine editorial highlighted this problem:

For, as they years went by, the star players were found to be aging very fast. And the difference between them and the young players was so great that a long transitional period would have to transpire before the young material could be sufficiently developed to take the place of the old timers.[46]

In fact the notably long careers of some MBBL stars had denied many good young players the opportunity to play in the professional league. Among these aspiring players was Gabriel Fajardo, who abandoned the game after realizing that the presence of the well-entrenched veterans made it very difficult to earn a spot on the national team. He decided to shift to basketball instead, and eventually became one of the best Filipino cagers of the 1940s, leading his collegiate team to several championships.[47] In 1948 he was chosen to be the co-captain of the Philippine National Basketball Team that participated in the London Olympics, the highlight of his illustrious sports career. The conditions that forced Fajardo's transfer from baseball to basketball reflected the widening gap between the plantation and industrial company–dominated MBBL and the country's basketball-playing higher educational institutions such as Fajardo's University of Santo Tomas. The baseball professional league's top players, who had risen to prominence from provincial and blue-collar backgrounds, had little regard for the young, urban-based, and well-educated players.

Popular Pastime vs. the Bourgeois Ballgame

The baseball-basketball schism also ran along the social class divide. Although this phenomenon manifested itself in different social settings, it was more evident in school athletics where sports were more systematically developed. Particularly, baseball tended to be popular in public schools while basketball was the favorite in many private educational institutions, which largely catered to students from middle and upper-class backgrounds.

Despite the widespread popularity of baseball in the early American period, the sport failed to expand from its stronghold in the interscholastic athletic meets. In fact it was reported that even after almost forty years of existence in the Philippines, "the majority of private educational institutions remained uninterested in the sport."[48] As for basketball, it failed to gain interest in public schools because it was introduced to the interscholastic level relatively late (1935), and it took some time for interest in the sport to grow, especially in the provinces.[49] As a result, baseball, with its large following in the provincial and rural areas, was immediately dubbed "the game of the masses"; in contrast basketball was mainly seen as a bourgeois sport due to its strong appeal among the educated urbanites. Baseball was said to have attracted popular interest "first among the poorer section of the community, who were not bothered with tanned complexion or roughened hands."[50] Such physical characteristics, which were generally abhorred by the elite and wannabe elite, were almost unavoidable in a sport played under the sun and by swinging wooden bats. In contrast, basketball, which was introduced as an indoor sport, favored the bourgeois with their access to the YMCA or to one of the private school gymnasiums.

As a result, varsity sports were increasingly regarded as a signifying feature of urbanity and cosmopolitan sensibilities. Being a member, or even simply a spectator, of the school varsity team was generally seen as a way of adopting a modern lifestyle for those who had the time and resources to spare. Such activities further defined their elite status and even served as venues for its conspicuous display.[51] Thus when a spate of violence marred the Manila Interscholastic Athletic Association baseball games in 1935, many were horrified at what they thought were blatantly barbaric acts. A sport magazine commentary noted that such incidents would have been "dismissed indifferently" had they occurred twenty-five years earlier, "or, if [they] happened in the provincial championships where the crowd is strongly partisan." The writer expressed his frustration by noting, "But in a cosmopolitan center like Manila . . . it is hardly conceivable that violence of this nature has been repeated with impunity, and without apprehending the culprits and giving them the punishment they deserve."[52] Such incidents were immediately taken to reflect the "uncivilized ways" of the baseball fans, who were largely migrant rural folks and blue-collar workers.

In comparison basketball was often cited for its genteel games where acts of hooliganism rarely occurred. One article described a typical basketball game in Manila, where people "have been accustomed to watching the [matches] as more or less a sporting and social event where the crowd applauds the good plays regardless of which team makes them, and where they keep silent when there is anything which does not merit their approval."[53] In 1949 a Philippine basketball team visiting the United States for a series of games against local California clubs failed to attract the interest of Filipino immigrants, a development on which poor ticket sales were largely blamed. The team's coach attributed the regrettable circumstance to the social class makeup of the migrant communities, pointing to the fact "that most of the Filipinos (majority-laboring class) had a preference for boxing and gambling."[54] Again, basketball was represented as a sort of a sophisticated game that did not appeal to the working-class Filipinos in the United States.

In summary, the various forms of unfavorable identifications of baseball—its connection to Filipinos' impression of the United States as an occupying force, its image as an agrarian game, its limited popularity with elementary and secondary students, and its constricting representation as the game of the masses—all contributed to its decline as the country's favorite sporting pastime. On the other hand, the positive associations of basketball, particularly its close link with the general conception of the United States as a harbinger of progress, its portrayal as a modern sport, its avid following on most college and university campuses, and the strong interest it attracted from the upper and middle classes generally helped elevate it to the pinnacle of the Philippines' sports hierarchy toward the end of the American colonial regime.

Sports and the Nation

Baseball made a brief comeback during the Second World War when Japan, one of the world's staunchest baseball-playing nations, ruled the Philippines for about half a decade. During this period a baseball league was formed in Manila, comprising a couple local teams from different government offices. The Nanyo Kohatsu squad (the name assumed by the famed Canlubang Sugar Barons) and Nippon Club (composed of Japanese soldiers and civilian personnel) were the most popular teams during this period.[55] Some Japanese wardens even organized baseball competitions in the concentration camps established throughout the country.[56]

When the war ended, the Manila Bay Baseball League games were resumed and there were efforts to revive interscholastic baseball as a means of developing young players. In 1950 the Philippine Amateur Athletic Federation (PAAF) initiated the formation of a secondary baseball league open to both public and private schools. This was eventually replicated in major regional centers around the country. In the international arena, the Philippines was the prime mover in the establishment of the Asian Baseball Federation (ABF) and hosted its first tournament in 1954.[57] Thus the competition between baseball and basketball did not end in the 1930s, continuing even after the country gained its independence from the United States following World War II.

Sport Participation and International Recognition

The emergence of basketball as the country's premier sport was primarily ushered in by the greater opportunity to participate in international competitions, which consequently granted more chances to gain international recognition for the country. This was almost impossible to attain in baseball because of the absence of major international tournaments due to the sport's limited growth in the global arena. Baseball only became an official Olympic event in 1992 and was removed from the list of events for the 2012 Olympics in London because of its lack of global appeal. The growth of the sport has been limited to North America, East Asia, and the Caribbean. In contrast, basketball's Olympic debut in 1936 preceded baseball's by more than fifty years. Even in the Asian Games, baseball was only included in 1994 whereas a basketball championship has continuously been held since the inaugural games in 1951.

Major sporting events such as the 1936 Berlin Olympics provided an international showcase for the Philippines, which only two years earlier had obtained some autonomy from the United States through the establishment of a commonwealth government. It was the first time that the country was able to participate in any major international events under its own flag. The country's relative success in basketball in Berlin was replicated almost twenty years later when the Philippines won the bronze medal in the 1954 World Basketball Championship in Rio de Janeiro, Brazil. This accomplishment remains notable for being the highest honor that an Asian country has ever achieved in a major international basketball competition. As a result, basketball became an important venue for obtaining valuable international publicity for the emerging nation-state, especially since its earlier attempt to proclaim independence from Spain in 1898 faltered after the revolutionary government failed to receive foreign recognition.

This story parallels the history of basketball in postwar Israel, where the sport played a role in helping the volatile and vulnerable nation-state gain the support and respect of other countries.[58] Elsewhere, basketball had likewise influenced the formation of national identity in Lithuania, where the sport became a potent "expression of national identity and resistance."[59] Like the Philippines, the Eastern European country also experienced colonization when it came under the imperial rule of the Soviet Union. In Lithuania, "basketball provided its fans with iconic national heroes and heroines who promoted Lithuania throughout the world by virtue of their excellence and successes. These players have played a major part in the creation of the nation as a political entity."[60] In the same way, the Philippine national team was lavished with a celebratory parade and a reception at the Presidential Palace of Malacañang upon their return from the Olympics in 1936.[61] The team's achievement not only focused the attention of the spectators in Berlin to the country's progress in basketball, but to the overall progress of the Philippines as well.

Apart from gaining international recognition, participation and success in major sports events could also help foster a sense of national pride and unity among people. The result of the Philippine National Basketball Team's participation in the Berlin Olympics invoked a sense of collective frustration at the questionable ranking system that awarded the country only a fifth-place finish despite it having the second-best record.[62]

Because of this event, basketball started to evolve from a parochial pastime—one that consisted of playing for or supporting one's school, neighborhood, or provincial team—to a national passion that engrossed much of the population. Hence, the impact of the event validates Vilma Cingiene and Skaiste Laskiene's assertion that "a nation is not only bound together through its common territory, history, and ideologies but also through the collective symbols, experience, and memories" that sports could provide.[63] The notable performance of Philippine National Basketball Team in the 1936 Berlin Olympics "provided the inspiration and gave the impetus that spurred the promotion of basketball in the Philippines."[64] After this milestone, the sport's influence spread from its historical niches (urban, college, private school, upper class) to the rest of the population. This development allowed basketball to attract a widespread following across different sectors of society, turning the Philippines into one of the world's few "basketball republics."

Games and Geopolitics

Beyond the initial empire-colony matchups, the institutionalization of regional competitions also helped shape the development of national sports in the Philippines. These competitions resulted in keen rivalries among the neighboring nations along the Pacific Rim, most notably Japan, China, Korea, and the Philippines. These rivalries were highlighted in the 1973 Asian Basketball

Confederation Championships held in Manila, during which, despite the presence of eight other national teams from the region, the games between these four countries were especially noted for being the most well-attended and with the most eager spectators.[65] These momentous rivalries emerged due to the following factors: 1) the logistical advantage provided by their geographical proximity; 2) the countries' parallel experiences in the introduction of modern sports during the late nineteenth century by American military personnel and Protestant missionaries; and 3) their own histories of economic and political disputes. Countries tend to excel in their favorite sports largely because of the willingness to put in more resources, the players' relatively long exposure to top-flight competition, and the motivation that they get from their supporters. In addition, national pride seems to be more at stake when teams compete in their country's national sport.

Over time this trend led to a kind of "competitive advantage" (based on the concept of comparative advantage), wherein countries claimed specific major sports almost as their "areas of excellence" and tried to achieve dominance in competitions. For instance, during the baseball competition at the first FECG, one observer noted how "the Japanese were clearly superior to the best Filipino team obtainable."[66] On the other hand, the Philippines was well-known for winning every FECG Basketball Championship from 1913 to 1934, with the exception of the 1921 Shanghai Games. In 1954, the coach of the University of Oregon's basketball team wrote after his team's Asian tour that "the Philippines has the best teams in the Far East." He pointed out that "it was only in Manila that the barnstorming American cagers suffered their three defeats in their whole tour of the Far East. They won all their games in Hongkong, Japan, Singapore, Bangkok and Taipei."[67] On the other hand, China was recognized as a formidable football country, with its teams dominating regional competitions.[68]

This perception was further reinforced during the Second World War when the ruling Japanese imperial regime promoted baseball among Filipinos and even organized matches in which

Table 5. Winners of the Asian Baseball and Basketball Championships, 1950s–60s

ASIAN BASEBALL CHAMPIONSHIP		ASIAN BASKETBALL CHAMPIONSHIP	
YEAR	WINNER	YEAR	WINNER
1954	Philippines	1960	Philippines
1955	Japan	1963	Philippines
1959	Japan	1965	Japan
1961	Japan	1967	Philippines
1963	South Korea	1969	South Korea
1965	Japan		
1967	Japan		
1969	Japan		

Sources: *The Filipino Athlete*, vols. 12–22; research data.

Japanese soldiers and other colonial personnel actively participated. As a result, baseball also became closely associated with the brutal regime, which likely reinforced the conception that baseball "belongs" to Japan. Adding to this perception is the fact that in the 1950s and 1960s Japan ruled the Asian Baseball Championships, while the Philippines made its mark in the Asian Basketball Championships (see Table 5). After World War II the idea that football belongs to China, baseball to Japan, and basketball to the Philippines was already well-entrenched in the mind of most Filipinos, and arguably for most Asian sports fans as well.[69]

Since the 1970s, however, this idea of "competitive advantage" among the three countries has started to wane. Until its reemergence in the twenty-first century, football lost its footing as a popular regional sports event. Japan continued to produce excellent baseball teams with its former colonies Korea and Taiwan following closely. After taking the Asian Games basketball championship in 1974, China emerged as the uncontested leader in Asian basketball during a run that only ended in 2010. The Philippines follows closely, along with South Korea, Iran, and a number of other Middle Eastern countries, which since the turn of the twenty-first century have sent excellent teams in Asian basketball tournaments.

3 The Hollywoodization of Hoops

Basketball, Mass Media, Popular Culture

> Sporting entertainments is one branch of show business.
> —Pierre Bourdieu

This chapter examines the influence of American popular culture in Asia during the late Cold War era (1975–91) in the context of Philippine basketball. During this time, the influence of visual mass media and American show business transformed the professional basketball scene in the Philippines from an exclusively sporting spectacle into a popular entertainment industry. Referring to the process as the "Hollywoodization of hoops," this chapter argues that this crucial shift transformed the overall character of basketball fandom into a multifaceted enterprise that transcends sports, reaching into the realms of television, film, music, apparel, and other consumer goods. In addition, the discussion also looks at how the Philippine Basketball Association (PBA), the country's premier league, helped maintain the popularity of the game despite the Philippines' unremarkable record in international competitions by capitalizing on its popularity as a celebrity-studded multimedia spectacle.

Although much has been written on the role of sports in international politics during the Cold War era,[1] the impact of the period on local sporting culture, particularly in the Asian context, largely remains unexplored. Thus instead of highlighting how sports became a "weapon" or a "battlefield" between conflicting nations, this study emphasizes how specific cultural practices like sports evolve during such critical periods. An analysis of how the advance of American popular culture from the mid-1970s to the early 1990s transformed the basketball scene in the Philippines provides a more pertinent picture of the enduring impact of the Cold War period. Moreover, it also gives us an idea of how the relationship between the United States and the Philippines, and Asia in general, has developed over time. Finally, this case can offer some valuable insights into the bigger picture of the "Americanization of Asia"[2] and how it is related to the larger discourses on neocolonialism, cultural imperialism, geopolitics, and globalization.

Cold War, Fiery Games

The year 1972—literally the longest in history[3]—provided ample time to thaw the global tensions that had escalated during the Cold War period. The year's two Olympic Games in particular provided venues for some less bloody confrontations between the United States and the Soviet Union and their respective allies. From February 3 to February 13, the Winter Olympics was held in Sapporo, Japan, the first time the event was hosted by a non-European or North American country. The Soviet Union and its satellite East Germany bagged the top two places in the medal tally, flaunting their socialist might against archrivals the United States and West Germany, which finished a distant fifth and sixth, respectively.

The Philippines became the first tropical nation to participate in the Northern Hemisphere–dominated event by fielding two athletes in the slalom and giant slalom competitions. The skiers' unremarkable performance on the slopes paralleled the downhill movement of the country's political condition. Seven months after the Sapporo Olympics, Washington-backed president Ferdinand Marcos declared martial law, citing the country's escalating communist insurgency as the rationale behind the move. This declaration ushered in fourteen years of heavy-handed dictatorship that steered the Philippines onto a steep slope that eventually crumbled in an avalanche of economic, political, and social crises.

The 1972 Winter Olympics, however, mainly served as an overture to its much-heralded sibling the Summer Olympics, which was held in Munich, West Germany, from August 26 to September 5. Although much of the event was overshadowed by what has come to be known as the Munich Massacre,[4] Cold War issues were not to be completely eclipsed. Of particular note was the basketball final between the United States and the USSR, which ended in one of the most controversial finishes in Olympic history. After a raucous ending that saw the Soviet team win 51–50, the Americans immediately filed a protest, which the five-member FIBA jury of appeal eventually denied.[5] There was speculation that the jury voted based on Cold War alliances and not on basketball rules, with representatives from Italy and Puerto Rico voting to uphold the protest while the jurors from Hungary, Cuba, and Poland voted to deny it.[6]

In Asia the paths of athletics and Cold War politics converged during a number of sporting events. One of those events, the controversial Games of the New Emerging Forces (GANEFO), was held in Jakarta, Indonesia, on November 10–22, 1963. The games were organized with the support of socialist states, particularly the USSR, China, and North Korea, to counter "the old and well-established Western tradition of the Olympics."[7] The event was planned by Indonesia primarily as a reaction to its suspension from the Olympic Games by the IOC (International Olympic Committee) for failing to provide travel visas to the delegates of Israel and Republic of China (Taiwan) when the country hosted the Fourth Asian Games the previous year. Under similar circumstances, FIBA had suspended the Philippines a few months earlier for refusing to provide entry visas to the Yugoslavian squad and other teams from socialist countries when the country was preparing to host the 1963 World Basketball Championship. As a result the country was excluded from the competition, the Basketball Association of the Philippines (BAP) was fined two thousand dollars, and the responsibility for hosting the event was passed to Brazil.[8] Almost twenty years after those incidents, Cold War–era ideological and political divisions were again highlighted during the boycotts of the 1980 Olympiad in Moscow. The boycotting nations included the Philippines and other Asian countries that were associated with the United States. In reprisal, the region's USSR-aligned socialist states refused to send delegates to the Los Angeles Olympic Games in 1984.

Cold War politics heightened some preexisting international sports rivalries, resulting in a number of highly publicized match-ups between opposing Asian countries. As one of the most ubiquitous team sports in the region, basketball was often transformed into a battleground where national teams fought it out for regional supremacy. The Asian Basketball Confederation (ABC, now FIBA Asia Championship for Men or simply FIBA-Asia) often turned into a spectacle not only of sheer sporting drama or national pride, but a symbolic showdown between the Cold War's opposing ideological paradigms.[9] Specifically, this regional basketball tournament saw the rise of China as a sporting powerhouse, reflecting its emergence from decades of isolation to its rise as a major global political and economic player in the twenty-first century. After its debut in 1975, China was able to suppress the basketball supremacy of the U.S.-aligned countries such as South Korea, Taiwan, and the Philippines, and has been dominating the biennial tournament since.

Apart from using basketball and other sports in promoting its global relevance, China also used them to foster good relations with its neighboring countries. For instance it reopened bilateral relations with the Philippines with a much publicized "basketball diplomacy" effort in 1974. In April of that year, a basketball delegation from the Philippines visited China as "goodwill envoys" to play a series of games against local teams. In return, a group of Chinese officials and basketball players arrived in the Philippines the same month to play against Filipino clubs. Prior to this, the last time a sports delegation from China visited the country was forty years earlier, during the 1934 Far Eastern Games in Manila.[10] The event mirrored the "Ping-Pong diplomacy" that culminated in U.S. president Richard Nixon's visit to China two years earlier. This series of events marked the opening of more favorable relations between the socialist country and the Philippines as well as with the rest of the world.

In contrast, the Philippines had a more domestic focus on the sport during most of the Cold War period. There has been a long-circulating conspiracy theory linking the rise of the PBA as an immensely popular entertainment spectacle and the extended rule of former president Ferdinand Marcos's authoritarian regime. For one, some of Marcos's closed allies played important roles in the league. Pablo Floro, Ricardo Silverio, and Eduardo Cojuangco, three of the former president's most trusted allies, owned the circuit's best-known teams. The historic rivalry between Floro's Crispa and Silverio's Toyota teams in particular has been credited with fueling the intense basketball fanaticism that is found not only on the hardwood but also deep within most Filipino homes.[11] In addition, the PBA games were shown on a television channel controlled by Marcos's top crony, Roberto Benedicto, while the network's most prominent anchor, Ronnie Nathanielz, was another noted Marcos loyalist. During this volatile period in Philippine history, the league arguably became useful to the regime's larger aim of diverting the attention of Filipinos from the transgressions of Marcos's dictatorial rule. Like the proliferation of pornographic films during the martial law period, PBA games became a titillating spectacle of physical prowess and melodramatic subplots.

Although this assertion remains to be explored further, there is another area where the link between the Marcos dictatorship and sports development is more evident. Two years after he declared martial law, Marcos dissolved the fifty-year-old PAAF, the country's sports governing body, and established the Ministry of Youth and Sports Development (MYSD). President Marcos himself wrote an article that was widely circulated to explain the philosophy behind the drastic change in the administration of sports in the country. Shifting from an externally oriented effort to gain international recognition, he emphasized the importance of sports in fostering a citizenry that is more subservient to the "nation." In particular he highlighted the values of a "team-man . . . who not only scores but helps others score."[12] During this period, mass calisthenics and physical exercise were widely promoted by the MYSD. Moreover, slogans such as *Sa Ikakaunlad ng Bayan, Ehersisyo ang Kailangan* (For the Progress of the Nation, Exercise Is Needed) were so widely circulated that they remain stuck in the minds of many people even decades later.

After five years of the MYSD program, the Marcos administration started to showcase its achievements in promoting healthier Filipinos by sending improved teams to international competitions. The Gintong Alay (Golden Offering) Program was established in 1979 to oversee the recruitment and training of athletes. The initial emphasis was on track and field, which offered more opportunities to win medals, although the program was eventually expanded to encompass all other sports.[13] The program achieved some success, and a number of the track and field stars who gained prominence in the Asian Games and other international competitions remain in the memory of many Filipino sports fans. Hence athletics, which afforded more opportunities for Filipinos to succeed, replaced basketball as the Marcos regime's channel for gaining international recognition.

Apart from Marcos, sports was also a favorite propaganda tool throughout Cold War Southeast Asia, where most of the countries were under authoritarian rulers.[14] Across the region, major sports events were used to bring large numbers of people together as audience not only to athletic competition but also to the conspicuous display of the state's power and its promotion of development plans and other national rhetoric. For instance the then newly independent country of Laos held its National Games in 1961 and 1964 to put its new military leader in the limelight and present a counternarrative of unity and progress at a time when the country was racked by conflicts and uncertainties.[15] On a larger scale the history of the Asian Games during this period shows how the staging of the event was dominated by political figures who shared the publicity with the sporting heroes.[16]

Basketball, Cold War, and the Americanization of Asia

The two Olympic events in 1972 illustrate how Cold War politics turned sports into symbolic battlefronts where high-profile victories or the boycott of major international sporting events were considered important diplomatic tactics.[17] Sports, however, was just one of the fronts in a larger cultural theater that included television, film, music, and other media. For instance, the Soviet Union's emphasis on sports was evident in its dominance of the Summer Olympic Games during the Cold War era; between 1952 to 1992, the communist superpower won the medal count six times, while the United States only did so three times. The USSR's supremacy was even more striking in the series of Winter Olympic Games in the same period, with seven medal-count victories.

The United States, in contrast, initially focused on film and mass media. Hollywood released its first Cold War–themed movie, *Invasion u.s.a.* in 1952, and it was followed by more than thirty films depicting the threat of nuclear war, espionage, and communist conspiracies.[18] Cold War themes also started appearing in books, television, music, and other media. As a cultural phenomenon, Hollywood quickly transcended the film industry, making its mark in other fields like professional sports. As a result, Cold War propaganda eventually penetrated the entire American entertainment industry, taking advantage of the favorable reception these cultural products received in many parts of the world. In particular, the use of new audiovisual technologies—initially developed for film and television productions—in broadcasting sports events allowed this popular pastime to expand its influence.

As the battlefront shifted to Asia after the outbreak of the Korean War in 1950, the region was subjected to a bombardment of American anticommunist-themed films and other means of propaganda. In the political context, the inroads made by American popular culture were part of the "containment" policy of the United States, which was a comprehensive plan devised to check the advance of communism by exposing its "evils" and by promoting the "goodness" of American ideologies such as democracy, capitalism, and individual freedom.[19] This American influence extended to the cultural and economic fronts. The corroding effect of deindustrialization in the United States beginning in the 1970s had many American companies looking overseas for expansion.[20] Corporate planners saw the consumer potential of the large Asian population and considered it an ideal place to market their products and services. Thus the raucous era of rock and roll, Hollywood blockbusters, and "Showtime" sports came to Asia as the Vietnam War and other lesser-known "proxy wars" between the United States and the USSR were being waged. The United States' major-league sports were promoted as a contrast to the rigid, military drill-like Soviet sporting model. The American sports represented a more free-flowing entertainment spectacle that resembled a Hollywood production.

Interestingly the entry of Hollywood did not suppress local Asian film industries, instead serving as a stimulus by introducing new production technologies and narrative themes. Several Asian film industries thrived, retaining their strong domestic followings while increasingly attracting the attention of international film viewers. New genres such as Westerns became popular in the 1970s, especially in the Philippines. In return Hollywood began accommodating Asian themes and settings into its own movie productions, especially in the animation and martial arts genres.[21] Likewise the inroads made by Anglo-American music and its attendant subcultural trends catalyzed the emergence of local popular music.

American cultural products, despite their growing influence in Asia, still met obstacles. Until the late 1980s, American television shows and films were strictly censored in many Asian countries, especially in those not aligned with the United States, because of suspicions that films and other visual media were being used for propaganda. In the same way, rock-and-roll and pop music were usually branded either as subversive or too progressive, and were largely deemed to be damaging, especially to the values of those in younger generations. Sports were not met with the same obstacles. Unlike television, film, and music, American sports not only flourished in U.S.-aligned countries but also thrived in most socialist countries. While the cultural context within which sports developed in socialist countries was quite different from the rationalities and values conveyed by major league sports, their presence nonetheless provided sporting entertainment with an essential link to the people's sensibilities.

Basketball, for instance, continued to flourish in communist China because of its strong association with the military and rural workers, which redefined its "popular" quality in Maoist terms.[22] Moreover, with China's opening up to the capitalist world beginning in the late 1970s, there was a dramatic upsurge in the following of professional basketball, closely resembling what was happening in the Philippines. Television also helped the game grow; one of the main factors behind basketball's appeal in China was "the ever tighter mutual dependency of sports and broadcast media, the reach of cable TV and its bottomless appetite for programming, and the overall trend of growing prosperity in East Asia through the last quarter of the 20th century."[23] Furthermore, compared with other U.S. sports, basketball was largely associated with American modernity due to its "scientific" origins and strong urban ties.[24] Thus basketball's promotion in the region was largely understood as "an extension of American moral, political, and commercial ambitions."[25] Judy Polumbaum, who studied the rise of basketball in China, noted the compatibility of the sport with contemporary popular culture, which is mainly dominated by the American entertainment industry. She remarked:

> Basketball is fairly easy for viewers and players to understand. At higher levels of play, especially, it incorporates a range of elements—speed and muscular skill, "quick thinking, resourcefulness, coordination, courage"—that provide players with varied challenges and spectators with drama and excitement . . . Evidently, as with action-adventures and violence from Hollywood, these properties travel across cultures.[26]

As a result the NBA was able to easily penetrate the Chinese market, now its biggest outside the United States. In addition the American league also tried hard to bring Chinese players to play in the United States to strengthen the NBA's link with its new frontier. Ultimately, the rise of Yao Ming into a league superstar after being drafted first overall by the Houston Rockets in 2000 gave the NBA a celebrity who bound the league even more closely with Chinese basketball fans.[27] The game has evolved into what Polumbaum called "a marker of Chinese modernization and world status," adding how in "political terms, the sport already is a vehicle for Chinese regional assertion through the Asian Games, with men's and women's teams regularly taking regional championships over the past two decades."[28]

The "Hollywoodization" of Philippine Basketball

In the Philippines, the late Cold War era saw basketball undergo another stage of "Americanization" as the professionalization of elite basketball in the mid-1970s unfolded a series of crucial changes that added a new chapter to the colorful history of the sport in the country. The period between the end of the Vietnam War in 1975 and the collapse of the Soviet Union in 1991 saw further inroads made by American popular culture, which resulted in a crucial shift in the national sports scene in the Philippines.

A number of developments in Philippine basketball defined this crucial period. First, the attempt to replicate the United States' NBA by a group of Filipino business leaders resulted in the establishment of the Philippine Basketball Association (PBA), the first professional basketball league in Asia. Second, the increasing influence of mass media, more specifically television, allowed the PBA to expand from a mere professional basketball league into a multifaceted entertainment enterprise. Finally, the evolution of the PBA into a mass-media spectacle resulted, in turn, in the rise of local sport celebrities. This group of athletes distinguished themselves from their predecessors by the reach of their appeal beyond the realm of sports; apart from displaying exceptional basketball skills on the hardwood, this new generation of sport celebrities was also involved in commercial endorsements, television shows, and films, and it received the media attention typically afforded showbiz personalities.

Play for Pay: Mimicry, Identity, Professionalization

> Your country is just great. In a country so far from America, I am amused by your [life]style . . . We have more [or] less the same mode of living. Your music, your fashion, movies and television shows, etc. are the same as ours. I'm surprised that you have lots of American programs on TV.[29]

Such were the words of Nate Stephens as he marveled at the unexpected familiarity of his new social environment a few weeks after he arrived in Manila in 1976. Stephens, a professional basketball player from the United States, was one of the "imports" hired to "spice up" the PBA games that year. However, he and a couple of other compatriots were not the only "foreign" aspects of the PBA. The same could be said of the league itself, with almost every facet of it copied from the NBA, the premier American basketball league. "Indeed men behind the local pro cage league have done almost everything and revived rules to make the league resemble the NBA," wrote one Filipino journalist.[30] Apart from tournament rules, mimicry was also evident in the way the local league formulated and organized its competition format, team management, and media broadcasting. Finally, bringing in the American cagers not only added taller and more athletic players to make the games more exciting, but also raised the league's overall level of play closer to that of the NBA.

Despite the evident influence of the NBA, the local league also had its own unique features, which could be attributed to the long history of basketball in the Philippines. For one, the PBA was entirely organized by Filipinos and it originated from a local amateur league called MICAA (Manila Industrial and Commercial Athletic Association). This commercial outfit was established in 1938, several years before the NBA started in 1946. Initially MICAA players consisted of employees holding day jobs, eventually evolving into a semiprofessional league featuring the country's best basketball athletes. By the 1970s, however, various issues plaguing the league divided its member teams into two camps—one aspiring for the professionalization of the league, the other wanting to keep its amateur status. The problems stemmed from the occasional drafting of MICAA players to the Philippine national team, which disappointed some team owners because the practice disrupted the league's schedule. In addition there were also questions about the amateur standing of MICAA players because most of them were already full-time athletes. There were also allegations that the players were actually paid via under-the-table deals to circumvent the rules that barred amateur cagers from receiving salaries.[31] Eventually this difference in opinion led some teams to bolt the MICAA to establish the PBA.

The second feature that set the PBA apart from the NBA was its geographical organization of franchises. Instead of having each team based in a particular city or province like the NBA, logistical limitations compelled the PBA to have all its teams based in Metro Manila. This setup especially suited the overall economic structure of the Philippines at that time, when large-scale facilities such as arenas were located in the country's capital. The large population concentrated in and around the metropolis provided the league with a strong base of followers. In addition the high logistical cost of regularly transporting teams from one city to another was just too much of a financial burden for a league whose pockets were not as deep as those of the NBA.

Third, the prominence of corporate sponsors of the league's teams likewise distinguished the PBA from its American counterpart. NBA teams are named after the city or the state where they are based, hence team names like Boston Celtics, New York Knicks, and Los Angeles Lakers. In comparison, PBA teams are named after the companies that own them, thus the names San Miguel Beermen, Alaska Milkmen, and Sta. Lucia Realtors. This is a reflection of the league's origins as an amateur commercial league. When the league started, a PBA official noted how it "was not a moneymaking operation," highlighting that "the value [for the PBA teams] was exposure for companies that had products to sell, of using their advertising budgets to finance their teams."[32] Lastly, the PBA also instituted some distinctive rules of play, the most notable of which was the introduction of the three-referee system, which aimed to prevent dirty plays and on-court melees that had become a fixture amid the startup league's intense competition and hostile rivalries. This rule was eventually adopted by the NBA in 1978 and has since become a permanent feature of America's top basketball league.[33]

Through these unique attributes, the PBA developed into a distinctly Filipino cultural icon despite its close resemblance to the NBA. The long history of the Philippines as a U.S. colony and post–World War II ally had created strong ties that made the United States' cultural practices an essential piece of the local cultural fabric. Thus unlike most other Asian countries, the inroads made by American popular culture in the region during the Cold War period did not really came as a novelty in the Philippines. The "professionalization" of the top basketball league in Philippines in 1975 was largely seen as a milestone in the continuous evolution of the sport in the country rather than as a product of the larger wave of "Americanization" that was, at that time, sweeping across the Asian region.

When Filipino basketball fans watched the PBA games, nothing about them seemed distinctly "American" to them apart from the presence of "imports" who would come to play for the local teams. Although these foreign reinforcements for the most part ended up as the game's best performers, they were not able to capture the same attention that was accorded popular Filipino cagers. In comparing the contributions of the American imports to those of the local players, a league official noted how they "only lend color to the tournaments . . . games in the PBA are won and lost by the local boys."[34] To underscore this distinction, only Filipino players are qualified for most of the prestigious year-end awards such as Most Valuable Player, in contrast to the NBA's practice of giving locals and foreign players equal footing in vying for individual honors. In consolation the foreign players compete among themselves for the far less heralded "Best Import" award. Finally, the league maintains an All-Filipino Conference where only locals can participate. Thus the PBA ensures that Filipino superstars shine the brightest.

When the PBA was established in 1975, many believed that the formation of the league was good for Philippine basketball. One proponent was Ramon Fernandez, one of the top players at that time who eventually went on to have an illustrious professional career. He noted how the establishment of the professional league would help the Filipinos improve their knowledge of the game. Moreover, Fernandez also thought that with the PBA, "young collegiate players would aspire to play a better brand of basketball to serve as their passport to the pro league where there is a higher standard of competition."[35] Indeed, with the availability of advanced facilities, well-trained coaches, and ample exposure to highly competitive games, the league was able to nurture the best basketball talents, most of whom later figured prominently in the local basketball scene. However, apart from the lure of being a professional athlete it provided, the PBA had also been attracting young players because of the public attention and the glamour that came with playing on the biggest stage of hoopsdom in the Philippines.

Basketball in a Box: Sport, Television, Mass Media

The professionalization of basketball in the Philippines was not simply a historical development confined to the field of sports. The advancement in mass-media technologies, particularly the widespread use of television, also contributed to the growth of the PBA. "For more than 50 years, Filipinos have been hooked on basketball," a veteran journalist wrote, "and with the television and radio broadcast of the games, our love for it has grown even more."[36] Television in particular contributed to the emergence of sports celebrities. David Andrews and Steven Jackson noted that television's "innate predilection for human intimacy, coupled with live sport's telegenic qualities, secured sport's place in the schedule during the early years of network television."[37]

Although sports have long been a regular feature of the local print media since the turn of the twentieth century, and have been broadcast on radio since the 1920s, it was only during the expansion of television broadcasting in the 1970s that the visual spectacle of sporting competitions was able to transcend the limited confines of the arena. The print media could only provide news or feature stories of sporting events and personalities. Radio afforded listeners more immediate information but they were still limited to the accounts and analysis of broadcasters, who were spectators themselves. The coming of television, however, enabled the audience not to only to know what happened but also, in a way, to experience the action themselves.

Television was not yet widely available in the Philippines when the PBA was established in the mid-1970s, with radio still being the most useful medium for reaching a nationwide audience. But television's era as the primary medium of mass entertainment was already beginning to dawn. Despite its limited reach, television earnings already contributed a significant part to the league's total revenue in its first year of operations.[38] A journalist's description of the role of television in the growing popularity of American professional basketball in the 1970s also proved to be true in the Philippines. He pointed out how television "made the game more potent commercially," expanding its audience base and allowing for more money to be made than before.[39] Unlike American professional basketball, however, the PBA was still largely influenced by its origins as an amateur intercorporate league and was still leagues away from the NBA's multibillion dollar business brand. The PBA was still unprofitable and remained reliant on subsidies from member companies to sustain operations.[40] This support from some of the country's top business conglomerates helped nurture the PBA during its years of infancy, but it did not take long before television helped the league to grow and achieve self-sustainability.

By the 1980s local media surveys showed that the PBA had developed into a widely viewed primetime television program. This transformation generally followed a larger global trend, which saw a reinforced relationship between professional leagues and television.[41] The 1981 television ratings placed the PBA fifth with a 17.3 percent audience share among multiweekly programs over a six-month period; it ranked behind two famous soap operas and two primetime news programs. The much-anticipated encounters involving the league's most popular teams could get as much as a 50 percent viewership share. As a result, television emerged as the PBA's top revenue source, especially with commercial outfits fighting it out for advertising spots during the game broadcasts. The broadcasting company that received the exclusive rights to show the PBA games on television in 1981 paid four million pesos, a huge amount of money at that time.[42]

Nonetheless increased revenue from television rights and advertisements did not dissuade the league from further improving its TV coverage format the following year. Indeed the number of innovations launched in the PBA's 1982 season led local sportswriters to dub it "The Year of Change."[43] Some of the most notable modifications were in technical production where new equipment, a more dynamic broadcasting style, and new expert analysts were introduced to make the PBA games more appealing to television viewers. The idea was to veer away from traditional play-by-play reporting of the events that transpired on the court. This outdated technique was a spillover from the radio era in which a detailed account of the play-by-play action was necessary for listeners to visualize what was going on during the game. With television this type of broadcasting became redundant because audiences were given direct visual contact to the action. The PBA adapted its broadcast style by bringing in three former coaches—two Filipinos, one American—as color commentators who provided expert analysis. These new game analysts helped the PBA come up with "lively, intelligent, and interesting" television coverage by providing "more insights into the game" and by making adjustments to "tone down on the obvious."[44] Noting how these changes would impact the overall philosophy of the country's premier professional basketball league, a league official noted, "We will be more analytical. We will use more cameras . . . It will be like the NBA, more professional."[45]

Generally these improvements in the television coverage of the PBA games enabled the league to bring basketball out of the arena and into the comfort of every follower's home. With high-tech, more probing, and portable cameras, the viewers could take a closer look at every play, or even see them from different angles. Instead of watching panoramic shots of vague moving figures, the new technology allowed fans to see their favorite basketball stars up close. Likewise, the technology that enabled the replay of the game's highlights prolonged the audience's excitement, which could have quickly dissipated given the fast pace of the game. Finally, the analytical reporting provided deeper, more informative, and more exciting coverage that relied not only on the commentator's expertise but also on well-researched and systematically compiled team statistics, individual profiles, and interesting trivia. Moreover it also became common practice for the game announcers to sensationalize and exaggerate their reactions to exceptional plays, regularly blurting out interjections to underscore slam dunks and other crowd-pleasing performances. These innovations made basketball more thrilling, action-packed, and full of drama—in short, they incorporated into the PBA games the distinctive qualities of a Hollywood show.

These changes proved effective: a 1988 survey ranked PBA games as the country's top multiweekly program, a significant improvement over their fifth-place ranking in 1981. In addition, "the All-Filipino Conference best-of-five championship series amass[ed] 65.6 percent on the average and [drew] a regular audience of over 3.2 million in Metro Manila" alone.[46] Moreover the rise of PBA as a prominent entertainment spectacle benefited the league's corporate sponsors both directly through their share of team and league revenues and indirectly through better exposure of their brands. "Without a doubt, our involvement in the PBA has improved the awareness of [our] brand. The championships that we've won have translated into improved sales," admitted the owner of a large food-processing company whose team was among the most successful in the league. He added, "There have been times right after a championship . . . when we saw improvement in sales. Our participation in the PBA has had a positive impact on the business as a whole."[47]

The growth of the PBA was continued over the next decade and the 1990s was marked by more innovations, not only in the broadcasting of the games but also in the sports arenas where the games were played. In order to make the games more exciting, the league held basketball-related contests for the audience, played lively music, and introduced different kinds of sideshows. "We give away T-shirts, we have performers, we have dancers, at the same time we have attracted glamorous personalities . . . We really want to promote the league as a vehicle of entertainment," Wilfred Uytengsu, PBA's former chairman, noted.[48] Moreover the lifting of FIBA's restriction against professionals in 1989 allowed the PBA to organize the national team and represent the country in international competitions. Similar to the United States' "Dream Team," the top PBA players selected to the national team became fan favorites, especially when they competed as a separate squad in PBA tournaments.

From Cagers to Celebrities

The development of the PBA during the late Cold War period also resulted in the ascension of basketball celebrities in the country's entertainment scene. Although highly popular athletes have been attracting huge numbers of followers since the early twentieth century, their prominence rarely went beyond the context of sports. The first Filipino basketball celebrity is undoubtedly Luis Salvador, a successful stage and film actor who played for the Philippine National Basketball Team from 1921 to 1925. Internationally he is best remembered for breaking the single-game point record (116 points) in an international basketball competition when he led the Philippine team to the championship against China during the 1923 Far Eastern Championship Games in Osaka.[49] However, the first professional basketball player to appear in a movie was Robert Jaworski, who in 1971 joined another famous basketball star, Freddie Webb, to top-bill *Fastbreak*, also the first basketball-themed film in the Philippines. Jaworski appeared in a few more film productions during his remarkable twenty-three-year professional basketball career. After suffering a critical injury, Webb dabbled in coaching PBA teams; however, he is more known for his stellar television acting career. Interestingly enough, both players became senators later in their lives.

A number of other basketball players eventually tried to follow their footsteps into the entertainment industry. However, with the Hollywoodization of Philippine basketball many of the more recent hoops stars did not even have to dabble in movie and television acting to achieve celebrity status. With the evolution of the PBA into a primetime television spectacle, many of its athletes have captured the type of media attention previously accorded only to famous movie and music personalities. Just like Hollywood celebrities, PBA stars were created through a combination of talent and the insatiable media attention that amplified their personalities. As one of its marquee players so aptly stated during the early years of the professional league:

> Makikilala ba ako kung hindi sa TV, sa magasin, sa diaryo? Maski maglaro ako araw-araw, maghapon, at magbumabad sa coliseum kung walang maglalagay sa peryodiko at sa TV, wala rin ako!

> [Would people know me if not for TV, the magazines, and the tabloids? Even if I play every day and stay in the coliseum from morning till late in the afternoon, if my name doesn't appear in the newspapers and on TV I would still be nobody!][50]

Few of the superstars that the league has churned out in its more than three decades of existence have attained the remarkable success of the "Glamour Boys."[51] Coming to the forefront of the PBA in 1988, the group was part of the "second generation" of Filipino basketball superstars who arrived as the celebrated pioneers of the league were losing their luster. They started a new era in the annals of the PBA and the history of Philippine basketball with their meteoric rise in the local entertainment scene. What distinguished the Glamour Boys from previous PBA superstars was their ability to shine beyond the world of basketball, a feat that only a few others have achieved. Apart from being decorated professional players, the Glamour Boys were also well-known as commercial models and product endorsers, and had cameo roles in television and movie productions. Stories and gossip regarding their professional and personal lives regularly graced the pages of local tabloids, magazines, and other print media. In short, they were more like showbiz personalities than mere basketball players. For the PBA, the importance of these celebrities was highlighted later on when a new professional league emerged to challenge its supremacy as the Philippines' premier basketball organization. The PBA responded by highlighting its well-known players and by marketing itself as "Bayan ng Superstars" (The Nation of Superstars).

The rise of professional basketball players as celebrities, however, has engendered its fair share of criticism. Many believe that the glitter and glamour of Tinseltown can be a distraction that affects an athlete's on-court performance. When Atoy Co, one of the PBA's earliest superstars, scored way below his average in a game in 1976, many writers were quick to blame his subpar performance on his overexposure to the showbiz lifestyle. The writers had good reason: while playing in the league that year, Co was also busy shooting his first movie appearance and taking time to look after a new restaurant that he opened with his actress girlfriend.[52] Stories like Atoy Co's have become commonplace throughout PBA's existence, as many of its players continue to receive enormous public attention as entertainment celebrities and pop-culture icons.

Beyond the glamour and its trappings, however, playing in the PBA has in itself been an immensely rewarding profession. When the league was established in 1975, players were just happy to get a stable salary, which was a considerable improvement over the meager allowance that they received during their amateur days. However, incomes have steadily increased as players' personalities have become more central to the existence of the league. By the early 1990s, the first multimillion contracts were being signed and many PBA players have been receiving similar compensation since then. Given the other benefits that could be derived through bonuses and endorsement deals, a PBA player's average income stands out as one of the highest among local entertainment celebrities.

Professional sports—especially basketball—is arguably the only avenue of social mobility in the country, in which talent alone is enough to get one from the bottom to the pinnacle of society. Not even the local film industry, whose stars often come from a number of "showbiz clans," can compare to this uncommon structure of meritocracy. Rags-to-riches stories abound, and the history of the

PBA is filled with tales of people overcoming great adversity. The league is "like a long-running television soap opera" according to its former commissioner; "To the ordinary fan, the PBA offers an escape from the clutches of endless politics, the troubles around the world, the pangs of hunger, and the litter of broken dreams."[53] As Garry Whannel points out, "Sport is presented largely in terms of stars and narratives: the media narrativises the events of sport, transforming them into stories with stars and characters; heroes and villains."[54] Through the years, the league's success has not only been evident in its effort to provide a widely accessible form of entertainment to its millions of followers; with the remarkable rise of its celebrated protagonists from the abyss of poverty and obscurity, it has also done its fair share of giving inspiration and hope to the millions of suffering and marginalized Filipinos.

The League and the Nation

The Hollywoodization of hoops has also served as a bridge that spans the chasm between social classes in the Philippines. This trend was especially apparent during the height of PBA's popularity in the early 1990s when the basketball arena became a trendy place for people "to see and to be seen." A sports journalist pointed out, "Whereas before, we had a crowd that was predominantly *masa* [from the masses], today the rich and beautiful, famous actors and actresses, and big-time like senators and congressmen mingle freely with our regular customers. Even presidential daughter Kris Aquino came in almost regularly at the Ultra [indoor stadium] for the games."[55] This turn of events was evident even beyond the arena: in the countryside or in urban slum areas, it became common for better-off families to open their doors and even windows so their less-privileged neighbors could watch basketball games from their television sets.

Moreover, the presence of President Cory Aquino's daughter among the crowd of fans also illustrated the expansion of interest in basketball to a group that in Philippine society was largely deemed to be uninterested in following sports: women. Although women have long been actively participating in various sports since the turn of the twentieth century, the avid following of spectator sports, with their propensity for violence and pervasiveness of gambling, has long been the reserve of men. However, with the Hollywoodization of hoops, basketball became not just a sport but also a star-studded spectacle that appealed even to those who did not know much about the game. "It was entertainment because the public enjoyed watching the game and you could see them get involved in the game, cheering, and so on," noted one former league executive. He added, "You met all kinds of people going to the games, women, young people, men. It was a healthy form of amusement."[56] In particular, the rise of the Glamour Boys in the late 1980s attracted a legion of female fans that were eager to get a glimpse of their beloved basketball superstars. To add more showbiz flavor to it all, the president's daughter was rumored to be dating one of the Glamour Boys at that time, which may have explained her frequent appearances at PBA games.

Aside from these notable changes, the Hollywoodization of hoops has also reshaped the overall character of hoop fandom in the country. Previously, Filipino basketball followers only intermittently came together as a collective body, typically when they supported the national team during international competitions. In the absence of these major sporting events, Filipino basketball followers generally retreated back to their own communities to follow the local or municipal leagues. However, this void was filled with the establishment of the PBA, as its thrice-a-week schedule spanning a ten-month period provided an extended attraction for the Filipino basketball fans.

In addition the television broadcasts of the games made the professional league accessible even to the most remote parts of the country. In this way, the convergence of basketball and mass media created a pervasive cultural phenomenon that, following Benedict Anderson, "created the possibility of a new form of imagined community."[57] Thus when a basketball player from the central Philippines distinguished himself during the early years of the

PBA, the media pointed out that he not only pleased the people of his province but the entire nation as well. A sports magazine article summarized one player's achievement, noting that "Manny Paner, that sturdy, most dependable hoopster who is [the] pride of most Cebuanos. Not only Cebuanos but Filipinos of all regions as well."[58] Arguably the rise of the game as a popular mass-media spectacle further unified Filipino basketball followers, if not an entire nation that has long been fragmented by geographical, ethnolinguistic, and other social divisions.

From National to Popular

With the increasing Hollywoodization of popular culture, the late Cold War period saw the Philippines' favorite pastime soar to new and greater heights. Ironically, this period also marked the time when the country struggled to make its mark in international basketball competitions. After decades of dominating the Asian basketball scene and making a number of notable showings in the Olympics and the World Basketball Championship, many local basketball followers were disappointed when the country started to suffer a long string of losses. The 1972 Munich Games gained significance as the last Olympic event for which the Philippine National Basketball Team qualified. Forgotten amid the drama of the USA–USSR championship game, the Philippines won games against Senegal and Japan to place thirteenth among sixteen participants. The country failed to win a game in any of the most prestigious international basketball tournaments until the recent 2014 FIBA World Cup in Spain.

In regional competitions, the Philippines bagged four of the first seven ABC crowns, with the last one coming at the 1974 tournament in Seoul. It went twelve years before winning the 1986 championships in Kuala Lumpur. It was another twenty-seven years before the Philippines made another notable showing, placing second to Iran in the 2013 FIBA-Asia tournament in Manila. The country has been even more unfortunate in its attempts to win the Asian Games basketball championship. After winning the first four championships at the prestigious regional sports event, the Philippine national team has repeatedly fallen short in its multiple attempts to reclaim the title. The last time it came anywhere close to taking the gold medal was in 1990 when the country placed second to the host Chinese team.

There are two obvious reasons behind the mediocre record of the Philippine National Basketball Team, particularly in regional basketball competitions, over the past three decades. First, the inroads made by American popular culture during the Cold War era and the promotion of basketball in socialist states (as a venue for the USSR and its satellites to play off their rivalry with the United States[59]) resulted in the rise of the sport in many Asian countries, thereby making the regional tournaments more competitive. As early as 1958 an American coach whose college basketball team came to play a series of games against Asian teams noted how the region had already shown greater interest in the sport:

> [Our] team traveled through 8 different countries in the Orient and found basketball improving at almost every area where we were privileged to play. The Philippines are still the leaders, but other countries are making rapid progress and we have found a real desire among some of the Asiatic basketball aspirants to learn everything possible about the game.[60]

Second, the professionalization of its top basketball league worked against the Philippines since important international basketball tournaments such as the Olympics, the World Basketball Championship, and the Asian Games were, until 1990, only open to amateur players. Hence the Philippines was forced to send second-rate athletes or inexperienced collegiate players between 1974 and 1990. Those young players did not fare well against the vastly improved national teams of South Korea, Japan, Taiwan, and China. So when the rest of the region was busy preparing for the 1977 ABC tournaments, the Philippines was contemplating if it should even participate in the event. "Perhaps if our players for that ABC would include [PBA players], then that would be a different story. *Pero masyado tayong napilayan* [but we were really crippled] . . . and these [national players] are really raw," a local sports magazine article reported.[61] The country eventually decided to send a delegation but the haphazardly organized team only placed fifth behind China, Korea, Japan, and Malaysia.

The string of losses in international competitions caused much frustration among local basketball fans. Criticisms also began to set in, especially from those who tried to revive the long-standing issue of the unsuitability of the game to the Filipino physical makeup. A prominent Filipino senator's message to an athletic delegation that had just returned from an unremarkable stint at the 1966 Asian Games effectively captured the sentiment of those who believed that basketball in the Philippines was being accorded too much importance. In his speech, he pointed out how

> A great deal of disappointment had been aired about our not winning in basketball. Even this fact to me is not discouraging. It should result in a modification of our attitude toward our undue emphasis in basketball. Our natural limitation of height does not enable us to win or even expect to win international championships. It is my considered observation that we had had undue attention to basketball. I admit that it is an excellent game but it is unnatural for us to expect winning against six footers or even seven footers.[62]

Similar comments have since surfaced many times, especially whenever another national basketball team returns from an international competition empty-handed. All these criticisms, however, seem to have little impact on the overall standing of basketball in the Philippines, as the sport continued to attract more followers with each passing year.

How did basketball remain popular in the Philippines even after its teams' dismal performance in international competitions? The answer is in the Hollywoodization of hoops, which has continued to uphold the popularity of basketball in the Philippines even as the country has languished in the cellar of international basketball hierarchy. Clearly the general emphasis of local basketball during the late Cold War period had shifted from an externally oriented national symbol to an inward-looking and self-perpetuating aspect of local popular culture. Thus the evolution of basketball from a national pastime to a multifaceted icon of the local entertainment scene has managed to keep the people's interest in the sport. The excitement of the PBA games and the league's overall image of glamour have proven just too fascinating and consuming, leaving little time for the Filipino basketball fans to ponder the country's disappointing performance in international competitions. As one veteran journalist so aptly puts it:

> We will not win a world basketball crown, or relive the glory days of Brazil in 1954 [when the Philippines won a bronze medal in the World Basketball Championships]. But it's no longer a question of how high our national team can rise in international arenas. What makes basketball a perennial top-grosser is the way our superstars play it. Or, more aptly, how we think these living icons play the game.[63]

Nonetheless the Hollywoodization of hoops does not suggest that the Filipinos enjoy watching the local PBA games on television so much that they have completely forgotten about the rest of the basketball world. In fact local basketball's development has been connected to larger processes that had been going on in almost every part of the globe. The rise of the PBA as the paramount stage of Philippine basketball, as Giulianotti and Robertson put it, was a "sporting corollary of the general trend toward MNC [multinational corporation] economic domination [where] privately owned teams [are more prominent] than the nationally representative ones."[64]

Eventually the influence of American popular culture spread to the rest of the region—especially in China, whose relationship with the United States took a decisive shift during the last two decades of the twentieth century. In the context of basketball, the impact of this crucial transformation is evident in how the sport evolved from something that in the 1970s was generally defined by its popular socialist context into its current structure, where "the globalizing commercial forces of the NBA and Nike [have displaced] the center of Chinese basketball world."[65] The development of basketball in the Asian region, therefore, represents the impact of the "Americanization of Asia" as well as demonstrates how sport becomes an important agent of social change. Finally, apart from the external influence exerted by the advance of mass media and the American popular culture since the late twentieth century, the internal construction of Philippine basketball, particularly through the active following of the local fans, has also contributed to the growth of the country's favorite pastime.

FIG. 1. (*above*) The Internal Revenue Team, winner of the 1916 National Basketball Championship (Filipino Division) poses in front of the American flag. From the collection of the Jorge B. Vargas Museum and Filipiniana Research Center, University of the Philippines.

FIG. 2. (*below*) Champion Philippine Team, Far Eastern Games, Shanghai 1915. *Left to right*: Silverio, Alemany, Garcia, Ylanan, Gonzales, Rabaya, Wilson. From the collection of the Jorge B. Vargas Museum and Filipiniana Research Center, University of the Philippines.

FIG. 3. A Filipino player takes a shot during the game against Uruguay at the 1936 Berlin Olympics. The Philippines won 33–23 in a contest played under pouring rain (note the spectators under their umbrellas). From the collection of the Jorge B. Vargas Museum and Filipiniana Research Center, University of the Philippines.

FIG. 4. The Philippine National Basketball Team was met by Brazilian officials shortly after their arrival in Rio de Janeiro for the 1954 World Basketball Championship. The team subsequently took third place in the tournament, the highest international basketball finish the country has achieved. From the collection of the Jorge B. Vargas Museum and Filipiniana Research Center, University of the Philippines.

FIG. 5. (*above*) The Derby Ace Llamados and the Meralco Bolts are two of the current eight teams in the Philippine Basketball Association (PBA), the world's second-oldest professional basketball league. Photo courtesy of Glenn Michael Tan.

FIG. 6. (*below*) The Ateneo de Manila University and Far Eastern University varsity teams prepare for a game during the 2012 University Athletics Association of the Philippines (UAAP) Finals. Photo courtesy of Karl James Angeles.

FIG. 7. Two Filipino defenders look helpless as NBA superstar Kevin Durant dunks the ball during the 2012 Ultimate All-Star Weekend, which featured a group of top NBA players suiting up against a PBA all-star team. Photo courtesy of Glenn Michael Tan.

FIG. 8. Members of the Smart Gilas, the Philippines' national team, huddle before a game during the 2013 FIBA-Asia championships in Manila. Photo courtesy of Glenn Michael Tan.

4 Rooting for the Underdog

Sports, Spectatorship, Subalternity

Can you imagine playing in a place with empty seats?
—Robert Jaworski

Basketball has come a long way from its origin as a physical education regimen carried out inside confined gymnasiums to its
current status as one of the most popular spectator sports in the
world. Since the 1970s basketball has evolved into a huge public
spectacle, with many followers who do not even play the sport. In
the Philippines a nationwide survey shows that about 73.5 percent
of the total population aged eighteen years and older follow basketball, either as live spectators or television viewers, and about
34 percent mentioned the game as their favorite sport to play.[1]

Filipino basketball followers across the country readily come
together to witness their favorite teams and players. From the
glitzy arenas of the top professional league in Metro Manila to
the dusty makeshift playgrounds in far-flung villages, no game
seems to be complete without the spectators who come to watch
all the action and, in most cases, become part of the spectacle
themselves.

Filipinos were introduced to basketball as spectators. The local
population, it is said, learned the basics of the game by watching
U.S. soldiers put their rifles aside to shoot hoops for recreation
during the American colonial period.[2] Since then, basketball

followers—in their various manifestations as spectators, supporters, viewers, groupies, and die-hard fans—have continuously played an important role in making basketball an integral aspect of Filipino everyday life.

This chapter aims to provide a view of the historical and social significance of basketball in the Philippines from the perspective of sports fans during the last decade of the twentieth century, a period that is largely considered the country's golden age of professional basketball. It argues that the popularity of basketball in the Philippines partly hinges on the sport's evolution into a subaltern spectacle in which the struggles of ordinary Filipinos are symbolically played out. This argument follows the proposition of Vandello and others who have argued that the "motivation for supporting underdogs might derive less from abstract moral concerns about fairness and more from self-interested, rational calculations of one's own emotion."[3] Thus by "rooting for the underdog," local basketball followers are clearly not only cheering for their favorite team but also rooting for themselves, and for the many other real underdogs outside the playing court.

This discussion focuses on Ginebra, more popularly known in the Philippine Basketball Association (PBA) as the "team of the masses" for its strong fan appeal especially among the lower rung of Philippine society. The discussion is divided into three parts: The first section relates basketball with the practice of cockfighting, a form of entertainment and gambling that was prevalent during the Spanish colonial regime. The "fowl game" is often referred to as the predecessor of basketball since it was the most popular public spectacle in the country before the introduction of modern sports at the turn of the twentieth century. The second part traces the development of Ginebra from a mediocre squad into the most popular team in the history of Philippine basketball.

Finally, the last section centers on a textual analysis of a couple of novelty songs that portray the sentiments of an avid basketball follower. The object of the fans' affection is, of course, Barangay Ginebra. The songs "Kapag Natatalo ang Ginebra" ("When Ginebra

Loses") and "Kapag Nananalo ang Ginebra" ("When Ginebra Wins") were released during Ginebra's celebrated championship run in 1997, and both tunes became the "national anthem" of the team's millions of fans. Although the songs are riddled with hyperbolic representations, they nonetheless reflect the devotion and passion that many Filipinos have for their favorite pastime. As texts, these two popular songs can help us unravel the entanglements that bind basketball and culture so closely together. In addition, the textual analysis is supplemented by interviews with basketball fans from Metro Manila and Davao City on the southern island of Mindanao. The interview subjects were chosen based on their knowledge of the national and international basketball stages as well as for their involvement in local basketball leagues and informal pickup games.

From Fowl Game to Foul Team

Although basketball fandom only developed in the Philippines at the turn of the last century, spectatorship had been around long before the rules of any modern sport were codified. During the precolonial period, harvest festivals and other important community events provided opportunities for people to come together to witness and participate in various forms of competitions and other attractions. Many of these practices remained even during the Spanish colonial period, although they were often infused with new meanings that were associated with the hegemonic Roman Catholic religion.[4]

A common public spectacle that thrived under the friar-dominated Spanish regime was the popular pastime of cockfighting. Writers dealing with the history of sports in the Philippines before the twentieth century often refer to the ubiquitous cockpit as the site of public spectacle that can now be largely observed on the basketball court.[5] When the United States took power, however, American colonial administrators made a determined effort to curtail the influence of the traditional fowl game, which they saw as a degenerating vice and a source of other social evils. In a letter to the YMCA's New York Headquarters in 1912, J. M. Groves reported on the important role of the Christian organization in countering the negative influence of cockfighting in Manila:

> The Filipinos are notably social by racial instinct. Their love of getting together explains partly the hold of the cockpit and the "fiesta." They realize that to combat the cockpit, low dance balls and other evils that assail their youth, wholesome substitute recreation must be provided and for this they look to the YMCA.[6]

Diversion and Defiance in the Colonial Pastime

Apart from being major crowd-drawers, both the cockpit and the hardwood are subaltern spaces where the thrills of subversion and the possibilities of emancipation are fleetingly experienced by the subjugated. In his insightful work on the social significance of cockfighting in the Spanish Philippines, Filomeno Aguilar Jr. sees in the popular gambling activity the ludic incarnation of the "clash of spirits." He describes this concept as pertaining to the "overlapping world of the indigenous and the colonial" that often resulted in the "cultural entrapment" of the local people, with the natives attempting to evade the fatal consequences of their captivity through a calculated two-pronged strategy of submission and resistance.[7] In the same way, professional basketball, especially during the height of its popularity in the 1990s, is often seen as a microcosm of Philippine society.[8] The basketball arena is considered a subaltern site wherein the struggles of the people against the prevailing political and economic forces that are corrosively impacting their everyday lives are symbolically played out.

Moreover, aside from their appeal as spectacles, the cockpit and the hardwood have also enticed people with the promise of an easy solution to their predicaments. Gambling, although widely considered the undesirable underside of sport, allows people to dream and to hope for a better life, which seems impossible to achieve through the usual channels. Despite the wholesome image that basketball, and especially the country's professional league, has tried to cultivate, the game of "ending"—a form of illegal gambling based on the final scores of PBA games—came to prominence in the 1990s.[9] The game of chance was particularly popular in the countryside and among the lower classes despite strict government prohibition. This reflects the position of cockfighting during the Spanish colonial period when the rationalities held by the people who practiced the game conflicted with the values espoused by the influential Catholic Church. Hence, just as on today's hardwood, "the internal message of the cockpit," according to Aguilar, "was counterhegemonic." He explains:

> The indigenous red was not the underdog; it could be asserted and bet on as the favorite by the real underdogs outside the cockpit. Red could win, but so could white. Since the outcome was never truly predictable, the native at least had an imaginary fifty-fifty chance. And so whenever red and white clashed in the arena, the power encounter between the indigenous and the Hispanic realms was reenacted all over again . . . as though the historical outcome was totally unknown.[10]

The phenomenon of basketball fanaticism mirrors these subaltern qualities of cockfighting in the colonial Philippines. Filipino sports journalist Recah Trinidad has pointed out how basketball and Filipinos were a "bad match" because of the islanders' generally small physique. In addition, the game's origin as a winter game also runs in contrast with the country's tropical climate. Furthermore, Trinidad has suggested that the Filipinos' insistence on playing and following basketball is, in fact, a reflection of their long-established propensity for "defiance." He added:

> There is deep within the Pinoy [Filipino] cager . . . the heart of a rebel. And nothing could be sweeter, blood-pumping than to see our cager sneaking up and gracefully propelling himself in the air and scoring a basket against a tall, hulking foreign foe.

The ritual of defiance started in Cebu. If Lapu-Lapu, shorter and with inferior artillery, was able to topple and kill the imperious Ferdinand Magellan [considered as the Western "discoverer" of the Philippines], why can't our basketeer be allowed to relive and relish memories of the triumph at Mactan on the hardcourt?[11]

The reference to the 1521 Battle of Mactan was an attempt to place basketball in the larger narrative of the country's history of struggle against foreign aggression. This historic event has remained a popular representation of the possibility of a subaltern victory, although a recent study challenges the commonly held assumption that the natives' triumph relied mainly on their courage and unconventional warfare tactics.[12] The defeat of Spanish imperial forces by local warriors led by Lapu-Lapu (a chieftain in Mactan, a small island off Cebu in the central Philippines) was used by Trinidad, in the context of basketball, as an inspiration for the "small" Filipinos in their forays into the "game of the giants."

In the PBA, however, the dichotomy has moved from a distinguishable native-foreign or colony-empire binary into a haze of interchangeable identifications. In the absence of an immediately identifiable antagonist, the red-white distinction that characterized the colonial cockfight has become a blurred montage of symbols and representations. Often, identifying which team is the underdog varies according to different factors, such as the composition of players, the venue of the game, or the team's image as determined by the overall ethos of its sponsoring company.

Aside from these factors, the general socioeconomic background of its followers has also played an important role in determining the position of a particular team in the underdog-favorite binary. This trend follows the larger shift in Philippine society where the foreign-native dichotomy of the colonial period has been replaced by the current division between the elites and the masses. The PBA, the premier cockpit of the most popular spectator event in the country over the past three decades, becomes the site of this contemporary "clash of spirits." Although all teams have supporters from both sides of the social divide, each club tends to appeal more to certain groups of fans because of several factors, such as the consumer product they represent, the social backgrounds of their prominent players, the club's won-loss record, and most importantly, their style of play.

The Team of the Masses

From 1975 to the early 1980s, the elite-masses binary was evident in the historic rivalry between the PBA's two most popular teams: Toyota and Crispa. The Toyota Super Corollas largely appealed to the middle and upper classes, primarily because their prominent players were *mestizos* (Spanish Filipino or Filipino American) who usually belonged to or identified with the upper crust of Philippine society. In addition, the products of the car company that sponsored the team were beyond the reach of many poor Filipinos. In contrast, the Crispa Redmanizers were perceived as the team of the masses because of the working-class or provincial origins of their players. The company that supported the team also manufactured cheap, mass-produced clothing marketed mainly to lower-class consumers.[13]

Luisito Tabay, a company driver who lived near the Crispa factory in Pasig, Metro Manila, recalls how the Toyota players were mostly *tisoy* (the colloquial word for *mestizo*), *makinis* (smooth-complexioned), and *parang mga artista* (like film stars). Not surprisingly he attributes these qualities to the Toyota players' lack of exposure to sunshine (*di naiinitan*). More interestingly he refers to himself instead of the Crispa players when making a comparison with the Toyota players. He said, "*Di kagaya ng trabaho ko sa delivery, lagi akong nasa labas, naaarawan, at na-aalikabukan kaya medyo nognog ako*" ("Unlike my job as a delivery truck driver, I always stay constantly exposed to the sun and dust, that is why I am rather burnt."). By describing the Toyota players in these terms, he was implicitly contrasting them with the Crispa players, with whom he identified. Luisito's explanation shows an instance of ascription to a particular social class category fusing the bond between a fan and his favorite team.

Despite their immense popularity, both the Crispa and Toyota basketball teams disbanded during the economic turmoil that engulfed the country in the mid-1980s. Apart from the financial crisis that affected the sponsoring companies, many believed that their downfall was due to the strong connection between their owners and the ousted Marcos regime. Among the teams that emerged to take their place, the Ginebra franchise[14] garnered the most ardent followers. Although the club had been in the PBA since 1979, it was only during the mid-1980s that Ginebra also came to prominence as the overwhelming crowd favorite. Unlike Crispa and Toyota, however, the team's popularity was not built on a remarkable winning record or the exceptional talent of its players. (In less than ten years as PBA members, Crispa teams amassed thirteen championships while Toyota squads ran away with nine.[15]) Ginebra won the top prize only eight times in a span of thirty years. Ginebra's limited success can be directly attributed to the overall talents of its players. Compared to its legendary predecessor teams that consisted of basketball superstars, Ginebra was basically a ragtag squad of marginal stars and role players. In fact, almost half of the twenty-five all-time best players chosen for the PBA's Twenty-Fifth Anniversary All-Star Team in 1999 were from Crispa and Toyota;[16] only Robert Jaworski could be identified primarily with Ginebra, although three other players in the list joined the club briefly at some points in their careers.

How then did Ginebra become the most popular PBA team of the past two decades given its unremarkable winning record? The answer lies in the type of basketball they play. The team became well known for its tightly fought games and come-from-behind victories that were based on run-and-gun offense and bruising defense. Both tactics proved tremendously appealing to the fans. Despite having only marginal players during most of the seasons in the 1990s, Ginebra more than made up for it with its toughness and audacity. The team's "fight it out till the end" approach and its propensity to win (or lose) close games gained for the club numerous loyal supporters. Just like Crispa, most of Ginebra's avid fans belonged to the lower rung of Philippine society, and they could relate to the club's hardworking and sometimes brutish style of play.

Even though they exude a blue-collar image, the team's color is red. This color is a reminder of the scarlet fighting cock that represented the natives, the social underdog in Spanish colonial society. The color also represents life and robustness, if not magical endowments,[17] which some supporters believed enabled Ginebra to carve out victory even if its players were badly mismatched against their opponents. Because their "never-say-die" style of play enabled them to attract a huge following despite their mediocre winning record, Ginebra came to be known in the PBA as a perennial underdog and, consequently, "the team of the masses."

Play Basketball and Be a Senator

A discussion of the Ginebra team would not be complete without a note on Robert Jaworski. Widely considered the most popular Filipino basketball player ever, the highly charismatic Jaworski joined the team in 1984. Ironically he came from the disbanded Toyota, the team that was largely identified with the elites. The predominantly proletarian fans of Ginebra who used to despise him for his *mestizo* swagger eventually admired him for the aggressive and rough style of play that came to define the team's blue-collar identity. Despite his *mestizo* looks, which Jaworski got from his Polish-American father, he had humble beginnings growing up in a working-class district of Manila. His modest upbringing enabled him to connect well with the majority of Ginebra fans.

Jaworski was already thirty-eight years old and in the twilight of his playing career when he transferred to Ginebra. Moreover, he had never been considered an exceptionally talented athlete even when he was at the peak of his career. "As a player," one fellow PBA star explained, "Sonny [Jaworski's nickname] is ordinary, *walang* specialty [he has no special basketball skills]. It's his heart, his spirit that matters."[18] He brought to the team the toughness and fighting spirit he was known for during his heyday playing for the famed Toyota franchise. Ginebra's unrelenting style of play first caught the attention of Filipino fans in a game in 1985 when Jaworski had to be rushed to a hospital because of an injury. Instead of merely calling it a day, he decided to return to the arena after getting treatment. With Ginebra's opponent enjoying a sizeable lead late in the game, Jaworski's decision to return and play despite his injury inspired his team and they rallied to a dramatic victory that resulted in wild celebration among the spectators. Just as the Battle of Mactan is to Philippine nationalism, this event became the watershed of Ginebra's status as one of the most celebrated teams in the history of Philippine basketball.

In 1986 team management recognized Jaworski's strong leadership qualities and appointed him as player-coach. He remained in that position until he left the league in 1998 after his election to the Philippine senate.[19] However, even as a coach Jaworski was not really known for his basketball acumen. A fellow PBA coach noted that he was really "not technical and scientific" but "knew how to draw the most from his players"; the coach added, "The one thing you knew about Sonny Jaworski's teams is that they came out and played hard every night."[20] In 1988 Jaworski led his squad to the league's All-Filipino championship. The team's achievement became one of the main stories in the 1988 PBA annual yearbook, which recognized Jaworski for "steering an Añejo [the name Ginebra used that year] squad that had no full-fledged superstar . . . With only a big fighting heart as high-octane fuel Añejo rode on the sheer madness of crowd support to beat the highly-favored Purefoods [team]" in the finals.[21] Jaworski's remarkable career spanned more than two decades, from 1975 until his final game when he was already fifty-one years old. This exceptional display of longevity is almost impossible to replicate in the grueling world of professional basketball. "The Living Legend," as Jaworski was fondly called, reluctantly left the PBA in 1998 after his successful foray into national politics.

It should be noted that Jaworski followed the footsteps of Ambrosio Padilla and Freddie Webb, former national basketball players who later served as senators of the Republic of the Philippines. Padilla, who was captain of the 1936 Philippine team that placed fifth in the Berlin Olympics, was elected to the Senate in 1957. Webb, who was part of the 1972 national team that participated in the Munich Olympics, was elected senator in 1992. Unlike Jaworski, however, Padilla was a prominent lawyer who had served as Solicitor General and in other prominent government posts. Meanwhile Webb was a long-tenured local politician before winning a post in the upper house of the country's legislative body.

Jaworski's popularity as a basketball celebrity was enough for him to amass almost nine million votes, which placed him ninth among the candidates vying for the twelve open seats. Unfortunately, his political career was largely unremarkable and he gained a reputation as one of the Senate's less eloquent members by shying away from parliamentary debates and from publicly airing his opinion on national issues. He eventually lost his reelection bid in 2004 after receiving 3.5 million fewer votes than the last-placed elected senator.[22] His failed reelection bid was taken by antipopulist groups as a sign of the Filipinos' "political maturity," with people starting to base their votes on candidates' political platforms and records of public service rather than on their popularity as media personalities. Robert Nestor Tan, a call-center employee, recalls how irked he was by the insistence of his father, a die-hard Ginebra fan, that he should support the reelection of Jaworski. Tan believed the former senator was not brilliant enough to deserve a seat among the highly esteemed members of the legislative body; his father, a fan, thought otherwise.

The Team of Fouls

Despite its relative success in the PBA, Ginebra also received its fair share of criticism. In particular the team's rough defensive style had been denounced repeatedly as bordering on outright dirty and unsportsmanlike. An analysis of Ginebra's defense during the 1989 PBA season noted that the team liked "to make you feel their defense. They play it rugged and physical. [The team] intimidates, threatens, scares but gets the job done."[23] One of their well-known players, Rudy Distrito, was nicknamed "The Destroyer" for his feared defensive tactics that had a couple opposing players suffering serious injuries.[24] Hence the "people's team" was also known as the "team of fouls" for its proclivity for committing excessive physical contact against their opponents. Furthermore, the fact that the name Ginebra was also the brand name of the best-selling gin in the country proved to be both a boon and a bane to the team. While the popularity of the alcoholic drink across the country enabled the team to connect with ordinary Filipino fans, the association with intoxicating spirits also highlighted the team's tendency for violence and rowdiness. This negative image was easily taken as a reflection of the socially disruptive behavior of the "uncivilized" masses with whom Ginebra, as the PBA's perennial underdog team, was mainly associated.

The Ups and Downs of Being a Fan

Understanding the phenomenal popularity of the Ginebra team, and more generally the profound influence of basketball in the everyday life of most Filipinos, can be difficult. Alexander Wolff, a well-known American basketball writer, describes the widespread practice and following of basketball in the Philippines simply as "madness."[25] Indeed, the term "fans"—used here interchangeably with spectators, supporters, and followers—refers to the "emotionally committed 'consumer' of sport events,"[26] who is generally viewed as "an obsessed individual: someone who has an intense interest in a certain team" or celebrity.[27] Nevertheless, despite the apparent irrationality of their actions, a study of fandom reveals a perceptive view not only regarding the contours of basketball as a "hegemonic sporting culture"[28] but also of the larger cultural landscape of the society in which it is situated.

Because of Ginebra's widespread popularity as the "team of the masses," an examination of the experience and rationalities of its loyal fans reveals certain points that can help us understand the popularity of basketball in the Philippines. Because "spectators not only watch games but also identify with the team themselves,"[29] their experiences can provide what historian Reynaldo Ileto refers to as an "opportunity to study the workings of the popular mind."[30] In this context we shall look into two novelty songs that were written as Ginebra's "fan anthems" in the wake of its celebrated championship run in 1997. These songs provide valuable insights into the mentality and the worldview of basketball's most avid followers. Essentially they provide a basis for a phenomenological analysis of the historical and social significance of this sport in the Philippines. Excerpts of the two songs (with English translations) are quoted as reference points to the various themes that are covered by the discussion. Their melodic and lyrical structures follow the chronological order and the overall "rhythm" of a basketball game. In particular the verses contain an animated description of basketball actions from the opening tip to the second half, with the momentum gradually building up to the last few minutes of play.

When Ginebra Loses: Subaltern Struggle as Spectacle

The first song, "Kapag Natatalo Ang Ginebra" ("When Ginebra Loses") was written and recorded by Gary Granada, an award-winning folk singer and hardcore Ginebra fan. The storyline centers on a Ginebra fan pouring out his feelings while watching his favorite team struggle in a game. The fan starts by relating how he "religiously" attends every match—a faithful follower enchanted by the rituals of the game, the veneration of athlete-heroes, and the celebration of one's identity as part of a larger congregation. Allen Guttmann in his seminal work *Sports Spectators* notes how fans "experience something akin to worship."[31] The association of sport-following to religion is a common observation, and one that reflects the huge influence of sports in the contemporary world.

This was true for basketball in the Philippines in the 1990s, and certainly remains so even now. According to Recah Trinidad,

"Today's Filipino is basically a man of two religions. He is a god-fearing Christian and an irrepressible basketball devotee." He adds, "While he makes it a point to attend Sunday Mass, at times rather reluctantly, he willingly worships through most of the week in the national basketball temple or at his very home before the TV."[32] In the song, the faithfulness of the fan to his favorite team is seen in how he continues to attend its games even as it struggles to win.

> Kahit hindi relihiyoso
> Naaalala ko ang mga santo
> O San Miguel, Santa Lucia
> Sana manalo ang Ginebra

> [Even if I'm not religious
> I remember to call on the saints
> O, Saint Michael, Saint Lucy
> I pray that Ginebra wins]

The lyrics reveal a sense of contradiction in this Christian–basketball fan dualism that Trinidad argues is part of Filipino religiosity. The character in the songs readily admits that he is not really *relihiyoso* [religious] but nonetheless calls on the saints—San Miguel and Santa Lucia—to intercede so Ginebra will win. Wittily, San Miguel and Santa Lucia refer not only to the venerated Catholic figures but are also names of other PBA clubs. The San Miguel team is owned by San Miguel Corporation, the Philippines' largest conglomerate whose flagship enterprise manufactures beer, while the Santa Lucia team is named after its sponsor, one of the biggest real estate developers in the country. This comical play on words reflects the ubiquity of religious symbols and the prominence of the Catholic Church in Philippine society.

On the whole, religion, either literally as Catholicism or metaphorically as basketball, is a refuge from the challenges and vagaries of everyday life. The coliseum, just like the church, provides the basketball fan a sense of community and belonging, inspired by rituals that celebrate suffering and sacrifice, and a promise that underdogs will have a chance to redeem themselves in the end. In addition, in this knowledge-driven age the coliseum and the church are among the few places where science or even rational thinking is not necessary in order to make sense of the world.

If basketball is indeed a religion, its games are far from mere solemn rituals. On the contrary, they resemble major fiestas (feast-day celebration) where the crowd, the revelry, and an overall atmosphere of gaiety prevail. In fact, the cheering and taunting borders on and occasionally spills over into raucous celebration and hostility between opposing camps. In contrast to the actions of European football fans, however, these confrontations rarely result in violence. One of the main reasons for the absence of hooliganism lies in the nature of fandom in the PBA: Since the teams are not rooted in a particular city or aligned with any other geographical or political division, the connection among fans is held together by their *symbolic* interest in a particular team and not by a *real* bond that results from a common ethnic background, geographical identification, or a shared community experience. The word *barangay* mentioned in the fifth line of the verse refers to the smallest political unit in the Philippines, often a cluster of small villages believed to have had a tradition of strong communitarianism. However, this term has also been used since the 1990s to refer to the throng of loyal fans that attend every Ginebra game. The characterization became so popular that the team officially changed its name to Barangay Ginebra in 1999. The *barangay* in the context of fandom in the PBA, therefore, is an "imagined community" whose temporal and geographic coordinates transcend the confines of a locality.[33] This absence of geographical rootedness has spared the league's fans from the inherent animosity between localities that can result from a history of conflicts and other forms of rivalry both real and imagined. More often the taunting and the disruptive behaviors mentioned in the song are not meant to incite a fight with rival fans but to provoke aggression and a more physical contest between the opposing players. Hence, just like the colonial cockfight, violence remains mostly as a spectacle that rarely spills out of the playing court.

Moreover a number of studies have underscored how modern sports offer a sense of belonging that is fading from other aspects of contemporary life.[34] In his seminal work *Consuming Sport*, Garry Crawford observes that as "'traditional' sources of community have begun to decline, such as those based upon family and local networks, the sense of community offered by contemporary sport becomes increasingly important."[35] Along the same lines, Sean Brown suggests that one's affiliation with a sports team is a way of dealing with "the incongruences of a world seeking more freedom whilst lamenting the loss of a secure world."[36] Among the Ginebra followers however, being a fan is seen mainly not as a replacement for a lost sense of community but as a venue for the continual expression and celebration of communitarian values and relations. Andrew Chua, an avid Ginebra fan, sees his frequent attendance at his favorite team's games as an opportunity to unwind with the officemates who have turned into some of his closest friends over their seven years of working together.

The absence of affiliation of the PBA clubs with a particular locality has left them with no immediate support base, a peculiarity for a professional sports league. Instead, teams largely gather their core of loyal supporters from among the employees of their sponsoring companies. For instance, employees of San Miguel Corporation (SMC), the Philippines' largest conglomerate and the owner of the Ginebra franchise, have access to free or discounted tickets to games. The company even regularly provides uniforms, banners, and other cheering materials that distinguish the employees from other supporters during Ginebra matches. Apart from tickets and other freebies, however, many workers consider cheering for their company's team an expression of pride and loyalty to their employers. Chua, an SMC employee, related how going to Ginebra's games made him feel honored to be part of a prestigious company. Wolff observed similar behavior in Japan, "where workers at Nippon Express [a company that owns a baseball club] . . . dutifully filled the stands and sang the company anthem" during home games.[37] These cases reflect the origins of many professional sports league as amateur intercompany tournaments organized to promote physical fitness among factory workers as well as to provide entertainment to offset the drudgery of working on the assembly lines.

Apart from having a more direct affiliation with the team, employee-fans also form an actual community based on the shared experiences of its members as fellow workers, or as long-term supporters occupying the same spot in the rafters. Employees serve as the core residents of the *barangay*, the imagined village that refers to the large number of followers that flock to Ginebra's every game. The energy of the cheering crowd often emanates from the core group and reverberates around the coliseum throughout most of the contest. With the incomparable support from the *barangay*, the team in effect enjoys a "home-court advantage" in each of its matches. Thus the song's reference to the other teams/companies (i.e., San Miguel and Santa Lucia) shows how boundaries are defined and identities are marked out in a league that lacks the usual categories of differentiation, such as community or regional affiliation.

> Ang barangay ay nagdiriwang
> halftime ay kinse ang lamang
> Cameraman, huwag mo lang kukunan
> Si senador at congressman
>
> [The barangay is celebrating
> At halftime we are ahead by fifteen
> Cameraman, just steer away
> from the senator and congressman]

Like basketball, following the spectacle surrounding electoral politics has long been a favorite pastime in the Philippines.[38] These two popular attractions converge in the PBA—as the last part of the stanza above suggests. In the 1990s the widespread popularity of the country's premier league caught the attention of the nation's political leaders, who eventually became fixtures at the league's games. One of the most notable attendees was former president Joseph Estrada, who during that decade made a remarkable ascent from senator to vice-president before making it all the way to Malacañang (the Philippines' presidential palace) largely by presenting himself as "the hero of the masses."

Like Estrada, whose family owned a professional basketball team for a time, many of the politicians who made conspicuous visits during the matches were true basketball fans. However it was quite apparent that despite their interest in the sport, they also attended games to attract the attention of the live spectators and television audiences who constituted a large chunk of the voting population. League officials openly welcomed these VIPs because their presence helped to raise and legitimize the PBA's status as one of the country's top sport attractions. Most of the fans, however, thought that the politicians' limelight-grabbing presence desecrated their hallowed coliseum with excessive politicking, which was associated with corruption and the overall moral decay dragging the country into a deep social crisis. "*Sobra na! halos sa lahat ng isyu nandun na sila, pati ba naman sa basketball? Para na yan sa mga tao para makapaglibang naman sa kabila ng mga kaguluhan sa atin*" ["It is too much! You can find them in almost any issues, shouldn't they spare basketball? This is supposed to be for the people to enjoy and take a breather from the various social problems that we have"], explained Lucedillo Goser, a basketball fan from Marikina, Metro Manila. Thus the verse ends with the fan pleading to the cameraman not to train his lens on the senator and the congressman who came to see the game.

Part of the song describes the action in the second half of a basketball game, where the contest intensifies and becomes more exciting for the spectators. It features some of the most prominent Ginebra players from the 1997 PBA Commissioner's Cup championship team. However, instead of performing heroic maneuvers to lead their team to victory, they altogether fumble their plays, miss their shots, have their passes intercepted, and commit all sorts of violations. Apart from being a basketball-themed dramatization of a subaltern struggle, the verses also portray how the fans identify with the difficulties their basketball heroes face. Thus the lyrics describe how the protagonist's world comes "crumbling down" after the ball was stolen from Bal David, the team's most skillful dribbler, or how his "exasperation started to pile up" when Marlou Aquino and Wilmer Ong, their best defenders, were disqualified from playing the rest of the game after fouling out.

As in the cockfight, the basketball game turns into what Aguilar calls a "liminal period": a moment of disjuncture when "history and social structure can be momentarily suspended and phenom-enologically forgotten as players . . . make for a pure fantastic entertainment."[39] Sporting spectacles such as basketball are diversions not necessarily because they make their spectators momentarily forget their troubles; rather, they take their fans away from the anger, joy, and grief of everyday life by making them feel that their burdens are shared, albeit symbolically, by the heroes of the hardwood. A Ginebra game, therefore, is commonly por-trayed as a spectacle of subaltern struggle where the hardships of an underdog team courageously fighting it out against a more formidable opponent become an exciting public attraction.

The action-packed stanza is followed by a refrain that shifts the song's tone from confrontational to imploring for sympathy. The mood swing reflects the fluctuation of the spectator's emotional balance throughout the game. As a "fanatic" engaged in some kind of "madness" the avid basketball follower experiences some lucid moments that allow him to come to his senses. Like the downbeat tone of the refrain, a fast-paced basketball game is also interspersed with breaks for the halftime and potentially momentum-altering timeouts that give both players and fans opportunities to put all the action in perspective.

From a brief period of calm, the mood of the spectator swings back to aggression and belligerence. Fuming at the sight of his team on the verge of losing, his anger even brings back memories of a boy he had fought in primary school. The lyrics continue: *Bumabalik sa aking isip / ang manliligaw ko noong Grade Six* [I begin to recall / the boy who I fought with in Grade Six]. This nostalgic linking of his current frustrations with Ginebra to an unpleasant childhood experience shows how sports fandom is not just a liminal pastime detached from the "normal" flow of life. Rather, being a sports fan can have more profound meaning that is rooted deeply in one's psyche or life history. Within a larger context, this follows Trinidad's argument about the primordial link of Philippine basketball to the sixteenth-century Battle of Mactan as a symbol of "defiance" against external aggression.[40] With a simple act of remembering, an ordinary incident becomes an intrinsic aspect of one's biography, in the same way that a particular event was readily made part of a nation's history. The fan's sentiment reflects how the subaltern struggle is often driven by repressed emotions and subconscious desires that are occasionally awakened under extreme circumstances.

Galit ako sa mga pasista
Galit ako sa mga imperyalista
Feel na *feel* kong maging aktibista
Pag natatalo ang Ginebra

[I hate the fascists
I hate the imperialists
I relish being an activist
Whenever Ginebra loses]

The coda presents a more contemporary and increasingly common form of defiance, especially given the growing public displeasure over what is largely perceived as a dysfunctional state of governance in the Philippines. For instance, the first two lines mirror the usual content of protest placards or mass demonstration speeches. However, these slogans do not only call for reforms in the Philippine government but also blatantly express the objection of many Filipinos to the long-standing alliance of the country with the United States, which they believe is exploitative and, as the lines state, fascistic and imperialistic. Thus basketball, which is regarded as an unmistakable symbol and manifestation of American imperialism, has ironically evolved into a venue for its subversion.

When Ginebra Wins: Sports Victory as Symbolic Emancipation

The second piece, "Kapag Nananalo Ang Ginebra" ("When Ginebra Wins"), was also written by Gary Granada but sung by Bayang Barrios, an acclaimed female folk singer. That she was chosen to sing it shows how sports fandom, which has long been associated with masculinity, has crossed the gender divide and captured the interest of many female basketball followers. It is clear that the second song was composed as a more optimistic rendering of the first one. With the exception of the opening stanza and the refrain, the lyrics were altered to describe the other side of the story narrated in Granada's version.

Just like the earlier piece, this song also depicts a subaltern struggle. However, since the story portrays a Ginebra victory, the lyrics express mainly positive things and the song has a happy ending. The first lines lay down the baseline condition of poverty, affliction, and suffering from where heroes would rise to liberate themselves and their respective communities from a long period of suffering and oppression. The song appropriates the initial bad plays besetting the team to symbolize the deepening crisis that has befallen the nation.

nagkasundo kaming magkakampi
na ang labo kasi ng referee
Ang barangay parang napeste
Natambakan agad kami ng bente

Parang bansa'y nagkaleche-leche
At nare-*elect* ang presidente

[We the fans all agree
the referees' calls are inconsistent
The team looks pestilence-stricken
we're behind by twenty
The nation is mired in disasters
And the president has been reelected]

To add more drama, the lines suggest the referees have con-
spired to make the situation more difficult for the team. Tasked
with upholding the rules of the game, they instead commit mis-
takes or deliberately blow their whistles for doubtful calls that
exacerbate the predicament of the downtrodden team. In the context of the nation, the ultimate referee is the president who is
responsible for the welfare and protection of the people, and the
failure of the Philippine government to uphold the law, shield
them from various social ills, and promote a better life for its citizens are a betrayal of the people's trust in the highest elected
official of the land. Hence the verse ends with a portrayal of the
reelection of the president as a national disaster (President Fidel
Ramos at that time was heavily criticized for expressing a desire
to extend his term despite a constitutional prohibition).

These early trials, however, are viewed as a temporary condition
that merely sets the stage for the rise of the underdog. This parallels the modern history of the Philippines, which is often seen as
a young nation (with full independence obtained only in 1946) or
as a society that has recently emerged from the "dark age" of the
Marcos dictatorship and is currently enduring a crisis before it
ultimately emerges as a politically stable and economically developed country. The golden age of professional basketball in the
1990s, for instance, was also a time of great national optimism
when the country was dubbed as the new "tiger cub"[41] for record-
ing notable economic progress. Unfortunately this enthusiasm
was dampened by the 1997 Asian financial crisis and a political

crisis the followed Joseph Estrada's ouster from the presidency amid charges of massive corruption following the Second EDSA Revolution in 2001.

As in the Ginebra team's case, the big bad guys initially beat up the underdogs before the latter are able to gather all their remaining energy, fight back, and dramatically prevail over their more advantaged opponents. When asked about their tendency to win (or lose) in exciting, closely contested games, Jaworski answered, "I've noticed that when we're the underdogs, that's when we win the game. *Pag kami naman ang lumamang ng mga* [If we are ahead by let's say] 19 points, that's when I feel uneasy. *Kasi nawawala ang* [because we lose the essential] vitamins F and S. You know, Fighting and Spirit."[42]

Pagbigyan nyo na ako
Sa munting hilig kong ito
Kung hindi baka mag-away pa tayo

[Just let me do this
This small pastime that I love
Or, we might just fight over it]

The refrain allows the fan to refocus the story from its larger social inferences back to her personal sentiments. It presents Ginebra fandom as a pastime that can be consuming, even addictive, making it incomprehensible to people who are not sports followers. Hence the main character, in the last two lines, implores others not to mind what she is doing or they might just clash. This part sounds like a threat of a personal fight if she is not tolerated, but taken with the rest of the stanza it sounds more like an appeal for consideration to avoid conflict rather than a form of intimidation to force her will. Hence, it is a request to allow for her self-withdrawal than a warning to leave her alone.

The above stanza also brings to mind the story of Federico Ramon, a plantation worker from Davao City whose obsession in following Ginebra games on the family's lone television set is tolerated by other household members who are not basketball fans. On most evenings, his wife and three daughters would religiously follow their favorite soap operas while he retreated to his workshop. Inside the small room he often finds his hands full repairing electrical appliances, a "sideline" that he performs for extra income. However, once or twice a week when there is a Ginebra game, his wife voluntarily retreats to the kitchen while his daughters chat or do their homework so their father can indulge in his occasional time for leisure (*panagsa nga lingaw-lingaw*). Toward the end of our conversation, Federico proudly shared how his wife and daughters now join him from time to time in watching Ginebra games on TV. He showed great satisfaction in his family's sympathy even if, he added with a smile, "*tuyuon gyud nila nga modapig sa kalaban*" ("They deliberately cheer for the opposing team").

This situation shows that, despite its nature as a public leisure interest, sports fandom is also a highly personal pursuit, like a spiritual retreat that enables a person to find solitude. Sports psychologist Daniel Wann and others suggest that fandom is a way of escaping and its practice can be "particularly prevalent during personally difficult and/or stressful times," noting that historically, "many individuals have used sport spectating as a diversion during wartime."[43] Rather than just a fleeting pastime, sports fandom can be a form of symbolic emancipation, a coping mechanism that enables a person to conquer an overly distressing social condition such as prolonged armed conflict or abject poverty.

The song's lens refocuses on the on-court action as the game moves to its latter stages. By this time, the underdog is starting to experience a reversal of fortune as the team finally executes good plays and chips away at the lead of its opponent. Apart from sheer luck, this comeback rally is of course achieved through self-sacrifice, trust, and teamwork. In short the team has once again become the idealized *barangay*, a small community that faces adversities or any task as one cohesive unit of hardworking, unselfish, and dedicated individuals. "The difficult shot of Noli Locsin," "Marlou's alley hoop," "three-point shots of Hizon and Jarencio," "the hustle of Macky and Benny Cheng," "the interceptions of Flash David," and "Coach Jaworski's direction"—in all these portrayals the different members of the Ginebra team make use of their individual basketball skills to contribute to the team's success.

Aside from their cohesiveness, the team also achieves recognition for its resilience. Ginebra was well known for refusing to be discouraged by its opponent's big lead; it became legendary for fighting it out until the final buzzer. On the team, no one embodied the word resilience more than Jaworski himself. Of the pioneers from the PBA's inception in 1975, he was the last one to retire. Three years before Jaworski finally hung up his jersey in 1998, Ginebra picked his son Robert Jr. in the second round of the PBA Draft. Unfortunately the two were not able to play in a PBA game at the same time: Robert Sr. was already at the tail end of his career and largely concentrated on coaching, whereas Robert Jr. needed more training to improve his play. Many believed then that Robert Jr. was not really good enough to enter the professional league but had nonetheless been drafted so the father-son tandem could provide more publicity for the league. Thus the song highlights in the last line of the stanza the wild cheers erupting from the stands when Robert Jr. (more popularly known through his nickname, Dudut) seems to be checking into the game.

> Sa isang iglap nagpalit ng score
> Lamang na kami 99–94
> Bumabalik sa aking isip
> Ang manliligaw ko nuong Grade Six

> [In a flash the score changed
> We are ahead, 99–94
> In my mind I begin to recall
> My suitor in Grade Six]

This part of the song depicts the moment when the underdog catches up with the stronger adversary in the last few minutes of the game. Inside the arena, this is a frenetic moment, a climactic period when loud cheers echo from the live spectators to the millions of TV viewers watching the game from their homes, in pubs, and in many other places. Quoting from José Rizal's *Noli Me Tangere*, Aguilar describes a cockfighting scene during the Spanish colonial period where "an underdog red's victory became even more emotionally charged and imbued with patriotic fervor: 'a wild shouting greets the *sentencia* [the winner's proclamation], a shouting that is heard from all over town, prolonged, uniform, and lasting for some time,' so that everyone, including women and children, would know and share in the rejoicing that the underdog had won over the dominant power."[44] Just like the raucous cheering that comes with the victory of the underdog cock, the chanting of *Ginebra! Ginebra! Ginebra!* allows for "social catharsis at least in the fictive world of gaming."[45]

Leo Prieto, a former league commissioner, sums up the importance of the PBA as a form of popular entertainment by asking, "What else is there for the people besides the PBA? Going to the movies. The games are exciting and people can stay for hours. You get identified with the teams and you are free to insult the referees and call them all kinds of names, get all that pent-up feeling out of your system, which you cannot do in the movie house."[46] Thus the "hoops hysteria" that comes with the triumphant win of the underdog team becomes a symbolic emancipation shared by the many other underdogs outside the basketball court.

The coda is a humorous description of the fan's feelings whenever Ginebra wins. The team's victory gives her a profound sense of freedom: she herself feels liberated from the everyday troubles of keeping a marital relationship in contrast to the lighthearted attention that she received from her Grade Six suitor. In comparison, in the "Kapag Natatalo ang Ginebra" ("When Ginebra Loses") song, the fan recalled the boy he had a fight with in Grade Six. In the end, for many people being a basketball follower is not just a fleeting experience that fades as one leaves the arena or turns the TV off after a game. It lingers in their imaginations, in their conversations, in their relationships, and in their everyday lives.

Ginebra after Jaworski

In addition to winning the 1997 Commissioner's Cup in very exciting fashion (the victory that inspired these two songs), Ginebra previously had celebrated championship runs in 1986 and 1988, as well as a successful come-from-behind victory in the Open Conference Finals in 1991. After the turn of the millennium the team, anchored by some of the league's best players, won four championships between 2004 and 2008. This is a remarkable feat, one that took the twentieth-century Ginebra teams eleven years to achieve. Despite having superior talents and a vastly improved record, however, the recent teams cannot compare with the immense popularity of the Ginebra squads of the late 1980s and 1990s. A recent survey revealed that Ginebra now shares the honor of being the favorite team in the PBA with Purefoods;[47] the latter rose to prominence in the late 1980s as the team of the "Glamour Boys."

Perhaps many of Ginebra's loyal fans have also retired since the departure of Jaworski, their beloved hero. Surely the team has been affected by the overall decline of the PBA as the premier sporting spectacle in the country amid the emergence of other sports such as boxing and billiards, the increasing popularity of American professional basketball that can be viewed live via cable television, and the rise of local collegiate basketball leagues. The decline of the PBA also came as part of the overall social upheaval that was brought about by the advent of globalization at the turn of the millennium. More importantly, by having bona fide superstars and turning in dominant performances, Ginebra has become too good to be a perennial underdog squad, and consequently has gradually lost its image as the "team of the masses."

In sum, part of the appeal of Ginebra, and of Philippine basketball in general, lies in its representation as a "game of the masses" that embodies the ideals and sentiments of millions of poor and marginalized Filipinos. This was a major divergence from its early years during the American colonial period when basketball was regarded as the "bourgeois sport" because of its strong following among the educated middle class. This process of "popularization" is not unique to Philippine basketball since it is seen in almost every major sport around the world. For instance, cricket and soccer have undergone this crucial shift, which has served as the foundation of their widespread appeal. Beyond this important turn of events, however, this chapter has explored how the popularity of basketball in the Philippines partly hinges on the sport's evolution into a subaltern spectacle, an important arena where the struggles of ordinary people are symbolically played out. As they root for the underdog, whether in the arena or in front of the television, Filipino basketball followers are clearly not only cheering for their favorite teams but also for themselves, and for the many other real underdogs outside the playing court.

5 Basketball without Borders

Globalization and National Sports
in Postcolonial Context

> We are experiencing globalization . . . We must be honest
> enough to say that we are experiencing hard times.
> —former PBA Commissioner Jun Bernardino

Basketball without Borders (BWB), jointly organized by FIBA and
the NBA, is a basketball camp held annually in selected cities
representing the main continents outside North America. The
program serves as the global basketball development and community relations outreach program of these two major
international basketball institutions. Since 2001 thirteen camps
have been held in Europe, along with ten in Africa, eight in the
Americas, and six in Asia.[1] The events are well-publicized primarily because of the involvement of popular NBA players who act as
mentors to the young participants. Although the program is just
a minor event in the busy calendar of the NBA, BWB is perhaps
more reflective of the league's current ideals than any of its other
outreach programs.

Despite its primary objective of promoting international goodwill, the BWB program has played a crucial step in the "innovative,
involved, and intertextual promotional strategy engaged by the
NBA [to turn] a racially stigmatized and struggling sports league
into an energetic, expansive, and, most significantly, popular

American entertainment industry."[2] This strategy has resulted in an important shift that is immediately noticeable inside the arena, and even outside. Internally, the steady influx of foreign players since the 1980s has not only altered the U.S. league's racial and other demographic profiles but has also transformed team management strategies, playing styles, and its overall character.

Externally, the broadening reach of the NBA as a commercial brand is reflected in its rising international revenue: in 2006, while international operations' share of the league's total income was a modest 10 percent, it represented the fastest-growing part of its business enterprise, having risen by 30 percent from the previous year.[3] However, as the NBA continues to build its "borderless" empire, it increasingly impinges on the boundaries of other basketball spheres. These peripheral basketball domains are nevertheless compelled by the opportunities afforded by a more porous global economic system to embark on their own, albeit more modest expansions beyond their usual scopes of influence. The overlapping margins of these basketball worlds are worth investigating, especially by those who are interested in understanding some of the most crucial issues in contemporary global political, economic, and cultural arenas.

This chapter examines the impact of globalization on national sporting culture through the refractive lens of postcolonialism. It focuses on the phenomenon of "contemporary globalization" that arose around the turn of the new millennium when "globalization" emerged as the trendiest buzzword for describing the increasing interconnectedness of people around the world. The discussion centers on a set of trends marking a strong correlation between the rise of globalization and the declining popularity of the Philippine Basketball Association (PBA) since the turn of the twenty-first century. The expanding influence of the NBA in particular is a fitting representation of the far-reaching impact of globalization. From the PBA's vantage point, however, the NBA's growing empire is viewed as one of the factors contributing to the decline of Asia's first professional basketball league. Apart from discussing the increasing popularity of the NBA in the Philippines, the present analysis attempts to depict the overall impact of globalization on the PBA by also looking into the global expansion of the basketball talent pool in the country, the emergence of collegiate leagues, and the growing criticism against the mediocre performance of the PBA-led Men's National Basketball Team in regional competitions.

Beyond the PBA, the chapter also constructs a "local history of globalization" by highlighting some of the "global" elements that have shaped the development of basketball in the Philippines. It lays down a long-term analysis that links the trendy concept of globalization with the outmoded yet persistent notion of "Americanization." The latter broadly refers to the hegemonic influence of the United States, which is linked to its colonial and imperial legacies. From the YMCA to the NBA, the globalization of Philippine basketball seems to be an extension of the Americanization process, which has inundated the archipelagic nation since the late nineteenth century. Despite the historical continuity, however, the current global process demonstrates that apart from the continued American influence, Philippine basketball now draws inspiration and innovation from several sources, and Filipino basketball is itself making its influence felt in the global arena. Even with its continued engagement with the United States, the globalization of Philippine basketball highlights its transcendence of the American "sense of world historical centrality,"[4] which is rooted in the two nations' colonial and imperial relations.

Power Moves

Modern sports already featured some of the characteristics of globality even before the concept of globalization emerged. Long before it became a common buzzword toward the end of the last century, "the organizational structure for the globalization of sport has [already] been in existence for some time," according to Alan Bairner.[5] The standardization of rules, the migration of players, coaches, and other personnel, and the establishment of major events like the Olympics and other similar competitions had led to the global diffusion of many athletic disciplines. In fact, sport is not only one of the fields where globalization initially became prominent; it is also argued that because of the existence of fewer cultural and political obstacles to its development on a worldwide scale, sport became one of the most advanced cases of globalization.[6] In particular, the period around the end of the last century saw the rapid global diffusion of modern sports as characterized by "the movement of performers, coaches, administrators, and sport scientists within and between continents and hemispheres."[7] Apart from the intensification of labor migration, this large-scale dispersion of sports has emerged as a product of more liberal trade policies and other conditions that enabled people, ideas, and cultures to more easily travel across geographical and social boundaries.

Nonetheless, for some societies the early association of modern sports with imperial power remains an uneasy reminder of their colonial past. Hence the development of modern sports has largely been characterized by an ambiguous process of attraction and repulsion, and it is unsurprising that anticolonial sentiments have partly motivated the revival, or even the invention, of indigenous sporting traditions. Most countries, including the Philippines, have a separate, formally established "national sport" with precolonial or premodern origins. Often, this sport is modernized to resemble current sporting forms and is actively promoted through schools and state-sponsored programs. These sports are developed to counter the continued advance of modern sports, which are considered threats to the cultural traditions and the overall identity of the nation. On the other hand, the rejection of the imperial origin of modern sports has also resulted in their indigenization. As discussed earlier, there are numerous examples of this phenomenon: the Indianization of cricket, the Japanization of baseball, the Israelization of basketball, to name a few. These cases show how, after a long and complex process, certain Western sporting traditions have been appropriated by some countries as part of their own cultural traditions.

More recently the rise of globalization and the increased influence of sports have protracted the debate on how they perpetuate neocolonial relations.[8] Echoing earlier pronouncements, critics highlight how the promotion of major league sports allows major corporations such as Nike, Spalding, and Gatorade greater headway in penetrating local markets. Much has been written about how home-grown enterprises are eaten up by the predatory expansion of multinational corporations; however, global sport brands not only displace local businesses but also play a central role in the construction of identities, thereby transforming local cultures.[9] Patterns of consumption in particular underscore not only one's social class background but also reveal much about a person's generational affiliation, lifestyle choice, and other identity determinants.

Due to the leading role of the United States in world politics as well as in global economic and cultural affairs, the rise of globalization in recent decades has been interpreted as a mere intensification of the Americanization process.[10] The work of Yair Galily and Ken Sheard provides one of the most straightforward analyses of the relationship between these two concepts within the context of basketball. Their analysis underscores the close ties between Israel and the United States that have been forged since the creation of the Israeli nation-state in 1948. Just as Israel has relied heavily on American military and economic aid, its professional basketball league has also been reliant on various inputs from North America. In particular, the arrival of Jewish American players, the hiring of seasoned U.S. coaches, and the experience gained from regular matches between U.S. and Israeli teams has been crucial to the development of the local professional basketball league. Because of this unidirectional movement of people and ideas, Galily and Sheard concluded that "the term Americanization is more suitable for explaining developments in that sport than the more general term 'globalization.'"[11] In fact this experience is not unique to Israel: given the evidence on how American basketball has transcended various national boundaries, one can just as well say that the game had already been borderless long before "Basketball without Borders."

The Global Sport and the National League

"We are experiencing globalization . . . We must be honest enough to say that we are experiencing hard times."[12] PBA Commisioner Jun Bernardino's downbeat outlook on globalization was made at a Senate inquiry specially convened to investigate a high-profile controversy involving the PBA's foreign-born players, a major crisis that enveloped the Filipino professional basketball league in 2003. Some of these athletes had been found to have falsified documents to support their applications for Philippine citizenship, a requirement for them to suit up as full-time players in the country's premier basketball league.[13] But even before the controversy surfaced, the league had already been suffering from dwindling revenue due to decreasing tickets sales and advertising contracts and an overall decline in interest in the PBA. The root of the problem had been traced to the advent of globalization: within a relatively short span of time, the sharp increase in the number of domestic and international competitors, including those from other sports, had lured public interest away from the league. The league's top official was trying to use this "economic consideration" to justify PBA's move to hastily recruit foreign-born players who are eligible for Filipino citizenship. Along with most team owners and league officials, Bernardino viewed the arrival of the Filipino-foreign players as an effective response to the challenges posed by globalization. The commissioner generally shared the overall enthusiasm that this new type of player would embody the stimulus needed to help the moribund league keep up with changing times. However, in the rush to acquire some of the best players, some PBA teams had become imprudent in complying with proper citizenship registration procedures for their recruits.

The new millennium brought a cloud of uncertainty over the Philippines' premier basketball league as the luster from the previous decade waned. Ticket sales dropped from the 5,562 average game attendance in 2001 to 4,481 in 2002. This trend would continue in the next two years as per-game ticket sales further dipped to 4,259 in 2003 and 4,187 in 2004. These numbers were particularly alarming when considered against 1989—one of the league's best years—when the league's average paid attendance was 7,364.[14] These numbers are backed up by the accounts of those who believed that the PBA was indeed losing its appeal among Filipino basketball fans. In Metro Manila most informants related that, unlike a few years earlier, they now only knew a few family members and friends who still actively followed the PBA. According to them, the sheer number of alternative basketball leagues and other popular sports that could be followed had led people to focus on those with better talents (e.g., the NBA) or more media coverage (e.g., the Olympic Games, Grand Slam tennis events), with the PBA falling to the bottom of the sports list because the level of competition was not considered "world class." This turn of events mimicked the trend in the United Kingdom in which the American basketball league was met with immediate cultural acceptance because of the perceived high standards of play.[15] At the southern end of the archipelago in Davao, where the PBA continued to attract a sizeable number of avid fans from among the rural residents, people were quick to add that the level of interest had considerably decreased over the past ten years. A couple of informants admitted that they hardly recognize most of the present crop of local professional players because they seldom took the time to watch televised PBA matches anymore. Many thought that the PBA games were boring, especially when compared to the NBA.

Given these numbers and narratives, the succeeding section explores some of the factors that have contributed to the decline of the PBA. Generally both groups of key informants, along with secondary data from some of the country's leading national periodicals, noted the following issues as factors behind the decline of the Philippines' professional basketball league: 1) the increasing popularity of the NBA; 2) the failure of new players, particularly those that are foreign-born, to connect with the fans; 3) the rise of local collegiate leagues; and 4) the PBA-led national team's failure to regain the Philippines' former position as one of the top basketball nations in Asia.

NBA Madness

In an effort to supplement its domestic supply of athletes and increase its market size, the NBA turned its focus overseas.[16] In the Philippines, various promotional activities were organized to make the U.S. league even more visible in the basketball-loving country. Apart from a multimedia promotional campaign, some initiatives were undertaken to bring the American pastime physically closer to its increasingly valuable followers in various overseas markets. In the Philippines, NBA Madness, an interactive event aimed at bringing the fun and excitement of the league to local fans, has been held in the country thrice, most recently in Metro Manila from September 28 to October 2, 2011. The attraction featured NBA legend Clyde Drexler and the Orlando Magic and Portland Trailblazers dance teams. The presence of these personalities and the various programs conducted during the five-day event allowed many Filipino NBA fans to get a closer look at their favorite celebrities. In addition to NBA Madness, the Junior NBA Camp, an annual training program for ten- to fourteen-year-olds, was also launched in 2007. The program is simultaneously held in different venues across the country and benefited around five hundred schools and seventy thousand students, parents, and coaches since its establishment.[17] Apart from the sheer popularity of the NBA, both events have been successful partly because local media depicted these developments as symbols that the Philippines was once again making a lasting imprint in the global basketball map.

The increased local exposure of the NBA resulted in an upsurge of local television ratings, an increase so notable that the Filipino market has become one of the biggest followers of the American basketball league in Asia. Since the turn of the millennium, two live games are shown every week on national television whereas before there was only one delayed telecast of an NBA match per week. The availability of cable television has also afforded many Filipinos access to all the NBA's daily games. Aside from sports channels like ESPN and StarSports, viewers can also check the NBA TV channel where live games and other basketball programs are shown. Marketing executive of NBA Asia Carlo Singson Jr. noted how "The fans are passionate, the percentage of people who play is awesome. NBA players who come here are amazed at how much Pinoys [Filipinos] know about NBA teams and NBA players," adding, "the Philippines is definitely a priority market for the NBA."[18] In a survey assessing the marketability of the league in the Philippines, it was found that 99 percent of the population was aware of the NBA. In addition, "During the [2008] NBA Season, 62 percent of the population watch[ed] the NBA games on TV at least once a month and about 40 percent of the population watch[ed] the NBA on TV at least once a week." Lastly the survey showed that "33 percent intend[ed] to buy NBA-branded items within the next year, rising to 44 percent (significantly more than the Asia and global averages) among men."[19]

The notable growth that the NBA has gained in the past decade has greatly affected the overall influence of the Philippines' own professional basketball league. In the abovementioned survey, it was also noted that only 48 percent of the population followed domestic basketball, considerably less than the 75 percent who considered themselves NBA fans.[20] From being a big primetime attraction during most of the latter part of the last century, the PBA games now shown on television are merely second-class basketball acts that fewer and fewer people are interested in watching. Inocencio Ogos, a village official in Davao, confirmed this trend when he explained that compared to the PBA, "*mas gwapo gyud ang dula sa nba, lahi gyud ang lihuk, plays, ug strategies*" ["the NBA is better, their moves, plays, and strategies are really different"].[21]

From Fil-Ams to Fil-Shams

Players with mixed Filipino-foreign ethnic backgrounds have been an important part of the local basketball scene since the early twentieth century. The *mestizos* (Filipinos with European and American ancestries) have been fixtures throughout the history of basketball in the Philippines. In fact, some of the most notable Filipino basketball players (Luis Salvador, Charles Borck, Carlos Loyzaga, Kurt Bachman, Robert Jaworski) come from this category. The common view is that these athletes excelled, apart from their basketball skills, because of racial backgrounds that made them a few inches taller than the average Filipino.

The number of Filipino-foreign players, particularly the Filipino Americans (Fil-Ams), has significantly increased since the 1990s because of an improved scouting network that has enabled PBA teams to scour American and other overseas talent pools for promising players. The resulting huge influx of Fil-Am athletes even spilled over to the amateur leagues and collegiate teams. This reflects the global propensity for greater mobility of human resources, particularly in professional sports where athletes freely cross national boundaries to showcase their talents abroad. Nowhere is this more evident than in the NBA where surnames such as Mutombo, Nowitzki, Ilgauskas, Stojakovic, Turkoglu, Ginobili, and Yao are largely taken as a sign that the American league is increasingly becoming "a melting pot of hoops."[22]

Initially the entry of these new talents into the PBA was met with great enthusiasm and acknowledged as providing the stimulus needed to push the league beyond its current quality and popularity. They became novel attractions that enhanced the appeal of the PBA, with fans marveling at their height, athleticism, and NBA style of play. Leo Adan, himself a former inter-*barangay* (village) basketball star, sees the important contributions of Filipino-foreign players to the sport:

> Okay sad ang mga Fil-Ams, doble ang techniques nga nahibal-an. Naay ideas nga wala sa atoa; daku ang kahibalo kontra sa ordinaryo nga Pinoy. Usa pa, tangkad pud, American height man gyud na sila.

[The Fil-Ams are okay, they are familiar with both local and American techniques. They have ideas that we don't have; they have more knowledge than the ordinary Filipino players. Another thing is that they are really tall, they have the typical American height.][23]

Unlike Adan, however, many local fans have lamented the transformation of their beloved league into something that is noticeably foreign. Over the years, the term Fil-Ams, frequently used as blanket reference to the foreign players, has become a misnomer as players from Australia, Europe, Africa and even from countries in the Polynesian, South Asian, and Arab regions are making themselves visible, even prominent, in the Philippine basketball scene. Eventually, the PBA fans' initial skepticism at the alarming increase of Fil-Ams turned into major disappointment during the "Fil-Sham controversy," in which a number of Filipino-foreign players were found to have falsified documents to support their citizenship claims. Consequently, a high-profile investigation that even involved the Philippine Senate tainted the clean and conscientious "family entertainment" image that the league was trying to project. "They were the shams that shamed the Philippine Basketball Association," wrote one journalist, "a stigma on the league that was marking its 30th season and a period of transition as the oldest play-for-pay loop in Asia."[24] The controversy even reached the esteemed hall of the country's highest legislative body; as one senator put it, "what is at stake . . . is not only the credibility and integrity of the [PBA]. It's also the sanctity and honor of having Filipino citizenship."[25] After a series of highly publicized investigations and trials, six players were eventually deported, of which four were considered among the league's new superstars.[26]

Then came the more controversial issue of illegal drug use. As the media trained their lenses on the questionable Filipino roots of some PBA players, the league received another blow when a number of its players tested positive for illegal substances during a random checkup. After an inquiry, five players were meted suspensions; of the five, three were Filipino-foreign players who were among the league's top sports celebrities.[27] As a result of these scandals, many fans believed that the once-admired Fil-Ams had become frowned-upon "Fil-Shams." The players who were supposed to bring the PBA to greater heights were the very ones pulling the league further down.

To make matters worse, all these scandals came after some local players and sports journalists criticized the Filipino-foreign players for getting higher salaries and enjoying more perks than local-born players. Their swelling ranks also created sentiment that these new players were taking jobs that should have gone to homegrown athletes. After all these issues were considered, there were debates as to whether the entry of Filipino-foreign players should be continued. Although some Filipino-foreign players had become popular with the fans, many people still believed that they were "not really Filipinos," and that teams should instead concentrate on developing "pure" Filipinos than on recruiting "half-breed" or "hybrid" players from abroad. One former league official suggested that for the league to recover from its current slump it should lessen its emphasis on Filipino-foreign players, recalling the "glory days" of the PBA in the 1970s and 1980s when homegrown players took center stage. He explained:

> There's a lot of difference when you talk about foreigners with Filipino roots [Fil-Ams, etc.] and the heroes who were raised here and learned the game in sandlots or in local schools. Fans have an easier time relating with players whom they have seen in television from the time they started their careers. These homegrown players have a built-in fan base and they add weight to a marketing strategy. Fellow alumni and provincemates of these players embrace them as their own.[28]

Clearly the controversy surrounding the status of Filipino-foreign players transcends the legal technicalities of citizenship acquisition. First, it is a question of national loyalty: What motivated these individuals to come to the Philippines? Often these hybrid cagers were primarily attracted by the financial benefits that come with playing professional sports. How strong was their prior interest in coming to the country? The ultimate goal for most of these athletes when they were still in college was to play in the NBA or in one of the major overseas leagues, with the PBA serving as a convenient backup plan once their aspirations of playing in the United States or Europe failed to materialize. These are some of the questions that many Filipino basketball fans have when judging the loyalty of Filipino-foreign players, particularly when fans believe the players' main motivation is money. Playing in the Philippines is generally not their first choice, and most of them return to their home countries after they retire from the PBA.

This matter becomes even more controversial when these athletes are chosen to wear the national colors and represent the country in international competitions. Recently the Philippine national team was caught in a controversy exposing an issue on the commitment of foreign-born players on the national team during the 2014 Asian Games basketball tournaments. Marcus Douhit, an American-born player who became a naturalized Filipino citizen in 2011, was benched during a crucial match after he was singled out by Chot Reyes, the country's head coach for "quitting" on the team after a subpar performance that saw them lose to Qatar, a lower-ceded team. "I don't think it was an issue of fatigue. I think it was more of an issue of desire," Reyes said.[29] Without Douhit, the team's main big man, the Philippines was narrowly beaten by South Korea in the following game, resulting in their elimination from the medal rounds.

The incident, again, raised the long-standing issue on the rationality of bringing in foreign-born and naturalized citizens to play for the country in international tournaments. Can these Filipino-foreign players exhibit the same sense of belonging and loyalty that homegrown players are assumed to have by default? Are they ready to "die" for their country as the exalted "heroes" of millions of Filipino basketball fans? Indeed, athleticism is necessary and their excellent basketball skills are even essential, but in top-level competitions where athleticism and talents abound, a game is often decided by the amount of dedication and sacrifice that players give to their teams. Some supporters of the displaced homegrown players equate the recruitment of Filipino-foreign players to hiring mercenaries. Thus a victory with these "paid" heroes is often seen as something hollow, falling empty on its perceived significance as a source of inspiration and as a symbol of emancipation for the subaltern nation.

Apart from the question of national loyalty, the issues surrounding the influx of Filipino-foreign players in the PBA are mainly about their "cultural difference." For instance, many local fans are appalled by what they generally see as the too flashy or overbearing on- and off-court antics of the league's new breed of stars.[30] Likewise foreign-born players who are mostly unfamiliar with Filipino cultural nuances have struggled to reach out to local basketball fans. In short, as the PBA becomes more globalized, it is also evolving into a foreign-dominated league—an "alien nation" that leaves many of its avid supporters alienated.

The Rise of Local Amateur Leagues

Apart from the rise of the NBA, the growth of basketball at the collegiate level has also diverted a large part of the public attention away from the PBA. These related trends reflect Kinichi Ohmae's analysis of the impact of globalization on the nation-state. He argues that the current global upheaval results in the "hollowing out" of the nation as local and external forces continue to erode the state's long-held influence.[31] In the context of Philippine basketball, the increasing popularity both of the NBA (external) and the local amateur leagues (internal) represents this process of hollowing out that leaves the PBA, a national league, struggling for its survival.

Of particular note is the rise of the collegiate leagues into a major live and televised attraction. Before the new millennium, most collegiate basketball games in the Philippines were held in stuffy university gymnasiums with limited audiences and little media coverage. However, the recent years have seen the commercialization of the NCAA (National Collegiate Athletic Association) and the UAAP (University Athletic Association of the Philippines) basketball games. With these developments, both interscholastic leagues have successfully expanded college basketball's fan base beyond their campuses. While some PBA games could hardly fill half of the Araneta Coliseum (one of the PBA game venues), tickets to a game between rival universities could be sold out in a couple of days.

For example, the matchup between the teams of the Ateneo de Manila and the De La Salle universities has evolved into a highly popular rivalry attracting an enormous fan following and media attention. One Saturday evening, after a two-hour basketball game and before a late dinner and a few rounds of beer with his *barkada* (circle of friends), interviewee Paul Urdaneta showered and put on a T-shirt celebrating his alma mater's championship victory of a few years earlier. At the group's usual haunt, they discussed the chances of their beloved Ateneo Blue Eagles in the upcoming season, scrutinizing the talents of the team's new players and its coach's game strategies, and sizing up its matchups against other UAAP teams. Notably the group's discussion of the PBA generally refers to the 1980s, which one of Paul's friends used to point out an "outdated" method of coaching that they thought the current Ateneo mentor disastrously insisted on using.

The rising interest in college basketball has even resulted in regular live broadcasts of its games, with viewership steadily increasing in recent years. A local sports journalist observed how "Ratings have been very high, and the UAAP in particular has helped in pulling down [the] ratings [of] and attracting sponsors away from all other basketball leagues."[32] Clearly the country's premier professional hoops league is one of those affected by the surging popularity of college basketball. Students and alumni are kept posted of the schedule of upcoming games during televised matches featuring their alma mater, not like in the PBA where it takes more effort to relate to company-sponsored teams. Apart from holding games in big venues and getting national television coverage, the commercialization of the amateur collegiate leagues has also included the entry of corporate sponsorship, the marketing of varsity apparel, and the rise of some college athletes as entertainment celebrities.

In addition many university teams, instead of settling for the services of their physical education instructors, now hire high-profile coaches who have professional experience. The former coach of the Ateneo Blue Eagles, the team that grabbed a series of five championships between 2008 and 2013, was Norman Black—an accomplished American-born professional player and coach who briefly played in the NBA. Furthermore, schools no longer simply enlist into teams students who excel in intramural tournaments; rather, most colleges have aggressive recruitment programs, with coaches scouring the entire country and even schools abroad for the best basketball prospects. This is why most collegiate teams are now manned by foreign players who have come from the United States as well as from "faraway" countries such as Nigeria and Serbia.

Reclaiming the Asian Basketball Crown

"I could be wrong," one Filipino sports journalist wrote, "but statistics showed that PBA attendance suffered after each debacle in the Asian Games." He added:

> Since 1990, have we beaten China in basketball? In the last Asian Games, the national team, composed of PBA players, lost to China, Korea and Kazakhstan in the medal race. And in this year's ABC (FIBA-Asia) tournament, the Philippines finished a dismal 15th, second to last. It was the country's worst ever in the 43-year-history of the Olympic qualifier. In my opinion, those embarrassing setbacks are some of the major reasons why the Filipino fans have been slowly shying away from most of

the PBA games despite all the media hype and hoopla. The fans want winners, not certified losers.[33]

After dominating the Asian basketball scene in the first three quarters of the twentieth century, Filipino fans have placed strong pressure on the national team to regain its regional superiority in the sport. Since the PBA took on the responsibility of representing the country in major international competitions in the 1990s, successive reincarnations of the national team have come close to winning the Asian Games basketball championship, arguably the region's most prestigious basketball crown: they finished second in 1990, fourth in 1994, third in 1998, and fourth again in 2002 before the Philippines was suspended by FIBA in 2006 and therefore was unable to participate in the quadrennial event that year (see Table 6). But this track record is clearly not enough.

Most local basketball fans expect better performances, and their lukewarm-at-best response to the national team's effort suggests that anything short of an Asian championship is a failure. Given the national team's shortcomings in attaining this lofty goal, many critics are declaring that the people should simply take this inadequate showing as a sign that basketball is not really for Filipinos. Many question the practicality of spending huge amounts of money on a mediocre team that has almost no chance of winning the Asian championship. Instead, they suggest that the country should instead concentrate on other sports such as boxing, bowling, billiards, and chess where height is not a premium and national players would therefore have better prospects. "We are even lower than Laos in the ranking," was how Mario Periquet described the current position of the Philippines in Asian basketball. He was exaggerating the country's international ranking, but his view nevertheless reflects the overall disappointment of Filipino fans with their national basketball team.

Despite its recent debacles, the Philippines remains one of the top teams in Asia. Proof of this is in the Philippines' second-place finish in the 2013 FIBA Asia Championship, which enabled the

Table 6. Basketball results in the Asian Games

YEAR	LOCATION	PHILIPPINE TEAM FINISH	CHAMPION	RUNNER-UP
(1st) 1951	New Delhi	First	Philippines	Japan
(2nd) 1954	Manila	First	Philippines	Taiwan
(3rd) 1958	Tokyo	First	Philippines	Taiwan
(4th) 1962	Jakarta	First	Philippines	Japan
(5th) 1966	Bangkok	Sixth	Israel	Thailand
(6th) 1970	Bangkok	Fifth	South Korea	Israel
(7th) 1974	Tehran	Fourth	Israel	South Korea
(8th) 1978	Bangkok	Fifth	China	South Korea
(9th) 1982	New Delhi	Fourth	South Korea	China
(10th) 1986	Seoul	Third	China	Korea
(11th) 1990	Beijing	Second	China	Philippines
(12th) 1994	Hiroshima	Fourth	China	Korea
(13th) 1998	Bangkok	Third	China	South Korea
(14th) 2002	Busan	Fourth	South Korea	China
(15th) 2006	Doha	Suspended, DNP	China	Qatar
(16th) 2010	Guangdong	Sixth	China	South Korea
(17th) 2014	Incheon	Seventh	Iran	South Korea

Sources: Dayrit, *Olympic Movement in the Philippines*; research data.

country to earn a slot in the 2014 World Cup in Spain. Moreover, the amateur squads that represent the country in the SEA (Southeast Asian) Games have been dominating the basketball competitions in that biennial event for years. However, the country's superiority in Southeast Asian basketball is almost unremarkable given that the Philippines is the only nation in the region where amateur basketball is a popular pastime. Ultimately the goal of the PBA is to put together a team that will qualify for the major international tournaments such as the World Cup and the Olympics. After earning a berth in the 2014 World Cup in Spain, the challenge is how to improve on this achievement, which many basketball followers downplayed since it was attained when the Philippines hosted the regional qualifier. This task seems to be herculean given that the regional tournaments have become more competitive in recent years. Attaining this objective now requires more than simply beating China, since many of the national basketball teams in the region have improved tremendously in the past twenty years. Even the Chinese, with a team boasting four current or future NBA players (one of them, Yao Ming, made the NBA All-Star Game eight times in his career), was beaten by crowd favorite South Korea in the 2002 Asian Games in Busan, South Korea; in 2006, Iran surprised everyone by bagging the basketball championship in the 2006 Doha Asian Games. The Iranian team won again at the 2013 FIBA-Asia Championship after beating a pesky Filipino team. Fielding a younger team, China could only finish fifth, a disappointing finish considering the country had won more than half of the championships in the tournament's history.

Playing with Globalization

In order to cope with some of the adverse effects of globalization, the PBA has implemented a number of programs to make its operation sustainable, and more importantly, to regain its strong appeal among Filipino basketball fans. Since the turn of the millennium there has been a strong effort to bring the PBA closer to the people by scheduling more games in urban centers around the country. This strategy aimed to strengthen the league's fan base in the provinces, which for a long time had been marginalized by the PBA's concentration in Metro Manila. Aside from holding regular-season games in the provinces, the PBA has held its annual midseason highlight, the All-Star Game, outside the Philippine capital nine times in the past ten years. The PBA All-Star Game has also moved beyond a mere basketball spectacle featuring the season's best players. Like the NBA, the PBA has started to conduct civic-oriented activities such as visits to schools and charitable foundations and other community-based outreach programs in the cities where All-Star Games are held.

Moreover, the country's premier basketball league has also made attempts to increase its international visibility by holding official games overseas. On March 8, 2005, the first PBA match outside of the Philippines was held in Jakarta, Indonesia, pitting the Shell Turbochargers against the Talk 'n Text Phone Pals. Since then, professional Filipino basketball has been showcased in Hong Kong, Guam, Dubai, and Singapore. In addition, the PBA Legends Tour, a series of exhibition games featuring former league superstars, visited several cities in Australia in 2005 and the United States in 2008. These international games were primarily aimed at capturing the interest of the large number of Filipino expatriate communities in these foreign cities, although the league was also hoping to attract the attention of local basketball fans.

Fortunately for the league, these initiatives have made an immediate impact. By April 2004, it was reported that revenues from PBA attendance rose to over 132 million pesos in Metro Manila (a 12.1 percent increase from the previous year, and a 29.56 percent increase from two years earlier). This development pushed the league's gross revenue to over 16 million pesos, an increase of 7.1 percent, and reflected a dramatic 80.3 percent improvement over two years. The provincial results were even more impressive: for the first six out-of-town games, the average attendance was 5,000 (a 44.94 percent increase from the previous year). Ticket sales brought in 6.4 million pesos for a staggering 116.17 percent increase.[34] The figures three years later were even more promising. From a balance of about 60 million pesos in 2006, the league reported 47 percent growth the following year, amounting to net income of 86.9 million pesos. On the whole, ticket sales went up by 17 percent and total revenue by 10 percent.[35]

Nonetheless, PBA Chairman Ricky Vargas warned that "figures don't mean a thing if the PBA isn't geared for the future." He added, "[A] vision propelled by a passion for the game is what will take Asia's first play-for-pay league to the next level."[36] Despite the favorable performance of the PBA in 2004 and 2007, fluctuations occurred during the intervening years. This apparent instability of the PBA demonstrates the necessity of more long-term measures to ensure its relevance and viability. A low attendance record, for instance, can be remedied by a well-planned marketing strategy such as the expansion of its market base in the provinces and even overseas, something the league has already successfully exploited. The sustainability of these initiatives, however, hinges on its capability to strengthen its cultural anchor, which has been increasingly weakened by the corrosive impact of globalization.

Outside the PBA, the globalization of sports has also given Filipino basketball talents the opportunity to showcase their skills abroad. For instance, the Indonesian Basketball League (IBL) features a number of Filipino players. This is a welcome development particularly for those Filipino players—mostly former professional players and amateur standouts—who are unable to earn spots on PBA teams. On the coaching side, Filipinos Geraldo Ramos and David Zamar are mentoring IBL teams. Ramos led Aspac Jakarta to a Grand Slam championship in 2004 and was eventually hired to handle the Indonesian national basketball team. A couple of years later, Zamar crossed the border to man the bench of the Melaka Chinwoo club in the Malaysian National Basketball League (MNBL). One of his top players, Jay Gabonada, is Filipino. In 2007, Melaka Chinwoo lost the MNBL Champions Cup to Klang WCT Land Berhad, a team coached by Daniel Advincula, another Filipino. Apart from Indonesia and Malaysia, Filipino basketball players are also in professional leagues in Saudi Arabia, Mexico, Germany, Switzerland, and the Cayman Islands.

Finally, the establishment of the ASEAN Basketball League (ABL) in 2009 has further expanded the influence of Philippine basketball as well as the opportunities for Filipino professional basketball players. The Philippine Patriots won the inaugural championship by besting five other teams from various Southeast

Asian nations, all of which had one to three Filipinos on their rosters. The Brunei team was even mentored by Geraldo Ramos, the same coach who previously handled the Indonesian national team and a veteran of several Philippine amateur basketball leagues.

The PBA and a Local History of Globalization

The development of Philippine basketball, and of the PBA in particular, has shown that globalization is not an entirely new phenomenon. In fact, the league has arguably been "global" since its inception in 1975. First, despite its origin as a local amateur league, the establishment of the PBA involved a significant amount of external influence since its professional rules and organizational setup was partly patterned after the NBA. The knowledge acquired from the NBA further enriched local expertise and stimulated innovation, a process that reflects the rise of new spaces in the contemporary global-local nexus. The founding of the PBA thus resulted in a league and a widespread sporting culture that is very American yet somehow distinctly Filipino.

Second, multinational companies (MNCs), which are largely cited as the main architects of the contemporary global system, have also played a prominent role in the PBA. In fact many PBA teams have been under the ownership of MNCs since the league started in 1975. For instance, the first PBA champion was the Toyota Team, which, as its name indicates, was owned by the popular Japanese car-manufacturing company. Other MNC-owned franchises include the Shell Turbochargers, Fed-Ex Express, Coca-Cola Tigers, and the Burger King Whoppers. Lastly, the free movement of human resources that is one of the most notable consequences of globalization has been part of the professional sport scene for some time.[37] Foreigners, especially Americans, have been actively involved in the league as players and coaches from its inception. PBA teams have been getting the services of "imports," foreign players who have reinforced their lineups, since the league was established in 1975. Clearly, these global features of the PBA can be attributed to its transnational links, especially with the United States, which has long played an important role in most aspects of Philippine politics, economy, and cultural life.

The more recent ascent of globalization and its impact on the structure and the social significance of basketball are closely linked to the abovementioned series of crucial events that have shaped the development of the sport in the Philippines. In the context of Philippine basketball at least, globalization is not an entirely new cultural phenomenon but is manifested mainly as a recent surge of Americanization, a process that itself has been at work in the archipelago since the turn of the twentieth century. Thus a post-colonial analysis of how the historical processes of colonization, nationalism, and neocolonialism are related to the existing conceptions of identity politics, economic relations, and cultural dynamics reveals a more rooted and protracted history of globalization and its many consequences.

Finally, understanding the impact of globalization on Philippine basketball also invites the examination of local agents. The recent issues afflicting the PBA were not only products of supra-societal processes but also the result of internal social dynamics. In a way, the PBA was neither a passive recipient nor was it simply forced to adjust to the social conditions set by forces of globalization. On the contrary, the league itself sought to take advantage of the available resources and knowledge from abroad by relaxing its traditional boundaries.

In summary, the current social changes have brought about closer integration between agency and structure and demonstrate how individuals and organizations reorganize their resources to cope with changing economic and social conditions. Globalization, therefore, is not just an interruption caused by external forces striking nations from without but also is an internal process that transforms these societies from within.

Playing in the Periphery

"Everybody Should Visit Manila" was the title of U.S. basketball star Gilbert Arenas's blog entry on July 14, 2008. The piece chronicled his offseason world tour that brought him to the Philippine capital, along with other stops in Beijing, Shanghai, Berlin, and Barcelona, to promote a new line of sporting apparel. Of these cities, he highlighted his experience in Manila as the most memorable. "They made me feel like an NBA star," was how he summarized the well-attended mall shows and the "royal treatment" that was accorded to him in the few days he spent in the metropolis. The avid following that basketball receives in the Philippines impressed him so much that he enthusiastically shared a piece of advice with his fellow NBA players: "If you're having a bad day or having a bad career, go to Manila. They'll bring your spirits up, trust me. I felt like I just won an NBA championship, to be for real."[38]

The special attention that Arenas received in Manila and the larger social condition that made his global promotional tour possible reflect the recent rise in popularity of basketball around the world. This remarkable development did not come as a surprise to some sports scholars such as Michael Mandelbaum, who pointed out how "the character of the game was in tune with the salient features of the post-industrial world."[39] In particular, some analysts have noted how basketball benefited from the technological and creative advances made in the television industry in the 1980s, and the way in which its speedy and continuous "telegenic quality" fits the highly mobile and fast-paced lifestyle of the twenty-first century.[40]

The NBA's aggressive overseas marketing plan follows the path taken by major American entertainment conglomerates such as Disney and McDonald's. Partly pushed by the necessity to expand after the saturation of its domestic market and partly drawn to the opportunities afforded by a more liberal world economic system after the end of the Cold War, the league tried to expand "by developing a global market of its products."[41] In just over two decades after its players made their international debut at the 1992 Barcelona Olympics, the NBA has evolved to become one of the world's most visible transnational corporate entities. In 2003, a

Time magazine article reported that "The global appeal is filling the NBA's coffers," giving the following figures:

> About 20% of all NBA merchandise—including NBA Cologne in Spain and NBA school supplies in Latin America—is now sold outside the U.S., providing an extra $430 million in annual revenue . . . Nearly 15% of the league's $900 million annual TV revenue (excluding local broadcasts) is now derived from its 148 television partners in 212 countries and territories. Some 40% of visitors to NBA.com (which includes sites in Spanish, Japanese and, since mid-January, Chinese) log on from outside the U.S., and a million fans pay $10 a month to listen to streaming English or Spanish audio of almost any game.[42]

Consistent with its community-development projects in the United States, the league has actively forged partnerships with organizations such as Habitat for Humanity in order to organize civic-oriented programs. NBA Madness, NBA Jam, and Basketball without Borders, along with other lesser-known global promotional projects, have contributed in making the NBA, and the game of basketball in general, one of the fastest-growing sports in recent years. In China, for instance, Polumbaum noted how "the fast-moving flashy NBA game" was especially attractive among young people "looking for cultural markers that will distinguish them from their elders."[43] Basketball came to the Middle Kingdom not only as a new pastime but as an integral part of a new era that brought about a profound transformation in the everyday lives of many Chinese people. On the other side of the globe, Falcous and Maguire pointed out a similar trend in the United Kingdom where the NBA's popularity not only hinged on its status as the top basketball league in the world, but also on the certain appeal it conveys as a "global product," particularly to the younger generation.[44]

Both observations affirmed the trend that was presented in Walter La Feber's *Michael Jordan and the New Global Capitalism* more than ten years ago. This seminal work examines not only the rise of basketball as a global phenomenon but also more broadly considers the advance of American cultural imperialism. La Feber observed how multinational corporations like Nike harnessed postindustrial technologies to dominate world markets and how these new MNCs differ from the old ones not so much on the production of "goods" but on the use of "knowledge."[45] Hence, just like the corporate logos of the various apparel companies that they represent, NBA players—from Magic Johnson and Michael Jordan to LeBron James—are easily recognizable as contemporary global icons.

Despite its rapid growth, the impact of the NBA's expansion, the degree of local reception, and the overall entrenchment of basketball still varies across geographical and cultural locations. In fact, there are still regions such as South Asia where basketball is neither widely played nor has much following. Even in Europe, South America, Africa, and the Middle East—regions where the sport has recently shown remarkable advancement—basketball remains second to football in terms of participation and following. In addition, home-grown sports such as the various forms of Asian martial arts are also riding on this globalization bandwagon and are gaining popularity in different parts of the world.

Nonetheless, the increasing influence of the NBA around the world, as Arenas's tour would attest, creates much media buzz and attracts a great deal of attention from local fans. This attention generally reflects the kind of frenzy that rock-and-roll music, Hollywood films, and other foreign products have received after suddenly flooding many local markets during the advent of globalization. However, the question as to whether basketball can sustain its unprecedented rise, especially in areas that have long-entrenched sporting traditions, remains. In countries that are less receptive to capitalism and other expressions of Western culture, modern sports, along with other foreign products and ideas, are often met with skepticism and even criticism. On the surface, the interest in basketball might be more of a fleeting fad than something that will leave a lasting mark on sporting cultures in many parts in the world.

In the Philippines, however, the immense popularity of basketball is more deeply rooted and its history as a hegemonic sporting culture goes back more than a century. This "cultural embeddedness" can account for the more lavish reception that Arenas received in Manila compared to the other places that he visited. Unlike most countries, the mass appeal of basketball in the Philippines could not be solely attributed to the more recent surge of globalization, which only became prominent toward the end of the last millennium. In fact, local basketball is so deeply rooted that its branches hardly spread out, largely remaining domestically oriented until today. Philippine basketball runs the court as a mature national sporting culture; it is ubiquitous, all-pervading. The country's professional league is the second oldest in the world and it boasts a sizeable troupe of adored local basketball celebrities.

Despite the long-entrenched position of basketball in the Philippines, the country has been largely unknown in the global basketball scene in recent years. Notably the Philippines waited for thirty-six years to qualify for the 2014 FIBA World Cup and its national team's last successful campaign in major international competitions was in 1954. This is why Gilbert Arenas, the visiting NBA player, was completely amazed when he saw the immense popularity of the sport in the country. Although Arenas did write about how impressed he was with the knowledgeable Spanish fans or at seeing that many Chinese are actually taller than him (he stands six foot four), these observations apparently did not come as a complete surprise to him; Arenas should have been quite familiar with the status of the sport in these countries since both can boast of outstanding international records. Players such as Spain's Pau Gasol and China's Yao Ming had achieved NBA stardom just as Arenas had.[46] Their entry into the United States was largely made possible by the advent of globalization, which ushered in an important shift in the late 1980s when the NBA started to look for basketball talents overseas. This trend intensified after the start of the new millennium, making foreign players an integral part of the premier American basketball league.

Arenas's impression of the popularity of basketball in Manila was telling. Obviously, local basketball was unfamiliar to him, and he can hardly be blamed for this ignorance: compared to the other countries that Arenas visited, the Philippines is not an international basketball powerhouse and no homegrown Filipino player has ever made it to the NBA. Yet as Arenas suggested in his blog, why does basketball attract a much larger, more avid following here than in the former two countries? Clearly, the influence of football and other "traditional" sport practices are putting up a challenge to the advance of basketball in Spain and China. However, apart from this obvious reason there are still other trails that are worth exploring in understanding the dynamics of basketball diffusion, especially in the context of globalization. In looking at the case of the Philippines, one of the interesting threads to untangle is the close ties of basketball with the country's history, especially in its relationship with the United States, the global superpower whose political and economic influence is expressed in the increasing popularity of basketball around the world. Thus, the popularity of basketball in China and Spain, as the experience of Gilbert Arenas indicates, is a recent development that can largely be viewed as a product of the current global system.[47] The deep entrenchment of the sport in the everyday life of most Filipinos, however, is a product of the successful reappropriation of the American game within the Philippines' cultural border.

Conclusion

"As there seems to be little to indicate exactly when basketball was introduced into the Philippine Islands, it is possible that the natives gained their first information of the game through watching the American soldiers stationed there," wrote James Naismith, the sport's inventor.[1] Despite its present popularity, the early years of basketball in the Philippines are so shrouded in mystery that even the person who created the game was reduced to mere speculation in his effort to reconstruct its beginning. No precise date is given as to when the game was first played and no specific person can be credited for originally bringing it to the Philippines. Instead, available sources only offer broad approximations (circa 1905–10) and inconclusive profiles of the sport's pioneers in the country (such as soldiers or missionaries).

This genealogical void in the early history of basketball in the Philippines is in stark contrast to the general history of the game itself. Its uniquely well-documented past includes information on the location of the first basketball game at the International YMCA Training School (now Springfield College) in Massachusetts, biographical details on the game's well-known Canadian inventor, and an exact foundation date (December 1, 1891). A Japanese student at the training school even made a sketch of that first game—providing a concrete visual evidence of the event. Compared to the evolution of baseball or football from premodern games, basketball, due to its "scientific invention," has generally been considered the first truly modern sport. With its relatively recent origin, basketball's point of introduction in many countries can often be traced back to a particular time, place, and personalities. In China, for instance, the game was first played in Tienjin's YMCA on December 5, 1895, and was presided over by Dr. Willard Lyon.[2] The outbreak of the Philippine-American War in 1898 and the subsequent establishment of the U.S. colonial regime in the Philippines resulted in an influx of soldiers, teachers, administrators, missionaries, and other American personnel, a great number of whom had already been exposed to basketball. Their arrival in the Philippines co-opted the role of the YMCA as sole originator of the game, as it is in other countries.

This clouded origin, however, only adds a mythic appeal to the country's most popular game. Like other national and cultural symbols, the "stuff of legend" that surrounds its ambiguous beginnings only makes the game more attractive to its followers. Likewise, this lack of detail has become almost immaterial at the professional level where intrigue, rumors, and gossip, more than concrete facts, have made basketball a well-entrenched entertainment spectacle and popular culture icon in the Philippines. More importantly, this vagueness also enables Filipinos to emphasize other milestones in the development of basketball in the country, allowing for greater agency in their reinvention of the American game as an intrinsic part of national culture. Instead of merely taking account of the place, time, and personalities to indicate how the game was introduced by the Americans, the reconstruction of its past or even the simple act of reminiscing about its "glory days" draws attention to the long process that saw the Filipinization of basketball. Thus after one or two sentences that briefly account for its early years during the American colonial period, the popular narration of the history of basketball in the Philippines invariably shifts to the country's early success in international competitions, elaborates on the exploits of its basketball heroes, and highlights its meteoric rise to its current position as the nation's favorite pastime.

In comparison, the indigenization of basketball in China has taken an even more extreme and more contentious course. Some Chinese sport historians contend that the sport's beginnings in the Middle Kingdom date back far beyond that fateful day in Tienjin when a YMCA missionary organized the first basketball match. According to them, long before basketball became one of the most popular modern sports, "ancient China [had already] produced a precursor of the game in *shouju*, a form of Tang dynasty handball."[3] Similarly the recent history of cricket in India encountered an interesting new twist when postcolonial theorists (but more popularly expounded in the film *Lagaan*) claimed that the widespread popularity of this sport introduced in the British colonial period was actually bolstered by its likeness to the local game of *gulli-danda*.[4]

In the Philippines there are no alternative discourses that challenge the American origins of basketball despite the strong emphasis on the Filipinization of the sport in the construction of its history. Surprisingly nobody has even made reference to its similarity to the long-forgotten indigenous game of *sambunot*, where opposing teams try to score by landing a coconut into two separate goals, one at each end of a rectangular field, that consisted of holes dug in the ground.[5] Just like the case of Indian cricket, claiming that the popularity of basketball in the Philippines lends its similarity to *sambunot* would be a good measure to the length that Filipinos would take to claim the sport as their own.

Just like the effort to trace its exact origins, accounting for the different factors that have influenced the rise of basketball as the hegemonic sports culture in the Philippines has been equally challenging. From its sparsely chronicled beginnings the sport has had to live through the volatile periods of U.S. colonial rule and the Second World War, compete with the highly popular American game of baseball, endure a lengthy string of failures in major international tournaments, survive an equally long political and economic crisis, and struggle in mitigating the often detrimental impact of globalization. On top of these, basketball has been incessantly hounded by a large number of critics and skeptics who question the vertically challenged Filipinos' suitability to the game of the giants. Finally, the rising popularity of other sport disciplines such as badminton and football has likewise continued to challenge the long-term viability of basketball as the country's national pastime.

In essence this research began with two important goals: to uncover the exact origins of basketball in the country and to identify the various factors that have contributed to its meteoric rise to the pinnacle of Philippine sports. Although this work contributes little in achieving the first objective, it provides a more extensive engagement with the latter.

Why Is Basketball Popular?

"It is often said that 'baseball follows the [American] flag,'" Elwood Brown noted. "So far as the Philippines is concerned this statement is equally true of basketball."[6] The U.S. colonial era in the Philippines is often subject to an inquisitive query on the incongruous popularity of basketball in the country. The association of the sport with modernity and "the promise of progress" during this period endeared it to many Filipinos. With greater access to education and other opportunities, they saw in basketball the thrilling and emancipating possibilities of the democratic system that the American regime was trying to introduce. Ironically the game also became a venue for the Filipinos to challenge the hegemony of the colonial power. Hence basketball represents the contradicting sense of attraction and repulsion that characterizes the relationship of the Philippines with the United States, even long after the former gained independence.

Nonetheless, the strong American influence that was firmly established by almost half a century of colonial rule is not the only reason behind the widespread popularity of basketball in the Philippines. As such, each of chapters has been designed as a response to the question of *Why is basketball popular in the Philippines?* This broad question, therefore, serves as the study's point of orientation as the discussion moves from one theme to another, from one chapter to the next. First, the book expounded on how basketball served as one of the channels in the U.S. colonial regime's effort to "Americanize the Filipinos," thereby attracting an avid following, especially after building a reputation as the "modern sport." Second, the game forged a strong association with the emerging nation-state, which saw in its early success in international competitions symbols of national unity and a venue to gain foreign recognition. This turn of events resulted in the "Filipinization of basketball," a process highlighted by the juxtaposition of its development as the country's most popular sport with the decline of baseball, America's favorite pastime. Hence, within the span of these two historical periods basketball evolved from a little-known colonial tool to a pervasive national symbol.

Third, on top of the important achievements that basketball attained from the 1910s to the 1960s, the most important factor behind the sustained development of basketball beyond this period was its ability to adapt to the changing times. In "The Hollywood-ization of Hoops," this historical-sociological inquiry posited how the evolution of the sport into an important icon of popular culture enabled basketball to weather obstacles and ensure its long-term survival. After more than fifty years of notable showings in international competitions, the good fortune of the country's national basketball team started to diminish and the squad eventually went into a long free fall, hindering its full recovery to this day. During this time, frustration over the series of setbacks in the country's long bid to recapture its dominance in regional basketball tournaments resulted in numerous criticisms of what many thought was the undue emphasis on basketball in Philippine sports.

The consolidation of American popular culture's influence since the Cold War period has ushered in the rise of visual mass media and the subsequent influx of American cultural products in the country. The advance of Hollywood movies, rock and roll and other music genres, and major league sports transformed the local cultural landscape. With the establishment of the country's professional league in 1975, Philippine basketball evolved from an externally oriented national symbol to a domestically focused entertainment spectacle that parallels the local showbiz industry. Thus transpired the evolution from national to cultural, wherein the popularity of basketball ceased to be fueled by the country's success in international competitions but by the star appeal of its players in its "Hollywoodized" professional league. In becoming an entertainment spectacle, basketball not only maintained its position as the country's premier sport but also enabled it to further advance its influence in the country.

Fourth, part of the appeal of Philippine basketball lies in its representation as a "game of the masses," embodying the ideals and sentiments of the millions of poor and marginalized Filipinos. This represents a major divergence from the sport's early years during the American colonial period in which basketball was regarded as the "bourgeois sport" because of its strong following among the educated middle class. This process of popularization, is not unique to Philippine basketball; almost any major sport around the world (e.g., cricket, football) has undergone this crucial shift on which any sport's widespread appeal generally rests. Beyond this significant development, however, the study also contends that the popularity of basketball in the Philippines partly hinges on the sport's evolution into a subaltern spectacle, an important site where the struggles of ordinary people are symbolically played out in the basketball arena. As they root for the underdog in the arena (or in front of the television), the local basketball followers are not only cheering for their favorite teams but also for themselves, and for the many other real underdogs outside the playing court.

Lastly, the advent of globalization brought a surge of new ideas, technologies, and resources that swiftly spread around the world, reshaping the globe's entire economic, political, and cultural landscape. In Philippine basketball, globalization ushered in the rapid expansion of the NBA, a development feared for its neocolonial overtones and a stark reminder of the almost five decades of political and economic marginalization during the U.S. colonial regime. Nevertheless, the changes catalyzed a sagging professional league that was in dire need of fresh inputs. The entry of Filipino-foreign players in the PBA, for instance, made the league more exciting and competitive. Moreover, the greater accessibility of the NBA, America's premier basketball league, also added a new treat to the standard list of local hoops fare. Even the long-mothballed amateur basketball scene had a renaissance because of this global impetus. The intercollegiate competitions in particular started to fill both huge arenas and primetime television slots on a regular basis, feats that were previously only associated with the PBA.

Overall the process of globalization helped further boost the popularity of basketball in the Philippines at the turn of the twenty-first century. Interestingly an exception to this positive development was the detrimental impact of this extensive transformation on the country's top national league, the PBA. The NBA competed with the local league for television viewership share and for overall fan attention, the rise of the amateur leagues resulted in the saturation of the local basketball scene, and a number of popular Filipino-foreign players were involved in illegal drugs, fraud, and other high-profile controversies that tainted the self-promoted wholesome image of the league as family entertainment. In short, globalization was beneficial to basketball in general, but not to the national basketball league, which went into an unfortunate decline.

Basketball from Below

Despite the extensive coverage of this historical-sociological odyssey, practical and theoretical limitations meant that this study could not account for all the factors that contributed to the development of Philippine basketball. Primarily the previous discussions mainly cover macro-level issues: apart from the chapter on the Ginebra fans, limited attention has been paid to developments at the grassroots level. The analysis of "basketball from below" could highlight the experience and rationalities of the "small players" to yield an alternative perspective to our reconstruction of the development of the national sporting culture in the Philippines. This approach has gained favor with postcolonial and subaltern scholars as a way out of the theoretical trap that often arises out of the fixation on undoing the empire-colony binary.[7] Instead of getting stuck in analyzing the complex geopolitical dynamics of postcolonial structures such as basketball, the examination of everyday culture often reveals a more nuanced illustration of empire-colony relations. In particular, a view into the subaltern's sense of agency affords us a better understanding of the people's struggles to "shape their own world and make their own meanings" out of the dominant rationalities that encroach onto their daily lives.[8]

This perspective is crucial to this research because the popularity of basketball in the Philippines has been largely anchored not only on the success of its national team (it has not won any major international tournament titles in almost fifty years) or on the widespread appeal of its top commercial league (globalization has since threatened its long-term survival). Rather it is the continued practice and following of the sport by ordinary individuals that sustains its prominence in the country. In particular, the various personal and social meanings that have developed over the people's long engagement with the sport makes it difficult, if not downright impossible, to erode the game's popularity even in times of deep crisis. Thus basketball remains highly popular among many Filipinos despite fervent criticism that the sport is incompatible with the nation's physical makeup.

In Philippine historiography, the seminal work of Reynaldo Ileto on the subaltern origins of Philippine nationalism is an indispensable source of insight. His analysis of lower-class Filipinos' use of colonial literary forms such as the *pasyon* and the *awit* as mediums of resistance emphasizes the importance of mass-based, popular movements in the struggle for nationalism.[9] In the same way, people interpret basketball games as subaltern spectacles that mirror their predicaments, particularly the stories of struggles and triumphs that characterize the fates of their favorite players and teams. This display of excitement and drama (closely resembling a primetime soap opera) has made the sport more appealing to the Filipino masses, many of whom have long suffered from poverty and marginalization. Thus it is interesting to note that words such as "fanatics" and "irrational," which were used to emphatically dismiss the sentiments of the members of peasant movements in Ileto's work, are also the same terms employed to describe the most avid followers of basketball in the Philippines.

Basketball and Beyond

The preceding discussions presented the development of Philippine basketball not only to demonstrate the formation of the country's sporting culture but also to reveal its close connection to the processes of colonialism, nationalism, popular culture, subalternity, and globalization. In particular, it explored how basketball figured in the emergence of the Philippine nation-state, a sentiment that was recently captured by Gerald Gems:

> Filipinos labored under a long American occupation, accepting American tutelage and sport forms yet denying complete assimilation. Ultimately they rejected English in favor of Tagalog and a variety of local dialects, the Filipino government retained its traditional elitism despite the trappings of a democratic structure, and Catholicism remained intact against the widespread influence of the YMCA and Protestant missionaries. Filipinos eventually eschewed baseball and football, choosing basketball as their national sport. They adapted the Americanization efforts to their own needs and values to produce a new hybrid culture similar to yet distinct from that of the U.S.[10]

From its beginnings as a method employed to "Americanize the Filipinos" basketball has become a channel for its subversion. Theoretically this process directs us back to Bhabha's concepts of mimicry and hybridity, two postcolonial frameworks that can be used to articulate the decolonization of basketball and its incorporation into the local cultural milieu. For one, the concept of mimicry fittingly illustrates the general receptivity of the Filipinos to the colonial reproduction of American infrastructure and ideologies in the Philippines. But rather than a mere case of unidirectional replication of ideas and practices, the concept is interpreted here as a more complex process of subject positioning. The adoption of certain knowledge is often pursued as a form of defense mechanism, a way of dealing with external threats by absorbing them into the internal world of the subject where they can be neutralized or alleviated. As part of this strategy, basketball is just one of the areas where the Filipinos have tried to deal with the imperial power while keeping their own cultural traditions intact by appropriating new meanings into the game.

Hybridity refers to the emerging rationalities arising from the convergence of imperial and local cultures. The gradual integration of basketball into people's everyday lives and the cultural consciousness illustrates the incorporation of "new knowledge" that Filipinos used as a venue to construct and express their national identity.[11] As a result, basketball became as deeply ingrained in the Filipino culture as the once-foreign *fiesta* (religious feasts) or *jeepney* (a public utility vehicle initially built from World War II–era American military surplus), now both symbols of Filipino culture and identity.[12]

Despite the promise of emancipation, however, a sense of tragedy lurks behind the processes of mimicry and hybridity. In the case of Philippine basketball, this is exemplified in the lack of resources that prevents the local leagues from expanding their market base across the country like the NBA, or in the physical limitations that make it impossible for an aspiring Filipino basketball player to be on par with his or her American counterparts. These are examples of what Bhabha calls the "slippage"—the moment when the colonized recognizes that it will never be like the colonizer.[13] Thus the Filipinization of basketball places the colonized as a subject of a difference that is almost the same but not quite.[14] This tragedy is shown in the subaltern's frequent absurd attempts to replicate the foreign—attempts that ultimately fail. What is more disheartening, however, is that even if the subaltern succeeds in its replication, the product is always something that it could not completely claim as its own. Ultimately the subaltern comes to a realization that much of its own identity, as Vicente Rafael describes, "is founded on what it cannot [completely] comprehend, much less incorporate."[15] The dilemma of Philippine basketball parallels the case of baseball in the Dominican Republic. There, Alan Kline notes, despite the Dominican players' excellence in the sport, they still come up short once one considers that much of Dominican baseball continues to be controlled by American interests:

> Because baseball is the only area in which Dominicans come up against Americans and demonstrate superiority, it fosters national pride and keeps foreign influence at bay. But the resistance is incomplete. At an organizational level, American baseball interests have gained power and are now unwittingly dismantling Dominican baseball. Therefore, just when the Dominicans are in position to resist the influence of foreigners, the core of their resistance is slipping away into the hands of the foreigners themselves.[16]

Thus, sport—as instrument, product, and reflection of colonial and postcolonial history—is caught in a situation that Bhabha calls a "state of ambivalence." On the one hand it provides opportunities, moments, and promises of liberation from the shackles of colonial and imperial domination. On the other, sports enable the colonizer or the empire to develop and maintain the technical disadvantages and cultural dependency that deny the total emancipation of the colonized.[17]

As a way out of this theoretical conundrum, the study suggests a post-binary analysis that transcends the colonial fixation on disentangling the complex empire-colony relations. In general, this is achieved by emphasizing the influence of regional dynamics in the formation of postcolonial and subaltern spaces. This approach argues that the initial incorporation of certain knowledge and practices from the colonial power is not the end result, but only the beginning of further explorations of other relational possibilities. This is not merely an impassioned rejection of the colonial or hegemonic power but an examination of other possible orientations of comparison. Hence, instead of merely searching for spaces between oppositional entities for hybrid cultural forms, it delves into a broader range of comparisons to explain the persistence of certain colonial practices and rationalities even as they lose their meanings amid the current empire-subject dynamics.

Following this approach, the study explores a broader arena of comparison to account for the other "players" that contributed to the development of basketball in the Philippines, instead of merely constructing a narrow and unidirectional contrast between the Filipino to the American. Throughout the chapters of this book, particular attention has been given to the development of sports in the Asian region, especially in China and Japan, to further put into context the formation of the national sporting culture in the Philippines. This specific investigation has conclusively established the role of regional sports competitions in the overall growth of Philippine basketball. For instance, the Philippine teams' domination of the basketball tournaments at the Far Eastern Championship Games in the early twentieth century served as an important foundation for the widespread popularity of basketball in the country.

At the same time, the American presence in the Philippines, as well its growing influence in the region, has mainly met with strong antagonism and resistance. The United States did not fully gain the trust of the Filipinos until the Second World War, when the Americans were heralded as their liberators from the brutal Japanese regime. Despite some strong anti-U.S. sentiments, basketball, along with a few other American sports, continued to grow and thrive not only in many parts of the Philippines but also in the neighboring countries of Japan and China. In fact, the sustained popularity of the sport in the country, particularly during the Cold War era, can be more appropriately viewed as part of the broader "Americanization of Asia" rather than as an exclusive offshoot of Philippine-American relations. Finally, the recent effort to improve the state of Philippine basketball has been motivated not by the usual subaltern preoccupation with engaging and exacting revenge on the former colonial master. Rather, the primary goal in the effort to advance the quality of the game over the past two decades has been to regain its status as one of the top basketball-playing countries in Asia. Taking this multidimensional viewpoint in analyzing postcolonial and subaltern practices not only offers a more comprehensive approach but also accounts for some important elements that are lost in the narrowed juxtaposition of the hegemonic power and the subaltern.

NOTES

INTRODUCTION

1. Guha, *Corner of a Foreign Field*, 50.
2. See Appadurai, "Playing with Modernity"; Kline, "Culture, Politics, and Baseball"; Mangan, *Cultural Bond*; Mills, *Subaltern Sports*; and Stoddard, "Sport, Cultural Imperialism, and Colonial Response."
3. Gems, *Athletic Crusade*, 2.
4. Barrows, *Decade of American Government*; Jones, "Athletics Helping the Filipino"; and O'Reilly, "Filipinos Made Great Progress" were some of the notable publications in the early twentieth century that mentioned the importance of sports in the American colonial project.
5. Seymour, *Baseball*, 234–35. Also see Gems, *Athletic Crusade*, 49.
6. Afable, *Philippine Sports Greats*.
7. More popularly known as the Tydings-McDuffie Act, the Philippine Independence Act established the Commonwealth of the Philippines, a ten-year transitional government in preparation for full Philippine independence and sovereignty. Under this arrangement, the Filipinos were able to enact their own constitution and elect executive and legislative officials. Foreign policy and military affairs were the responsibility of the United States, and certain legislation required the approval of the American president. See Go and Foster, *American Colonial State*.
8. The International Basketball Federation is an umbrella association of national organizations that serves as the highest governing body for international basketball competitions. It was originally known through its French name of the Fédération Internationale de Basketball Amateur (hence FIBA). As part of its effort to expand and include professional players in international competitions, it dropped the word "Amateur"

from its official name in 1989 but retained the initialism; the "BA" now represents the first two letters of "basketball." The World Basketball Championship (renamed the FIBA World Cup in 2010), which started in 1950, is an international basketball competition contested by the men's national teams of the members of FIBA.

9. Gems, *Athletic Crusade*, 66.

10. In 1985 the Philippines won the FIBA Asia Championship in Kuala Lumpur, Malaysia, and qualified for the FIBA World Championship held in Madrid, Spain. However, due to the political crisis that culminated in the 1986 People Power Revolution, the country did not participate in the tournaments. Before 2014, the last year the country actually played in the FIBA World Championships was 1978, when it hosted the prestigious event in Manila. After more than thirty years, the Philippines returned to one of basketball's most prominent tournaments when it earned a spot in the 2014 FIBA World Cup in Spain after placing second in the FIBA Asia Championships.

11. This sanction was removed in 1990, allowing for the participation of professional players in the Olympics and World Championship.

12. The word "national sport" is often synonymous with "national pastime," which refers to a sport that has a widespread and fervent following in a particularly society. However, in the Philippines, it is necessary to distinguish basketball as a national sport (de facto) from the country's official national sport (de jure), which is arnis. Arnis is a traditional martial art in which a rattan stick is the primary weapon.

13. Bale and Cronin, *Sport and Postcolonialism*, 3.

14. "Hoopsphere" refers to the scope and influence of basketball as an element of popular culture. It is based on the word hoop, the round metal rim to which the net is attached to form basketball's goal. The word is also commonly used to refer to the game itself.

15. Guha, "On Some Aspects."

16. Mills, *Subaltern Sports*, 1.

17. Cullinane, "Basketball and Culture," 55.

18. Bartholomew, *Pacific Rims*.

19. Booth, *Field*, 16.

20. For a good example of how the post-binary approach is utilized to analyze the dynamics of postcolonial sport, see Appadurai, *Playing with Modernity*. Also see Bale and Cronin, *Sport and Postcolonialism*.

21. Markovits and Hellerman, *Offside*.

22. Markovits and Hellerman, *Offside*, 10.

23. Social Weather Stations, *Social Weather Report*, 100.

24. Mahar Mangahas, "It's World Pool Time Again," *Philippine Daily Inquirer*, November 3, 2007, 9.

25. Manolo Iñigo, "Basketball Boo-boo," *Philippine Daily Inquirer*, April 15, 2008, A22.

26. The 1966 Asian Games team largely comprised rookies, and was beaten by South Korea and Israel in the elimination round. They later lost to China in the consolation round and finished sixth overall. See "The Fifth Asiad in Bangkok: A Summary," *The Filipino Athlete* 20 (January–February 1967): 6–7.

27. The suspension was meted out because of the conflict between factions of the Basketball Association of the Philippines (BAP), the top basketball-governing body in the country. The conflict resulted from a disagreement between some groups in the BAP over the capability of the national team to carry the banner of the country in top international competitions.

28. Afable, *Philippine Sports Greats*, 2.

29. Philippine Amateur Athletic Federation, *Minutes of the Thirty-Second Annual General Meeting*, 71.

30. Reaves, *Taking a Game*.

31. Reaves, *Taking a Game*, 107.

32. Philippine Amateur Athletic Federation, *Minutes of the Thirty-Fifth Annual General Meeting*, 6.

33. Philippine Amateur Athletic Federation, *Minutes of the Thirty-Fifth Annual General Meeting*, 6.

34. It is important to note that Filipino leaders were not unanimous in their views regarding the "impending growth of the Filipinos." Later on, Senator Ambrosio Padilla led the effort of nineteen FIBA member countries to limit the height of players in international competitions to six feet two inches. The petition was made after the Rome Olympics in 1960, but because of strong opposition led by the United States, the petition was rejected (Cunningham, *American Hoops*). Padilla was the captain of the 1936 Philippine Olympic basketball team and went on to become a successful lawyer. He was elected to the Philippine Senate in 1957 while remaining active in basketball; he served as FIBA's Vice President for Asia (1956–64) and as the president of the Asian Basketball Confederation (1960–66).

35. Philippine Amateur Athletic Federation, *Minutes of the Thirty-Fourth Annual General Meeting*, 89.

36. B. Anderson, *Imagined Communities*.
37. Rafael, *Promise of the Foreign*, 5.
38. Pope, "Army of Athletes."
39. See Appadurai, "Playing with Modernity"; Kline, "Culture, Politics, and Baseball"; Mills, *Subaltern Sports*; and Stoddard, "Sport, Cultural Imperialism, and Colonial Response."
40. See for example, Jones, "Athletics Helping the Filipino"; Povich, "This Morning"; and Worcester, "Field Sport."
41. Rafael, *Promise of the Foreign*, 19.
42. Rafael, *Promise of the Foreign*, 19–20.
43. Rafael, *Promise of the Foreign*, 5.
44. Appadurai, "Playing with Modernity." A number of studies were recently conducted exploring how cricket and other sports like martial arts, polo, and football were utilized as venues for expressing local sentiments in postcolonial South Asia (Mills, *Subaltern Sports*). Writing on a similar theme from across the globe, Stoddard reports in *Sport, Culture and History* how cricket in Barbados emerged not simply as a form of colonial recreation, but also as an arena where the empire and the colony negotiated the results of cultural proselytism. Earlier, Roden's article "Baseball and the Quest for National Dignity in Meiji Japan" examined how the success of some high school students in the game of baseball against American sailors stationed in the port of Yokohama enhanced the geopolitical image of Japan as the country was breaking free from an unequal treaty that had opened its ports to American trade. These examples show how sport, which started as a colonial tool of political control, evolved into a means of local resistance and a medium for the expression of national identity.
45. Appadurai observed how "cricket became popular in the first three decades of the 20th century," and as the nationalist movement of Mahatma Gandhi and the Indian National Congress gathered momentum in the same period, cricket nationalism and explicitly nationalist politics as such came into contact in the ordinary lives of young Indians." Interestingly this period also saw in the Philippines the occasion of the nationalist movement against the American colonial regime and the emergence of basketball as a national sport. See Appadurai, *Playing with Modernity*, 90, 99.
46. Appadurai, *Playing with Modernity*, 102.
47. Aguilar, *Clash of Spirits*, 47.
48. Appadurai, *Playing with Modernity*, 112.

49. Mandelbaum, *Meaning of Sports*.
50. Appadurai, *Playing with Modernity*, 93.
51. Appadurai, *Playing with Modernity*, 112.
52. Appadurai, *Playing with Modernity*, 112–13.
53. E. Brown, *Annual Report*, 1911, 490.
54. Bhabha, *Location of Culture*, 114.
55. Gems, *Athletic Crusade*, 66.
56. Particularly, the Bancroft Library holds the papers and personal collection of David P. Barrows, who was Superintendent of the Bureau of Public Instruction under the American colonial government. His collection contains information on the introduction of physical education and modern sports in the Philippines. After his stint in the Philippines, Barrows went back to teach at the University of California, and eventually served as its president from 1919 to 1923. Likewise the Bentley Library contains materials from several American colonial administrators in the Philippines, including Dean Worcester (Secretary of Interior) and Walter Marquardt (Superintendent of the Bureau of Public Instruction).

1. SPHEROID OF INFLUENCE

Epigraph: Barthes, *What Is Sport?*, 3.

1. Merriam-Webster's Online Dictionary, http://www.merriam-webster .com/dictionary/exercise.
2. Wuest and Bucher, *Foundations of Physical Education and Sport*.
3. Wolters, *History, Culture, and Region*, 25.
4. May, *Social Engineering in the Philippines*.
5. Mechikoff, *History and Philosophy of Sport*.
6. Guttmann, *From Ritual to Record*.
7. Apter, "Subvention of Tradition," 214.
8. Olcott, *Life of William McKinley*, 2:111.
9. Buffington, *Physical Training for Filipinos*, vi.
10. E. Brown, *Annual Report of the Physical Director*, 1911, 490.
11. Joaquin, *Almanac for Manilenos*, 36.
12. E. Brown, *Annual Report of the Physical Director*, 1917, 291.
13. For a discussion on American colonial health, see W. Anderson, *Colonial Pathologies*.
14. England, "Physical Education," 3.
15. W. Anderson, *Colonial Pathologies*, 3.
16. E. Brown, *Annual Report of the Physical Director*, 1911, 4.

17. Nestled within a high-elevation area of the Cordillera Range, Baguio City was built by the American colonial government as the Philippines' summer capital. As with hill stations in other colonies, the city was established in an area with a cool climate that was favorable to the white colonial masters who originated from temperate countries. Early U.S. officials found the tropical heat in the Philippines degenerative to the health and overall well-being of white soldiers and civilians, thus Baguio was established as a place for recuperation. See W. Anderson, *Colonial Pathologies*.

18. E. Brown, *Annual Report of the Physical Director*, 1911, 4.

19. Atkinson, "Education in the Philippines," 832.

20. Morill, *Report of Secretary-General*, 1915, 1026.

21. Buffington, *Physical Training for Filipinos*, iv.

22. The idea of "Manifest Destiny" was popularized in the mid-nineteenth century during the United States' western expansion. The term's racial, class, religious, and gender connotations allow it to also be used to refer to the American imperial process. See Gems, *Athletic Crusade*. "The White Man's Burden," is a poem by Rudyard Kipling that is subtitled "The United States and the Philippine Islands." It is largely interpreted as a statement of Western racism and global supremacist ideology. See Miller, *Benevolent Assimilation*.

23. Kramer, *Blood of Government*, 2.

24. Gems, *Athletic Crusade*, 2.

25. Gems, "Anthropology Days," 197.

26. Worcester, "Field Sports."

27. Worcester, "Field Sports," 221.

28. Worcester, "Field Sports," 221.

29. *Moros* refers to Filipino Muslims, a collection of several ethnolinguistic groups that compose the largest non-Christian group in the Philippines. The word was used as a derogatory term by the Catholic Spanish colonizers of the archipelago in reference to shared Islamic beliefs between the groups from the southern island of Mindanao and the Moors of North Africa, who had previously conquered southern Spain.

30. Walter W. Marquardt, "A Trip through the Southern Islands on the S.S. Negros (July 24–August 18, 1918)," Unpublished Report, Bureau of Education, 1918, 89. Walter Marquardt Papers, BHL-UMI.

31. O'Reilly, "Filipinos Made Great Progress," 7.

32. Bureau of Education, "Inclusion of the Department of Mindanao and Sulu in the Bureau of Education," Circular No. 166, Series 1914; RG 350-E5-1887-44 US-NARA.

33. Frank W. Carpenter, letter to Vernon L. Whitney, April 21, 1914; RG 350-E5A-1887-1158 US-NARA.

34. O'Reilly, "Filipinos Made Great Progress," 7.

35. Gems, *Athletic Crusade*, 58.

36. Buffington, *Physical Training for Filipinos*.

37. Hornedo, *Culture and Community*.

38. Scott, *Weapons of the Weak*.

39. Groves, *Report of the Secretary General*, 1911, 476.

40. Speak, "China in the Modern World."

41. Tener, *Report of the Secretary General*, 387.

42. D. Goh, "States of Ethnography."

43. Jones, "Athletics Helping the Filipino."

44. Washington Post, "Headhunters Drop That Pastime for Football," 1.

45. Jones, "Athletics Helping the Filipino," 586.

46. Salman, *Embarrassment of Slavery*, 6.

47. Salman, *Embarrassment of Slavery*. The classic text is Lynch's "Social Acceptance Reconsidered," in Lynch and Guzman, *Four Readings*, 1–68.

48. Ironically, the American colonial regime collaborated with the elites in their effort to consolidate their control of the Philippines, which eventually led to the retention, if not the greater accumulation of economic and political power by the oligarchs. See B. Anderson, "Cacique Democracy in the Philippines" chap. 9, 192–226.

49. Jones, "Athletics Helping the Filipino," 589.

50. Jones, "Athletics Helping the Filipino," 586.

51. Jones, "Athletics Helping the Filipino," 589.

52. Jones, "Athletics Helping the Filipino," 591.

53. Hayden, *Philippines*.

54. Atkinson, *Education in the Philippines*.

55. Jones, "Athletics Helping the Filipino," 588.

56. Karnow, *In Our Image*. Also see Isaac, *American Tropics*.

57. Halili, *Iconography of the New Empire*, 168.

58. Pecson and Racelis, *Tales of American Teachers*, 191.

59. Bureau of Education, *Athletic Handbook*, 1911.

60. Jones, "Athletics Helping the Filipino."

61. Maria Clara is the main female protagonist in Jose Rizal's 1887 novel, *Noli Me Tangere* (*Touch Me Not*). Clara embodies beauty, grace, simplicity, and obedience–values that women were expected to exhibit in the Catholic-dominated Spanish Philippines. Because of the strong influence of Rizal's novel, Maria Clara's persona was eventually taken to represent the ideal Filipino woman.

62. O'Reilly, *Islanders Show Their Caliber*, 7.

63. Jones, "Athletics Helping the Filipino," 588.

64. Jones, "Athletics Helping the Filipinos," 588–89.

65. Halili, *Iconography of the New Empire*, 168.

66. Bloomers were a symbol of the women's suffrage movement in the late nineteenth century. In the Philippines, the suffrage movement started during the American Period with the establishment of the Asociation Feminista Filipina in 1905. The struggle for women's voting rights lasted for more than thirty years, culminating with the passing of a law allowing women to vote on April 30, 1937. See Kalaw, *How the Filipina Got the Vote*.

67. Bureau of Education, *General Instructions*.

68. Bureau of Education, "Recommendations of the Superintendents' Committee on Physical Training," Circular No. 90, Series of 1914, July 27, 1914; RG350-E5-1887-39, US-NARA.

69. Frank L. Crone, Director of Education, letter to the Department of Recreation, Russell Sage Foundation, May 19, 1916, 3; RG350-E5-1887-1216, US-NARA.

70. Bureau of Education, "Bloomers May Now Be Used without Skirts." Circular No. 19, Series of 1930, March 10, 1930; NARA 2698–90.

71. Morris, *Marrow of the Nation*, 88.

72. Barrows, *Decade of American Government*, 61.

73. Gems, *Athletic Crusade*, 47.

74. Horger, *Play by the Rules*.

75. Groves, *Report of Foreign Secretaries*, 1912, 1074.

76. Fraser, *Report of the Secretary-General*, 1914, 930.

77. Groves, *Report of the Secretary General*, 1915, 1.

78. Turner, *Report of the Secretary General*, 1916, 1074.

79. Villanueva, *History, Development, and Progress*.

80. Putney, *Muscular Christianity*.

81. Turner, *Report of the Secretary General*, 1916, 1078.

82. Maxwell, *Annual Report*, 1.

83. E. Brown, "Unpublished Biography."

84. White, "Education Report," 658–59.

85. Gems, *Athletic Crusade*, 60.

86. Gems, *Athletic Crusade*, 23.

87. Antolihao, "Far Eastern Games."

88. Morris, *Marrow of the Nation*, 12.

89. Brownell, *Training the Body for China*, 50.

90. Guttmann and Thompson, *Japanese Sports*, 133.

91. "The New Olympian," *Philippine Free Press* (February 1, 1913), 1. Also see Morris, *Marrow of the Nation*, 22.

92. Parezo, "Special Olympics," 111.

93. Go, "Introduction," 2.

94. O'Reilly, "Islanders Show Their Calibers," 7.

95. Gems, *Athletic Crusade*.

96. Jones, "Athletics Helping the Filipino," 591.

2. FROM BASEBALL COLONY TO BASKETBALL REPUBLIC
Epigraph: Reaves, *Taking in a Game*, 1.

1. Markovits and Hellerman, *Offside*, 15.

2. Markovits and Hellerman, *Offside*, 15.

3. Perez, "Between Baseball and Bullfighting."

4. Reaves, *Taking in a Game*, 109. Also see Gems, *Athletic Crusade*.

5. Mojares, *War against the Americans*, 22, 152, 211.

6. Brownell, *Training the Body for China*, 130–31. Also see Morris, *Marrow of the Nation*.

7. The area's name was later changed to Plaza Warwick to honor an American military officer who died in combat on a neighboring island. After Philippine independence, however, the public square was called Freedom Park, a name that remains today. See Mojares, *War against the Americans*.

8. Fraser, *Report of the Secretary-General*, 1911, 481; International Division/ Foreign Work Administrative and Program Records, YMCA-UMN.

9. Ylanan and Ylanan, *History and Development*.

10. Freer, *Philippine Experience of an American Teacher*, 273, 286.

11. Bureau of Education, *Athletic Handbook*.

12. Santiago, "Organization of the San Mateo Baseball Team."

13. Roden, "Baseball and the Quest for National Dignity."

14. Mason, "Football on the Maidan." Also see Guttman, *Games and Empires*.

15. E. Brown, "Far Eastern Olympic Games."

16. O'Reilly, *Islanders Show Their Caliber*, 7.

17. Ylanan and Ylanan, *History and Development*.

18. Walsh, "Babe Ruth Came to Manila."

19. Ylanan and Ylanan, *History and Development*, 62.

20. "Confirmed," *The Filipino Athlete* 5, no. 13 (February 1, 1940): 21.

21. "Comments," *The Filipino Athlete* 8, nos. 15, 16 (October 1947): 22.

22. Pantaleon, "25 Years of NCAA."

23. Lacsamana, "Hendon F.C. Spanish Football Club."

24. Llanos, "British Sailors Introduced Football."

25. Bureau of Education, *Athletic Handbook*, 40.

26. Melendres, "Decades in Basketball."

27. E. Brown, "Unpublished Biography."

28. E. Brown, "Unpublished Biography," 10. Also see Ylanan and Ylanan, *History and Development*.

29. Ylanan and Ylanan, *History and Development*, 71.

30. "Comments," *The Filipino Athlete* 1, no. 6 (October 16, 1935): 4.

31. Del Rosario, "Basketball Offense."

32. See Barrows, *Decade of American Government*; Freer, *Philippine Experience*; and Worcester, *Field Sport*.

33. *Filipino Athlete*, "Is Baseball Dead in the Philippines?"

34. Philippine Amateur Athletic Federation, *Minutes of the Thirty-Second Meeting*, 71.

35. Mandelbaum, *Meaning of Sports*, 40.

36. Block, *Baseball before We Knew It*.

37. Freer, *Philippine Experience*.

38. Shortly after the team's celebrated return to the Philippines, a local journalist published an article questioning the eligibility of some of the Little League champions. Eventually it was learned that the team violated some of the league's regulations on players' ages and residencies. As a result, their championship was forfeited and the ensuing scandal turned the victory from a source of Filipino pride to a cause of national shame. See Hoffer, "Fields of Schemes."

39. "In Canlubang . . . 50 Years of Organized Baseball," *The Filipino Athlete* 20, no. 4 (July–August 1967): 15–16.

40. Mandelbaum, *Meaning of Sports*, 199.

41. Reaves, *Taking in a Game*.

42. Department of Public Instruction, *Narrative Report*, 22.

43. "Where Have All the Ballparks Gone?" *Sports Weekly Magazine* 2, no. 78 (November 26–December, 5 1976): 36.

44. "Where Have All the Ballparks Gone?"
45. "Where Have All the Ballparks Gone?"
46. "Decline of Baseball," *Filipino Athlete*.
47. *Sports Weekly Magazine* 2, no. 61, August 1–8, 1975, 21.
48. "Is Baseball Dead in the Philippines?" *Filipino Athlete*.
49. "Basketball in the Philippines," *Filipino Athlete*.
50. Andolong, *Youth Development*. Also see Reaves, *Taking in a Game*.
51. For a similar example in Republican China, see Morris, *Marrow of the Nation*.
52. "Comments," *The Filipino Athlete* 1, no. 7 (November 1, 1935): 3.
53. "Editorial: A Regrettable Incident," *The Filipino Athlete* 2, no. 14 (February 16, 1937): 9.
54. Philippine Amateur Athletic Federation, *Minutes of the Thirty-Second Meeting*, 79.
55. Ylanan and Ylanan, *History and Development*.
56. Vaughan, *Community under Stress*.
57. Ylanan and Ylanan, *History and Development*.
58. Galily, "Playing Hoops in Palestine."
59. Cingiene and Laskiene, "Revitalized Dream."
60. Cingiene and Laskiene, "Revitalized Dream," 8.
61. Ambrosio Padilla, "Our Berlin Itinerary: Continuation," *The Filipino Athlete* 2, no. 7 (October 16, 1936): 3–6, 15. UPVM.
62. Giron, "Islanders."
63. Cingienne and Laskiene, "Revitalized Dream," 778.
64. Giron, "Islanders," 10.
65. Mamerto Miranda, "The ABC as the Treasurer Sees It." *Agenda of the Twelfth Annual General Meeting of the PAAF Board of Governors* (Manila: Philippine Amateur Athletic Federation, 1974).
66. E. Brown, *Far Eastern Olympic Games*, 166.
67. J. Balonso, "Oregon University Basketball Series," *The Filipino Athlete* 12, no. 19 (September 1954): 9.
68. R. T. Reyes, "Chinese Air Force Scores Near Sweep in Ten-Game Football Series," *The Filipino Athlete* 13, no. 12 (February 1956): 8.
69. "Has There Been Any Philippine All-Around Athletic Superiority?" *The Filipino Athlete* 12, no. 15 (May 1954): 19.

3. THE HOLLYWOODIZATION OF HOOPS

Epigraph: Bourdieu, "How Can One Be a Sports Fan?"

1. See Wagg and Andrews, *East Plays West*.

2. Surprisingly this concept has surfaced in academic literature only recently and has been limited to the discussion of the rise of some Asian economies in the late twentieth century. See Petras, "Americanization of Asia," and Emmerson, "Americanizing Asia?" In this book the concept is simply used to refer to the cultural influence of the United States that came to the Asia with the "Black Ships" in 1853. Its most profound manifestation is arguably more evident in the United States' former colony, the Philippines, than in any other country in the region.

3. Stephenson and Morrison, "Long-Term Changes in the Rotation of the Earth."

4. Five days before the closing of the Olympic Games, eight Palestinian fighters belonging to the Black September group broke into the Olympic Village and held Israeli athletes and staff hostage. The kidnappers demanded the release of hundreds of Palestinian prisoners held in Israeli jails. Eleven members of the Israeli Olympic team were killed by the hostage takers. Five of the attackers were killed by the police in a failed rescue attempt while the other three were captured. See Klein, *Striking Back.*

5. "In what many consider to be the freakiest finish to any athletic contest in history, the Soviet team eventually scored the decisive bucket, but only after the game's final seconds were played not once, not twice, but three times." (Elzey, "Film Review"). In the end, the United States team refused to accept their silver medals, which are now kept in the IOC's headquarters in Lausanne, Switzerland.

6. Elzey, "Film Review."

7. Pauker, "Ganefo I."

8. International Federation of Basketball, *FIBA-World Championship History,* http://www.fiba.com/ downloads/ v3_abouFIBA/mp/fiba_world _championships_history.pdf.

9. Bitong, "Year That Was."

10. "Sports Diplomacy," *The Filipino Athlete* 28 (March–April 1974): 11.

11. Trinidad, *PBA: 20 Years in Pictures,* 13.

12. Marcos, "Sports for Physical Fitness."

13. Andolong, *Youth Development through Sports.*

14. In Southeast Asia the list includes Suharto (Indonesia), Mahathir Mohamad (Malaysia), Lee Kwan Yew (Singapore), Sarit Thanarat and Thanom Kittikachorn (Thailand), Ne Win (Myanmar), Phoumi Nosavan (Laos), and Marcos.

15. Creak, "Sport and the Theatrics of Power."
16. Hong, *Sport, Nationalism, and Orientalism.*
17. Wagg and Andrews, *East Plays West.*
18. Shaw, *Hollywood's Cold War.*
19. Shaw, *Hollywood's Cold War.*
20. Giulianotti and Robertson, *Globalization and Sport.*
21. Kwok, *Multiple Modernities.*
22. Morris, "'I Believe You Can Fly.'"
23. Polumbaum, "Evangelism to Entertainment."
24. Mandelbaum, *Meaning of Sports.*
25. Polumbaum, "Evangelism to Entertainment," 179.
26. Polumbaum, Evangelism to Entertainment," 203.
27. Larmer, "Center of the World."
28. Polumbaum, *Evangelism to Entertainment*, 200.
29. "And Now Comes the Weathermakers."
30. Bonifacio, "How Pro Are the PBA Pros?"
31. Cantor and Barrameda, PBA: *The First 25*, 14.
32. Cantor and Barrameda, PBA: *The First 25*, 17.
33. Trinidad, PBA: *20 Years in Pictures.*
34. Micua, "No Longer Brittle," 20.
35. Bauto, "Mon Fernandez," 13.
36. Manolo Iñigo, "Overkill," *Philippine Daily Inquirer*, May 2, 2008, A30.
37. Andrews and Jackson, *Sport Stars*, 7.
38. "Toyota and Crispa-Floro Again and Again! A Dominance Can Spell Financial Disaster for the PBA," *Sports Weekly Magazine* 2, no. 79 (December 5–12, 1976): 4–5. PNL.
39. Polumbaum, *Evangelism to Entertainment*, 203.
40. Cantor and Barrameda, PBA: *The First 25*, 17.
41. Crawford, *Consuming Sport*, 130.
42. Eljera, "PBA League as Top TV Spectacular," 18.
43. Trinidad, "1982," 5–6.
44. Villafranca, "Philippine Basketball Association," 7.
45. Trinidad, "1982," 5.
46. Ronnie Nathanielsz, "Salud: PBA's New Czar," PBA *Annuals 88–89*, 16.
47. Cantor and Barrameda, PBA: *The First 25*, 32.
48. Cantor and Barrameda, PBA: *The First 25*, 156.
49. Bocobo and Celis, *Legands and Heroes*, 131.
50. Avendanio. "Making of a Basketball Star," 9. Also see Cantor and Barrameda, PBA: *The First 25*, 16–17.

51. The group includes Alvin Patrimonio, Gerry Codinera, Paul Alvarez, and Jojo Lastimosa.
52. Francisco Jocson, "Atoy's Career at a Skids," *Sports Weekly Magazine* 2, no. 98 (April 16–23, 1976): 12–13. PNL.
53. Eala, "Philippines' Basketball League," 49.
54. Whannel, "Reading the Sports Media Audience," 23. Also see Andrews and Jackson, *Sport Stars*, 7.
55. Mendoza, "Year of Firsts," 4.
56. Cantor and Barrameda, PBA: *The First 25*, 16.
57. B. Anderson, *Imagined Communities*, 46.
58. Max Baguio and Baby Alenton, "From the Orangemen," *Sports Weekly Magazine* 2, no. 67 (September 12–19, 1975): 22. PNL.
59. Wagg and Andrews, *East Plays West*.
60. Odle, "Basketball in the Philippines," 3.
61. Avendanio, "Should They Go to Bangkok?" 10.
62. Osias, "Filipino Athletes Deserve Praise," 30.
63. Trinidad, "Basketball Is Not the Name of the Game."
64. Giulianotti and Robertson, *Globalization and Sport*, 11.
65. Morris, "'I Believe You Can Fly,'" 15.

4. ROOTING FOR THE UNDERDOG

1. Sandoval and Abad, *Sports and the Filipino*, 1–4.
2. Bureau of Education, *Athletic Handbook*, 40. Also see Naismith, *Basketball*, 47.
3. Vandello et al., "Appeal of the Underdog," 614.
4. Wendt, "Philippine Fiesta and Colonial Rule."
5. Barrows, *Decade of American Government*. For more recent writings, see Gems, *Athletic Crusade*; Reaves, *Taking a Game*; and Ylanan and Ylanan, *History and Development*.
6. Groves, *Report of Foreign Secretaries*, 1912, 641.
7. Aguilar, *Clash of Spirits*, 47.
8. Eala, "Philippines' Basketball League."
9. "Ending" is a two-digit lottery where the result is taken by combining the last digits (hence the name) of a PBA game's final score. For instance, if the final score between two teams is 105–97, the winning number will be 57.
10. Aguilar, *Clash of Spirits*, 49.
11. Trinidad, "Basketball Is Not the Name of the Game," 5.
12. Angeles, "Battle of Mactan."

13. Bartholomew, *Pacific Rims*, 300–301.

14. Gilbey's Gin, St. George Whiskies, Añejo Rum 65s, Gordon's Gin Boars, and Barangay Ginebra Gin Kings.

15. From 1975 to 2003, the PBA was composed of three conferences (in 1993 these three conferences were named All-Filipino, Commissioner's, and Governors Cups). Thus there are three champions—one in each conference—in one year instead of the usual one annual champion.

16. Cantor and Barrameda, *PBA: The First 25*.

17. Aguilar, *Clash of Spirits*, 49.

18. Cantor and Barrameda, *PBA: The First 25*, 101.

19. Jaworski, however, left the PBA without formally announcing his retirement. There was a constant rumor that he would resume his professional basketball career.

20. Cantor and Barrameda, *PBA: The First 25*, 178.

21. Mendoza, "PBA 88," 10.

22. COMELEC (Commission on Elections), "2004 Synchronized National and Local Elections." http://www.comelec.gov.ph/?r=Archives/Regular Elections/2004NLE/Results/04senalp. Retrieved September 30, 2014.

23. Henson, "Team Profiles," 48.

24. Long after his retirement, Distrito's name resurfaced in the television news when he was featured in a story noting how he excelled in a basketball tournament inside a Nevada prison facility in the United States.

25. Wolff, *Big Game, Small World*.

26. Guttman, *Sports Spectators*, 6.

27. Crawford, *Consuming Sport*, 19.

28. Markovits and Hellerman, *Offside*.

29. Mandelbaum, *Meaning of Sports*, 31.

30. Ileto, *Pasyon and Revolution*, 11.

31. Guttmann, *Sports Spectators*, 178.

32. Trinidad, "Basketball Is Not the Name of the Game," 4–5.

33. B. Anderson, *Imagined Communities*. For a discussion on the relevance of Anderson's ideas to sports, see Nash, "Contestation in Modern English Professional Football."

34. Delaney, *Community, Sport and Leisure*. Also see Stone, "Role of Football in Everday Life."

35. Crawford, *Consuming Sport*, 52.

36. S. Brown, *Football Fans around the World*, 17.

37. Wolff, *Big Game, Small World*, 305.

38. Paras, "Nation Hooked on Hoops."

39. Aguilar, *Clash of Spirits*, 49.

40. Trinidad, "Basketball Is Not the Name of the Game."

41. This term was coined to refer to the countries that had shown potential for following the industrial growth of the Asian Tigers (South Korea, Hong Kong, Taiwan, Singapore) during the Asian Miracle years (1980s–90s). The Ramos administration even used the slogan "Philippines 2000!" to mark the turn of the millennium as the year when the country would achieve the status of a Newly Industrialized Country (NIC). Unfortunately the Asian financial crisis shattered this optimism. See Ramos, *Toward Philippines 2000*.

42. Cantor and Barrameda, PBA: *The First 25*, 101.

43. Wann et al., *Sports Fans*, 39. Also see Wann, *Sport Psychology*.

44. Aguilar, *Clash of Spirits*, 49. Also see Rizal, *Noli Me Tangere*, 259.

45. Aguilar, *Clash of Spirits*, 49.

46. Cantor and Barrameda, PBA: *The First 25*, 16.

47. Social Weather Station, *SWS Sports Survey: Purefoods and Ginebra Tie as the Most Popular in PBA*. http://www.sws.org.ph/pr080814.htm. Retrieved September 19, 2014.

5. BASKETBALL WITHOUT BORDERS

1. FIBA, "Basketball without Borders (BWB) camps." http://bwb.fiba.com /camps. Retrieved September 24, 2014.

2. Andrews, " (Trans)National Basketball Association," 77.

3. "NBA to Open First Overseas Store in China,"*Asia Times,* December 1, 2006. http://www.atimes.com/atimes/China_Business/HL01Cb01 .html. Retrieved January 18, 2011.

4. Guthrie-Shimizu, *Transpacific Field of Dreams*, 5. Also see Rodgers, *Atlantic Crossings*.

5. Bairner, *Sport, Nationalism, and Globalization*, 11.

6. Allison, *Global Politics of Sport*.

7. Maguire, *Global Sport*, 89.

8. Mills, *Subaltern Sports*. Also see Bale and Cronin, *Sport and Postcolonialism*.

9. Maguire, *Global Sport*, 23.

10. See, for example, Beck et al., *Global America?*; Mennel, "Globalization and Americanization"; and Pieterse, *Globalization or Empire?*

11. Galily and Sheard, *Cultural Imperialism and Sport*, 55.

12. Dave L. Llorito, "Fil-Pretenders Put Up Defense against Deportation," *Manila Times*, November 10, 2003, 19.

13. Although the league has been employing a limited number of foreign "imports" since its inception in 1975, the PBA has a rule that regular players should be Filipino nationals. Philippine law, in turn, requires foreign-born applicants to prove their Filipino lineage in order to receive Philippine citizenship. The accused foreign-born players were found to have falsified the documents used to prove their Filipino lineage. The Philippine constitution follows the citizenship idea of *jus sanguines*, which means Filipino citizenship is acquired by blood (being born to a Filipino parent) rather than *jus soli* (being born in the Philippines).

14. Joel Orellana, "Basketball Continues to Lose its Popularity," *Manila Times*, August 19, 2006, 19.

15. Falcous and Maguire, "Making It Local?"

16. Miller et al., *Globalization and Sport.*

17. *Jr. NBA Philippines 2014 Presented by Alaska.* http://ph.nba.com/local -events/83/jr-nbajr-wnba-philippines-2014-tips-off-january-18. Retrieved September 24, 2014.

18. Phillips, "Philippines Is the NBA's New Frontier."

19. Phillips, "Philippines Is the NBA's New Frontier."

20. Phillips, "Philippines Is the NBA's New Frontier."

21. Personal interview, June 25, 2007.

22. Walters, "International Conspiracy."

23. Personal interview, July 5, 2007.

24. Bong Pedralvez, "Fil-Shams Casts Shadow over Pinoy Sports Heroes," *Manila Times*, December 28, 2003, 19.

25. Llorito, "Fil-Pretenders Put Up Defense."

26. Pedralvez, "Fil-Shams Casts Shadow."

27. Agnes R. Cruz, "Torion Gets Green Light to Play Again in the PBA," *Philippines Today: Online Magazine*, August 3, 2003. http://www.philip pinestoday.net/2003/August/sports3_803.htm. Retrieved April 6, 2007.

28. Manotoc, "PBA Marketing."

29. Interestingly, comments on this online news have shown that many Filipino fans are supporting Douhit and are criticizing Reyes for his strategy and decisions as a coach. Some fans have pointed out how Douhit helped the Philippines qualify for the 2014 FIBA World Cup and humbly accepted the team's decision to replace him with Andray

Blatche for the tournament. The author pointed out that "Douhit can't be Kuya Marcus [big brother Marcus] when we win, and not a true Filipino when we lose." See Songalia, "Marcus Douhit Deserves Better."

30. Trinidad, "PBA at the Mercy of Bums?"
31. Ohmae, *End of the Nation-State.*
32. Velasco, "Boosting College Sports."
33. Inigo, "PBA Losing Its Appeal."
34. Henson, "PBA Back on Track."
35. Henson, "Time to Rethink PBA Constitution."
36. Henson, "Time to Rethink PBA Constitution."
37. Bairner, *Sport, Nationalism, and Globalization.*
38. Arenas, "Everybody Should Visit Manila."
39. Mandelbaum, *Meaning of Sports,* 278.
40. Polumbaum, *Evangelism to Entertainment.* Also see Larmer, "Center of the World."
41. Andrews, "(Trans)National Basketball Association," 79.
42. Eisenberg et al., "NBA's Global Game Plan."
43. Polumbaum, *Evangelism to Entertainment,* 203.
44. Falcous and Maguire, "Making It Local?"
45. LaFeber, *Michael Jordan and the New Global Capitalism.*
46. Pau Gasol was the third pick in the 2001 NBA Draft and eventually won Rookie of the Year honors, while Yao was the top overall selection in the 2002 draft. Overall, five Chinese and thirteen Spanish players are either currently on NBA rosters or have played in the league at one time. This trend, however, has dipped in recent years after a number of international players who were drafted high (e.g., Darko Milicic, Andrea Bargnani, Yi Jianlian) failed to live up to their potential.
47. For a discussion on the impact of globalization on Chinese basketball, see Morris, "'I Believe You Can Fly.'" For a piece on Yao Ming and globalization, see Larmer, "Center of the World."

CONCLUSION

1. Naismith, *Basketball,* 147.
2. Guttman, *Games and Empires.*
3. Polumbaum, *Evangelism to Entertainment,* 183.
4. Farred, "Double Temporality of Lagaan."
5. By the 1930s, a ball (such as a football, volleyball, or basketball) was more often used in place of a coconut husk. See Bureau of Public Schools, *Philippine Games.*

6. Spalding, *Spalding's Official Basket Ball Guide*, 189

7. Goh Beng Lan, "Redrawing Centre-Periphery Relations."

8. Goh Beng Lan, "Redrawing Centre-Periphery Relations," 83.

9. Ileto, *Pasyon and Revolution*.

10. Gems, *Athletic Crusade*, 150.

11. Bhabha, *Location of Culture*, 114.

12. Introduced by the Spanish, *fiesta* refers to the Catholic tradition of holding annual celebrations to commemorate feast days of saints and other important Church events. *Jeepney* is a popular mode of transport found all over the Philippines; it was initially made by refurbishing surplus military vehicles left by the Americans after the Second World War.

13. Bhabha, *Location of Culture*.

14. Bhabha, *Location of Culture*, 89 [emphasis included].

15. Rafael, *Promise of the Foreign*, xvi.

16. Kline, *Sugarball*, 3.

17. Bhabha, *Location of Culture*.

BIBLIOGRAPHY

ARCHIVE AND LIBRARY COLLECTIONS

Bancroft Library, University of California, Berkeley
    David P. Barrows Papers
Bentley Historical Library, University of Michigan
    John C. Early Papers
    Frederic S. Marquardt Papers
    Walter W. Marquardt Papers
    Frank Murphy Papers
    Dean C. Worcester Papers
College of Human Kinetics Library, University of the Philippines
    Dissertations and Theses Collection
Jorge B. Vargas Museum and Filipiniana Research Center, University of
    the Philippines (UPVM)
Kautz Family YMCA Archives, University of Minnesota (YMCA-UMN)
    Elwood S. Brown Papers
    International Division/Foreign Work Administrative and Program
        Records
    Alfred H. Swan Photograph Collection
Philippine National Library (PNL)
    Periodicals Section
Philippine Sports Commission Library
    Periodicals Collection
Rizal Library, Ateneo de Manila University (RL ADMU)
    American Historical Collection
    Periodicals Section
United States Library of Congress (US LOC)

United States National Archives and Records Administration (US-NARA)
Bureau of Insular Affairs Records (RG 350); quotations from records in US-NARA are generally in the following form: record group-subgroup-series-folder.
University of the Philippines Main Library
Dissertations and Theses Collection
Periodicals Section

INTERVIEWS BY AUTHOR
Adan, Leo. 05 July 2007.
Angeles, Karl James. 19 December 2007.
Austria, Claudia. 30 January 2008.
Bacong, Michelle. 17 December 2007.
Bello, Francis. 12 July 2007.
Bitanga, Rosauro. 03 July 2007.
Chua, Andrew. 10 December 2007.
Mosar, Lydia. 14 July 2007.
Ogos, Inocencio. 25 June 2007.
Ogos, Manuel. 09 July 2007.
Pepito, Necias. 05 December 2007.
Periquet, Mario. 17 January 2008.
Ramon, Federico. 19 July 2007.
Ramos, John Lucas. 08 July 2007.
Sabado, Nancy. 20 November 2007.
Santos, Bhert. 03 July 2007.
Tabay, Luisito. 17 December 2007.
Tan, Robert Nestor. 25 November 2007.
Urdaneta, Paul. 20 November 2007.
Villanueva, Divine. 22 January 2008.

PUBLISHED SOURCES
Afable, Jorge, ed. *Philippine Sports Greats*. Mandaluyong City: MAN Publishers, 1972.
Aguilar, Filomeno, Jr. *Clash of Spirits: The History of Power and Sugar Planter Hegemony on a Visayan Island*. Quezon City: Ateneo de Manila University Press, 1998.
Allison, Lincoln, ed. *The Global Politics of Sport*. New York: Routledge, 2005.
Anderson, Benedict. "Cacique Democracy in the Philippines." Chap. 9 in *The Spectre of Comparisons: Nationalism, Southeast Asia, and the World*. Quezon City: Ateneo de Manila University Press, 2004.

————. *Imagined Communities*. London: Verso, 1991.

Anderson, Warwick. *Colonial Pathologies: American Tropical Medicine, Race, and Hygiene in the Philippines*. Quezon City: Ateneo de Manila University Press, 2006.

"And Now Comes the Weathermakers: Nate Stephens." *Sports Weekly Magazine* 2, no. 62, (August 9–15, 1976): 13.

Andolong, Nerio. *Youth Development through Sports*. Manila: self-published, 1977.

Andrews, David L. "The (Trans)National Basketball Association: American Commodity-Sign Culture and Global-Local Conjuncturalism." In *Articulating the Global and the Local: Globalization and Cultural Studies*, edited by Ann Cvetkovich and Douglas Kellner, 72–101. Boulder, CO: Westview Press, 1997.

Andrews, David L., and Steven J. Jackson. "Introduction." In *Sport Stars: The Cultural Politics of Sporting Celebrity*, edited by David L. Andrews and Steven J. Jackson, 1–19. New York: Routledge, 2001.

Angeles, Jose A. "The Battle of Mactan and the Indigenous Discourse on War." *Philippine Studies* 55, no. 1 (2007): 3–52.

Antolihao, Lou A. "The Far Eastern Games and the Formation of Asian Identity in the Asia-Pacific during the Early Twentieth Century." In *Asian Communication and Media Studies: Sports, Globalization, Communication*, edited by Ding Junjie and Luo Qing, 214–30. Beijing: Asia Media Research Center, 2007.

Appadurai, Arjun. "Playing with Modernity: The Decolonization of Indian Cricket." Chap. 5 in *Modernity at Large: Cultural Dimensions of Globalization*. Minneapolis: University of Minnesota Press, 1996.

Apter, Andrew. "The Subvention of Tradition: A Genealogy of the Nigerian Durbar." In *State/Culture: State-Formation after the Cultural Turn*, edited by George Steinmetz, 213–52. Ithaca NY: Cornell University Press, 1999.

Arenas, Gilbert. "Everybody Should Visit Manila." *Agent Zero: The Blog File*, July 14, 2008. http://globalbasketnews.wordpress.com/2008/07/15/agent-zero-everybody-should-visit-manila/. Retrieved September 30, 2014.

Atkinson, Fred W. "Education in the Philippines." *The Outlook* 70 (January–April 1902): 832.

Avendanio, Salvador A. "Should They Go to Bangkok?" *Sports Weekly Magazine* 2, no.74 (October 31–November 7, 1976): 10.

————. "The Making of a Basketball Star." *Sports Weekly Magazine* 2, no. 100 (April 26–May 2, 1976): 9.

Bacobo, Christian, and Beth Celis. Legends and Heroes of Philippine Basketball. Manila: Christian Bocobo, 2004.

Bairner, Alan. *Sport, Nationalism, and Globalization*. Albany: State University of New York Press, 2001.

Bale, John, and Mike Cronin, eds. *Sport and Postcolonialism*. Oxford: Berg, 2003.

Barrows, David P. *A Decade of American Government in the Philippines, 1903–1913*. New York: New World Book Co., 1914.

Barthes, Roland. *What Is Sport?* New Haven, CT: Yale University Press, 2007.

Bartholomew, Rafe. *Pacific Rims: Beermen Ballin' in Flip-flops and the Philippines' Unlikely Love Affair with Basketball*. New York: New American Library, 2010.

Bauto, Bessie O. "Mon Fernandez: Toyota's Deadly Beanpole." *Sports Weekly Magazine* 2, no. 59 (July 18–25, 1976): 13.

Beck, Ulrich, Natan Sznaider, and Rainer Winter, eds. *Global America? The Cultural Consequences of Globalization*. Liverpool: Liverpool University Press, 2003.

Beran, Janice. "Physical Education and Sport in the Philippines." In *Sport in Asia and Africa*, edited by Eric Wagner, 147–64. New York: Greenwood Press, 1989.

Bhabha, Homi K. *The Location of Culture*. London: Routledge, 1994.

Bitong, Ernie T. "The Year That Was: Top Sport Stories of 1967," *The Filipino Athlete* 20, no. 6 (November–December 1967): 16–17.

Block, David. *Baseball Before We Knew It: A Search for the Root of the Game*. Lincoln: University of Nebraska Press, 2005.

Bonifacio, Bitoy. "How Pro Are the PBA Pros?" *Sports Weekly Magazine* 2, no. 122 (October 1–8, 1976): 34.

Booth, Douglas. *The Field: Truth and Fiction in Sport History*. London: Routledge, 2005.

Bourdieu, Pierre. "How Can One Be a Sports Fan?" In *The Cultural Studies Reader: Second Edition*, edited by Simon During, 427–40. London: Routledge, 1999.

Brown, Elwood. *Annual Report of the Physical Director*. 1911. Philippine YMCA, International Division/Foreign Work Administrative and Program Records, YMCA-UMN.

———. *Annual Report of the Physical Director*. 1917. Philippine YMCA, International Division/Foreign Work Administrative and Program Records, YMCA-UMN.

———. "Far Eastern Olympic Games." In *Athletic League Handbook*. 1913. Elwood Brown Papers, YMCA-UMN.

———. "Unpublished Biography." May 1922. Elwood Brown Papers, YMCA-UMN.

Brown, Sean, ed. *Football Fans around the World: From Supporters to Fanatics*. London: Routledge, 2007.

Brownell, Susan, ed. *The 1904 Anthropology Days and Olympic Games: Sport, Race, and American Imperialism*. Lincoln: University of Nebraska Press, 2008.

———. *Training the Body for China: Sports in the Moral Order of the People's Republic*. Chicago: University of Chicago Press, 1995.

Buffington, Frances C. *Physical Training for Filipinos*. Boston: D. C. Heath, 1909.

Bureau of Education. *Athletic Handbook for the Philippine Public Schools*. Manila: Bureau of Printing, 1911.

———. *General Instructions No. 29*, Series of 1918 (July 17). RG350-E5-2618-90 US-NARA.

Bureau of Public Schools. *Philippine Games for Physical Education*. Manila: Bureau of Printing, 1952.

Cantor, Jimmy, and Bong Barrameda, eds. PBA: *The First 25*. Quezon City: Philippine Basketball Association, 2000.

Carpenter, Frank W., letter to Vernon L. Whitney, April 21, 1914. Bureau of Insular Affairs Records. RG 350-E5A-1887-1158 US-NARA.

Cingiene, Vilma, and Skaiste Laskiene. "A Revitalized Dream: Basketball and National Identity in Lithuania." *The International Journal of the History of Sport* 21, no. 5, (November 2004): 762–78.

COMELEC (Commission on Elections). "2004 Synchronized National and Local Elections." http://www.comelec.gov.ph/?r=Archives/Regular Elections/2004NLE/Results/04senalp. Retrieved September 30, 2014.

Crawford, Garry. *Consuming Sport: Fans, Sport and Culture*. London: Routledge, 2004.

Creak, Simon. "Sport and the Theatrics of Power in a Postcolonial State: The National Games of 1960s Laos." *Asian Studies Review* 34 (June 2010): 191–210.

Cullinane, Michael. "Basketball and Culture: A Problem in Private Transitory Ownership?" *Philippine Quarterly of Culture and Society* 3, no. 1 (March 1975): 54–58.

Cunningham, Carson. *American Hoops: The History of United States Olympic Basketball from Berlin to Barcelona*. PhD diss., Purdue University, 2006.

Dayrit, Celso L. *The Olympic Movement in the Philippines*, Quezon City: self-published, 2003.

Delaney, Tim. *Community, Sport and Leisure.* New York: Legend Books, 2001.

Del Rosario, Alfredo. "Basketball Offense." *The Filipino Athlete* 1, no. 7 (November 1, 1935): 5, 11.

Department of Public Instruction, Commonwealth of the Philippines. *Narrative Report of the Department of Instruction as Required by Executive Order No. 861.* Manila, 1935: 22. Frank Murphy Papers, BHL-UMI.

Eala, Noli. "The Philippines' Basketball League," *FIBA Assist Magazine,* June 2004, 49.

Eisenberg, Daniel, Cathy Booth Thomas, Jackson Baker, Sean Gregory, Laura A. Locke, and Adam Pitluk. "The NBA's Global Game Plan." *Time,* March 17, 2003. http://content.time.com/time/magazine/article /0,9171,1004412,00.html. Retrieved September 28, 2014.

Eljera, Bert. "The PBA League as Top TV Spectacular." In *1981 PBA Annuals.* Pasig: Philippine Basketball Association, 1981.

Elzey, Chris. "A Film Review of George Roy's :03 Seconds from Gold." *Journal of Sport History* 29, no. 3 (Fall 2002): 518–22.

Emmerson, Donald K. "Americanizing Asia?" *Foreign Affairs* 77, no. 3 (May–June 1998): 46–56.

England, Frederick. "Physical Education." In Bureau of Education, *Athletic Handbook for the Philippine Public Schools.* Manila: Bureau of Printing, 1911.

Falcous, Mark, and Joseph Maguire. 2005. "Making It Local? National Basketball Expansion and English Basketball Subcultures." In *Sport and Corporate Nationalisms,* edited by Michael L. Silk, David L. Andrews, and C. L. Cole, 13–34. Oxford: Berg, 2005.

Farred, Grant. "The Double Temporality of Lagaan." In *Visual Economies of/in Motion: Sport and Film,* edited by Richard C. King and David J. Leonard, 85–128. New York: Peter Lang, 2006.

The Filipino Athlete. "Basketball in the Philippines." September 16, 1935.

———. "Editorial: Is Baseball Dead in the Philippines?" June 1, 1937, 8.

———. "Editorial: The Decline of Baseball." December 1, 1940, 10.

Food and Nutrition Research Institute (FNRI). *6th National Nutrition Survey.* Taguig City, Philippines: FNRI, Department of Science and Technology, 2003.

Fraser, H. C. *Report of the Secretary-General.* 1911. Philippine YMCA, International Division/Foreign Work Administrative and Program Records, YMCA-UMN.

———. *Report of the Secretary-General.* 1914. Philippine YMCA, International Division/Foreign Work Administrative and Program Records, YMCA-UMN.

Freer, William B. *The Philippine Experience of an American Teacher.* New York: Charles Scribner and Sons, 1906.

Galily, Yair. "Playing Hoops in Palestine: The Early Development of Basketball in the Land of Israel, 1935–56." *The International Journal of the History of Sport* 20, no. 1 (November 2003): 143–51.

Galily, Yair, and Ken Sheard. "Cultural Imperialism and Sport: The Americanization of Israeli Basketball," Culture, Sport, Society 5, no. 2 (Summer 2002): 55–78.

Garcia, Jaume, and Climent Quintana-Domeque. "The Evolution of Adult Height in Europe: A Brief Note." Economics and Human Biology 5, no. 2 (July 2007): 340–49.

Gems, Gerald R. "Anthropology Days, the Construction of Whiteness, and American Imperialism in the Philippines." In *The 1904 Anthropology Days and Olympic Games: Sport, Race, and American Imperialism,* edited by Susan Brownell, 189–216. Lincoln: University of Nebraska Press, 2008.

———. *The Athletic Crusade: Sport and American Cultural Imperialism.* Lincoln: University of Nebraska Press, 2006.

Giron, Eric S. "The Islanders." In *Philippine Sports Greats,* edited by Jorge Afable, 1–12. Mandaluyong, Rizal: Man Publishers, 1972.

Giulianotti, Richard, and Roland Robertson. *Globalization and Sport.* Malden, MA: Blackwell Publishing, 2007.

Go, Julian. "Introduction: Global Perspectives on the U.S. Colonial State in the Philippines." In *The American Colonial State in the Philippines: Global Perspectives,* edited by Julian Go and Anne Foster, 1–42. Pasig City: Anvil Publishing, 2005.

Go, Julian, and Anne Foster, eds. 2005. *The American Colonial State in the Philippines: Global Perspectives.* Pasig City: Anvil Publishing, 2005.

Goh, Daniel P. S. "States of Ethnography: Colonialism, Resistance, and Cultural Transcription in Malaya and the Philippines, 1890s–1930s." *Comparative Studies in Society and History* 49, no.1 (January 2007): 109–42.

Goh Beng Lan. "Redrawing Centre-Periphery Relations: Theoretical Challenges in the Study of Southeast Asian Modernity." In *Asia in Europe, Europe in Asia,* edited by S. Ravi, M. Rutten, and B. L. Goh, 79–101. Singapore: ISEAS and IIAS, 2004.

Groves, James M. *Report of Foreign Secretaries*. 1912. Philippine YMCA, International Division/Foreign Work Administrative and Program Records, YMCA-UMN.

———. *Report of the Secretary General*. 1911. Philippine YMCA, International Division/Foreign Work Administrative and Program Records, YMCA-UMN.

———. *Report of the Secretary General*. 1915. Philippine YMCA, International Division/Foreign Work Administrative and Program Records, YMCA-UMN.

Guha, Ramachandra. *A Corner of a Foreign Field: The Indian History of a British Sport*. London: Picador, 2002.

Guha, Ranajit. "On Some Aspects of the Historiography of India." In *Subaltern Studies I*, edited by Ranajit Guha. Delhi: Oxford University Press, 1982.

Guthrie-Shimizu, Sayuri. *Transpacific Field of Dreams: How Baseball Linked the United States and Japan in Peace and War*. Chapel Hill: University of North Carolina Press, 2012.

Guttmann, Allen. *From Ritual to Record: The Nature of Modern Sports*. New York: Columbia University Press, 2004.

———. *Games and Empires: Modern Sport and Cultural Imperialism*. New York: Columbia University Press, 1994.

———. *Sports Spectators*. New York: Columbia University Press, 1986.

Guttmann, Allen, and Lee Thompson. *Japanese Sports: A History*. Honolulu: University of Hawaii Press, 2001.

Halili, Servando D. *Iconography of the New Empire: Race and Gender Images and the American Colonization of the Philippines*. Quezon City: University of the Philippines Press, 2006.

Hayden, Joseph R. *The Philippines: A Study in National Development*. New York: Macmillan, 1947.

"Headhunters Drop That Pastime for Football." *Washington Post*, August 6, 1927, 1. RG350-E5-1887-52 US-NARA.

Henson, Joaquin. "PBA Back on Track," *The Philippine Star*, April 28, 2004, A30.

———. "Team Profiles." In *PBA Annuals 88–89*. Pasig City: Philippine Basketball Association, 1989.

———. "Time to Rethink PBA Constitution." *The Philippine Star*, November 4, 2007, A20.

Hoffer, Richard. "Fields of Schemes." *Sports Illustrated* 78, no. 2 (January 18, 1993). http://www.si.com/vault/1993/01/18/127893/field-of-schemes

-in-august-a-team-from-a-remote-corner-of-the-philippines-won-the
-little-league-world-series----then-the-victory-dissolved-in-deceit.
Retrieved February 15, 2012.

Hong, Fan. *Sport, Nationalism, and Orientalism: The Asian Games*. London: Routledge, 2007.

Horger, Marc T. "Play by the Rules: The Creation of Basketball and the Progressive Era, 1891–1917." PhD diss., Ohio State University, 2001.

Hornedo, Florentino H. *Culture and Community in the Philippine Fiesta and Other Celebrations*. Manila: University of Santo Tomas Publishing House, 2000.

Hughson, John, David Inglis, and Marcus Free. *The Uses of Sport: A Critical Study*. London: Routledge, 2005.

Ileto, Reynaldo. *Pasyon and Revolution: Popular Movements in the Philippines, 1840–1910*. Quezon City: Ateneo de Manila University Press, 1979.

Iñigo, Manolo. "Overkill." *Philippine Daily Inquirer*, May 2, 2008, A30.

———. "PBA Losing Its Appeal." *Philippine Daily Inquirer*, November 10, 2003, 31.

Isaac, Allen P. *American Tropics: Articulating Filipino America*. Minneapolis: University of Minnesota Press, 2006.

Joaquin, Nick. *Almanac for Manilenos*. Manila: Mr. & Ms. Publications, 1979.

Jones, O. Garfield. "Athletics Helping the Filipino," *Outlook*, August 1914, 585–92.

Kalaw, Pura V. *How the Filipina Got the Vote*. Manila: self-published, 1952.

Karnow, Stanley. *In Our Image: America's Empire in the Philippines*. New York: Ballantine Books, 1990.

Kaufmann, Jason, and Orlando Patterson. "Cross-National Cultural Diffusion: The Global Spread of Cricket." *American Sociological Review* 70 (February 2005): 82–110.

Klein, Aaron J. *Striking Back: The 1972 Munich Olympics Massacre and Israel's Deadly Response*. New York: Random House, 2007.

Kline, Alan. "Culture, Politics, and Baseball in the Dominican Republic." *Latin American Perspectives* 22, no. 3 (1998): 111–30.

———. *Sugarball: The American Game, the Dominican Dream*. New Haven, CT: Yale University Press, 1991.

Kramer, Paul A. *The Blood of Government: Race, Empire, the United States, and the Philippines*. Quezon City: Ateneo de Manila University Press, 2006.

Kwok, Jenny Wah Lau. *Multiple Modernities: Cinemas and Popular Media in Transcultural East Asia*. Philadelphia: Temple University Press, 2003.

Lacsamana, Jimmie T. "Hendon F.C. Spanish Football Club." In *Manila Football League Program, Manila-Hongkong Interport Match, May 17–25, 1951*. Manila: Manila Football Club, 1951.

LaFeber, Walter. *Michael Jordan and the New Global Capitalism*. New York: W. W. Norton, 1999.

———. *The New Empire: An Interpretation of American Expansion, 1860–1898*. Ithaca NY: Cornell University Press, 1963.

Larmer, Brook. "The Center of the World," *Foreign Policy*, September–October 2005. http://www.foreignpolicy.com/articles/2005/08/30/the_center_of_the_world. Retrieved September 28, 2014.

Lim, T. O., L. M. Ding, M. Zaki, A. B. Suleiman, S. Fatimah, A. Tahir, and A. H. Maimunah. 2000. "Distribution of Body Weight, Height and Body Mass Index in a National Sample of Malaysian Adults." *Medical Journal of Malaysia* 55: 108–28.

Llanos, Ricky. "British Sailors Introduced Football in the Philippines." In *Manila Football League Program, Manila-Hongkong Interport Match, May 17–25, 1951*. Manila: Manila Football Club, 1951.

Llorito, Dave L. "Fil-Pretenders Put Up Defense against Deportation." *The Manila Times*, November 10, 2003, 19.

Lynch, Frank. "Social Acceptance Reconsidered." In *Four Readings on Philippine Values*, 4th ed., edited by Frank Lynch and Alfonso de Guzman II, 1–68. Quezon City: Ateneo de Manila University Press, 1973.

Maguire, Joseph. *Global Sport*. Cambridge: Polity Press, 1999.

Mandelbaum, Michael. *The Meaning of Sports: Why Americans Watch Baseball, Football and Basketball, and What They See When They Do*. New York: Public Affairs, 2004.

Mangan, J. A., ed. *Cultural Bond: Sport, Empire, Society*. London: Frank Cass, 1992.

Manotoc, Tommy. "PBA Marketing, Repackaging Go Hand-in-Hand," *Philippine Daily Inquirer*, March 20, 2009, A28.

Marcos, Ferdinand E. "Sports for Physical Fitness and Brotherhood." *The Filipino Athlete* 28, no. 2 (May–June 1973): 4.

Markovits, Andrei S., and Steven L. Hellerman. *Offside: Soccer and American Exceptionalism*. Princeton NJ: Princeton University Press, 2001.

Mason, Tony. "Football on the Maidan: Cultural Imperialism in Calcutta." *The International Journal of the History of Sport* 7, no. 1 (1990): 85–96.

Maxwell, J. Truitt. *Annual Report of the Physical Director*. 1925. Philippine YMCA, International Division/Foreign Work Administrative and Program Records, YMCA-UMN.

May, Glenn A. *Social Engineering in the Philippines*, Westport CT: Greenwood Press, 1980.

Mechikoff, Robert A. *A History and Philosophy of Sport and Physical Education: From Ancient Civilizations to the Modern World*. 5th ed. New York: McGraw-Hill, 2010.

Melendres, Teddyvic. "The Decades in Basketball." In *The Philippine Olympic Week*, edited by Enrique M. Gonzales, 22. Manila: Philippine Olympic Committee, 1989.

Mendoza, Al S. "PBA 88: A Big Smashing Party." In *PBA Annuals 88–89*. Pasig City: Philippine Basketball Association, 1989.

———. "Year of Firsts, Comebacks . . . Romance." *PBA Annuals 90–91*. Pasig: Philippine Basketball Association, 1991.

Mennel, Stephen. "Globalization and Americanization." In *The Routledge International Handbook of Globalization Studies*, edited by Bryan S. Turner, 96–113. New York: Routledge, 2010.

Micua, Leonardo V. "No Longer Brittle . . . The Noritake Festival." *Sports Weekly Magazine* 2, no. 65 (August 29–September 5, 1976): 20.

Miller, Stuart. *Benevolent Assimilation: The American Conquest of the Philippines*. New Haven CT: Yale University Press, 1982.

Miller, Toby, Geoffrey Lawrence, Jim McKay, and David Rowe. *Globalization and Sport*. London: Sage Publications, 2001.

Mills, James, ed. *Subaltern Sports: Politics and Sport in South Asia*. London: Anthem Press, 2005.

Ministry of Education, Culture, Sports, Science and Technology (MEXT). *Official Statistics 2004*. http://www.mext.go.jp/b_menu/toukei/001/022/2004/002.pdf. Retrieved September 28, 2014.

Miranda, Mamerto. "The ABC as the Treasurer Sees It." *Agenda of the Twelfth Annual General Meeting of the PAAF Board of Governors*. Manila: Philippine Amateur Athletic Federation, 1974.

Mojares, Resil B. *The War against the Americans: Resistance and Collaboration in Cebu, 1899–1906*. Quezon City: Ateneo de Manila University Press, 1999.

Morill, Alfred. *Report of Secretary-General*. 1915. Philippine YMCA, International Division/Foreign Work Administrative and Program Records, YMCA-UMN.

Morris, Andrew D. "'I Believe You Can Fly': Basketball Culture in Post-socialist China." In *Popular China: Unofficial Culture in a Globalizing Society*, edited by Perry Link, Richard P. Madsen, and Paul G. Pickowicz, 9–38. Lanham MD: Rowman & Littlefield, 2002.

——. *Marrow of the Nation: A History of Sport and Physical Culture in Republican China*. Berkeley: University of California Press, 2004.

Naismith, James. *Basketball—Its Origins and Development*. New York: Association Press, 1941.

Nash, Rex. "Contestation in Modern English Professional Football: The Independent Supporters Association Movement." *International Review for the Sociology of Sport* 35, no. 4 (2000): 465–86.

Odle, Don J. "Basketball in the Philippines." *The Filipino Athlete* 14, no. 22 (December 1958): 3.

Ogden, Cynthia L., Cheryl D. Fryar, Margaret D. Carroll, and Katherine M. Flegal. "Mean Body Weight, Height, and Body Mass Index, United States 1960–2002." *Advance Data from Vital and Health Statistics* 347 (October 27, 2004). http://www.cdc.gov/nchs/data/ad/ad347.pdf. Retrieved September 5, 2008.

Ohmae, Kinichi. *The End of the Nation-State: The Rise of Regional Economies*. London: Harper Collins, 1995.

Olcott, Charles S. *The Life of William McKinley*. 2 vols. Boston: Houghton Mifflin, 1916.

O'Reilly, P. S. "Islanders Show Their Caliber in the Olympiad." *The Bulletin: San Francisco*, March 25, 1913, 7. RG350-E5A-1887-118 US-NARA.

Osias, Camilo. "Filipino Athletes Deserve Praise." *The Filipino Athlete* 20, no. 1 (January–February 1967): 30.

Pantaleon, Virgilio. "25 Years of NCAA." In *NCAA 25th Anniversary Souvenir Program, 1949–1950*. Manila: National Collegiate Athletic Association, 1950.

Paras, Wilhelmina. "A Nation Hooked on Hoops: For Filipinos, It's the Top Game after Politics." *Asiaweek*, October 24, 1997, 47.

Parezo, Nancy J. 2008. "A Special Olympics: Testing Racial Strength and Endurance at the 1904 Louisiana Purchase Exposition." In *The 1904 Anthropology Days and Olympic Games: Sport, Race, and American Imperialism*, edited by Susan Brownell, 59–126. Lincoln: University of Nebraska Press, 2008.

Pauker, Ewa T. "Ganefo I: Sports and Politics in Djakarta." *Asian Survey* 5, no. 4 (April 1965): 171–85.

Pecson, Geronima, and Mary Racelis, eds. *Tales of American Teachers in the Philippines*. Manila: Carmelo and Bauermann, 1959.

Perez, Louis A. "Between Baseball and Bullfighting: The Quest for Nationality in Cuba, 1868–1898." *The Journal of American History* 81, no. 2 (September 1994): 493–517.

Petras, James. 1998 "The Americanization of Asia: The Rise and Fall of Civilization." *Journal of Contemporary Asia* 28, no. 2 (1998): 149–58.

Philippine Amateur Athletic Federation. *Minutes of the Thirty-Fifth Annual General Meeting of the PAAF Board of Governors.* Manila Hotel, June 7, 1952, UPVM.

———. *Minutes of the Thirty-Fourth Annual General Meeting of the PAAF Board of Governors.* Rizal Memorial Coliseum, July 13, 1951, 89, UPVM.

———. *Minutes of the Thirty-Second Annual General Meeting of the PAAF Board of Governors.* Rizal Memorial Coliseum, July 29, 1949.

Phillips, Aaron. 2009. "The Philippines Is NBA's New Frontier." *Dime Magazine*, September 2, 2009. http://dimemag.com/2009/09/ thephilippines-is-the-nbas-next-frontier/. Retrieved February 2, 2011.

Pieterse, Nederveen. *Globalization or Empire?* New York: Routledge, 2004.

Polumbaum, Judy. "From Evangelism to Entertainment: The YMCA, the NBA and the Evolution of Chinese Basketball." *Modern Chinese Literature and Culture* 14, no. 1 (Spring 2002): 178–230.

Pope, Steven W. "An Army of Athletes: Playing Fields, Battlefields, and the American Military Sporting Experience." *The Journal of Military History* 59, no. 3 (July 1995): 435–56.

Povich, Shirley. "This Morning," *Washington Post*, January, 24 1934, 15. RG 350-E5A-1887-52 US-NARA.

Putney, Clifford. *Muscular Christianity: Manhood and Sport in Protestant America, 1880–1920.* Cambridge MA: Harvard University Press, 2001.

Rafael, Vicente. *The Promise of the Foreign: Nationalism and the Techniques of Translation in the Spanish Philippines.* Durham NC: Duke University Press, 2005.

———. *White Love and Other Events in Filipino History.* Quezon City: Ateneo de Manila Press, 2000.

Ramos, Fidel V. *Toward Philippines 2000: A Resurgence of Optimism and Growth.* Manila: Office of the Press Secretary, 1994.

Reaves, Joseph. *Taking a Game: A History of Baseball in Asia.* Lincoln: University of Nebraska Press, 2004.

Rizal, Jose P. *Noli Me Tangere.* Reprint of Berlin edition (1886). Quezon City: R. Martinez and Sons, 1958.

Roden, Donald. "Baseball and the Quest for National Dignity in Meiji Japan." *The American Historical Review* 85, no. 3 (June 1980): 511–34.

Rodgers, Daniel T. *Atlantic Crossings: Social Politics in a Progressive Age.* Cambridge MA: Harvard University Press, 2000.

Salman, Michael. *The Embarrassment of Slavery: Controversies over Bondage and Nationalism in the American Colonial Philippines.* Quezon City: Ateneo de Manila University Press, 2001.

Sandoval, Gerardo A., and Ricardo G. Abad. "Sports and the Filipino: A Love Affair." *Social Weather Bulletin* 97, nos. 3–4 (February 1997).

Sands, Robert. "Anthropology and Sport." In *Anthropology, Sport, and Culture*, edited by Robert Sands. Westport CT: Bergin and Garvey, 1999.

Santiago, Luis. "The Organization of the San Mateo Baseball Team." *The Teachers' Assembly Herald* 5, no. 26 (1912): 142–43. RG350-E5A-15351-17 US-NARA.

Scott, James. *Weapons of the Weak: Everyday Forms of Resistance.* New Haven CT: Yale University Press, 1985.

Seymour, Harold. *Baseball: The People's Game.* New York: Oxford University Press, 1990.

Shaw, Tony. *Hollywood's Cold War.* Edinburgh: Edinburgh University Press, 2007.

Social Weather Stations. *Social Weather Report*, August 26–September 5, 2005.

———. *SWS Sports Survey: Purefoods and Ginebra Tie as the Most Popular in PBA.* http://www.sws.org.ph/pro80814.htm. Retrieved September 19, 2014.

Songalia, Ryan. "Marcus Douhit Deserves Better Than This." http://www.rappler.com/sports/by-sport/basketball/gilas-pilipinas/70313-marcus-douthit-deserves-better?utm_source=facebook&utm_medium=referral. Retrieved September 28, 2014.

Spalding, Albert G. *Spalding's Official Basket Ball Guide, 1913–14.* New York: The American Sports Publishing Co., 1914. US-LOC.

Speak, Mike. "China in the Modern World, 1840–1949." In *Sport and Physical Education in China*, edited by James Riordan and Robin Jones, 70–89. London: Routledge, 1999.

Stephenson, F. Richard, and Leslie V. Morrison. "Long-Term Changes in the Rotation of the Earth: 700 B.C. to A.D. 1980." *Philosophical Transactions*, Series A, 313, no. 1524 (November 1984): 47–70.

Stoddard, Brian. "Sport, Cultural Imperialism, and Colonial Response in the British Empire." *Comparative Studies in Society and History* 30, no. 4 (1988): 649–73.

———. *Sport, Culture and History.* London: Routledge, 2008.

Stone, Chris. "The Role of Football in Everday Life." In *Football Fans around the World: From Supporters to Fanatics*, edited by Sean Brown, 7–22. London: Routledge, 2007.

Sugden, John, and Alan Tomlinson, eds. *Power Games: A Critical Sociology of Sport*. New York: Routledge, 2002.

Tener, William A. *Report of the Secretary General, Philippine YMCA*. 1908. International Division/Foreign Work Administrative and Program Records, YMCA-UMN.

Trinidad, Recah. "1982: The Year of Change in the PBA," *1981 PBA Annuals*. Pasig: Philippine Basketball Association, 5–6.

————. "Basketball Is Not the Name of the Game." In *Dribblers: A Photographic Essay on Basketball Players of the Philippines*, edited by Marites Pardo-Panlilio. Manila: PT Picturehouse, 1990.

————. "PBA at the Mercy of Bums?" *Philippine Daily Inquirer*. http://sports.inquirer.net/inquirersports/inquirersports/view/20080722-149913/PBA-at-the-mercy-of-bums. Retrieved July 23, 2008.

Trinidad, Recah, ed. *PBA: 20 Years in Pictures*. Pasig: Philippine Basketball Association, 1994.

Tumonggor, Johan, and Hari K. Lasmono. "Youth Profile in Some Suburban Areas in East Java (Preliminary Survey of the Indonesian Youth Stature at the Fiftieth Anniversary of Indonesia)." *Folia Medica Indonesiana (FMI)* 39, no. 2 (April 2003). http://www.journal.unair.ac.id/detail_jurnal.php?id=1321&med=3&bid=3. Retrieved September 5, 2008.

Turner, E. Stanton. *Report of the Secretary General. Philippine YMCA*. 1916. International Division/Foreign Work Administrative and Program Records, YMCA-UMN.

Vandello, Joseph A., Nadav P. Goldschmied, and David A. R. Richards. "The Appeal of the Underdog." *Personality and Social Psychology Bulletin* 33, no. 1 (2007): 603–16.

Vaughan, Elizabeth H. *Community under Stress: An Internment Camp Culture*. Princeton NJ: Princeton University Press, 1949.

Velasco, Bill. "Boosting College Sports." *The Philippine Star*, January 31, 2011, A20.

Villafranca, Vic. "The Philippine Basketball Association in the Year of the Dog," *1982 PBA Annuals*. Pasig: Philippine Basketball Association, 1982, 7.

Villanueva, Pedro D. *History, Development, and Progress of Physical Education in the Philippines*. Bachelor's Thesis, YMCA College, Chicago, 1922.

Wagg, Stephen, and David L. Andrews, eds. *East Plays West: Sport and the Cold War*. London: Routledge, 2006.

Walsh, Thomas P. "Babe Ruth Came to Manila." *Bulletin of the American Historical Collection* 30, no. 3, (July 2002): 10.

Walters, John. "The International Conspiracy behind the Success of the San Antonio Spurs." Newsweek. http://www.newsweek.com/interna tional-conspiracy-behind-success-san-antonio-spurs-253711. Retrieved September 30, 2014.

Wann, Daniel, Merrill Melnick, Gordon Russell, and Dale Pease. *Sport Psychology*. Upper Saddle River NJ: Prentice Hall, 1997.

———. *Sports Fans: The Psychology and Social Impact of Spectators*. New York: Routledge, 2001.

Wendt, Reinhard. "Philippine Fiesta and Colonial Rule," *Philippine Studies* 46, no. 1 (First Quarter 1998): 3–23.

Whannel, Garry. "Reading the Sports Media Audience." In *MediaSport*, edited by Lawrence A. Wenne, 119–33. London: Routledge, 1998.

White, Frank R. "Education Report." In U.S. Department of Interior, *Education in the Territories and Outlying Possessions*: 658–59. U.S. Department of Labor, 1913. RG 350-E5-117-73, US-NARA.

Wolff, Alexander. *Big Game, Small World: A Basketball Adventure*. New York: Warner Books, 2002.

Wolters, O. W. *History, Culture, and Region in Southeast Asian Perspectives*. Singapore: Institute of Southeast Asian Studies, 1982.

Worcester, Dean C. "Field Sport among the Wild Men of Northern Luzon." *The National Geographic Magazine* 22, no. 3 (March 1911): 215–67.

———. *The Philippines: Past and Present*. New York: Macmillan, 1921.

Wuest, Deborah A., and Charles A. Bucher. *Foundations of Physical Education and Sport*. St. Louis: Mosby, 1995.

Yang, X. G., et al. *Study on Weight and Height of the Chinese People and the Differences between 1992 and 2002*. Beijing: National Institute for Nutrition and Food Safety, 2005. http://www.ncbi.nlm.nih.gov /pubmed/16334998. Retrieved September 5, 2008.

Ylanan, Regino, and Carmen Ylanan. *The History and Development of Physical Education and Sports in the Philippines*. Manila: self-published, 1965.

INDEX

Page numbers in italic refer to illustrations.

Advincula, Daniel, 169
Aguilar, Filomeno, Jr., 21, 124, 139, 146
All-Filipino Conference (PBA), 106, 110
"Americanization," 31–32, 181; adapted by Filipinos, 185; of Asia, 94, 120, 189; and globalization, 151–53; of Israeli basketball, 153; and Philippine basketball, 102–3, 106
Anderson, Benedict, 49, 115
Anderson, Warwick, 38
Andrews, David, 107
Appadurai, Arjun, 20–21
Apter, Andrew, 35
Araneta Coliseum, 163
Arenas, Gilbert, 171–72, 175–76
ASEAN Basketball League, 169
Asian Baseball Federation, 87
Asian Basketball Championships. *See* FIBA Asia
Asian Games: basketball championships, 4; Philippine

basketball performance, 165; 1951 Delhi, 17; 2002 Busan (South Korea), 167; 2006 Doha, 167; 2014 Inchon (South Korea), 13, 161
Ateneo de Manila University (Blue Eagles), 163–64
Atkinson, Fred, 50

Baguio City, 39, 69
Bairner, Alan, 151
Bale, John, 7
barangay, 135–37, 144
Barangay Ginebra. *See* Ginebra
Barrios, Bayang, 141
Barrows, David, 44, 55, 69, 77
Bartholomew, Rafe, 9
baseball: and the *bourgeoisie*, 84–86; and the colonial public school system, 79; decline of, 72–73, 81–82; during World War II, 86–87; embodied in nineteenth-century U.S. society, 78; "follows the

baseball *(cont.)*
American flag," 180; and
higher education, 82–84;
introduction in the
Philippines, 36; "language,"
69; role in colonization, 3; and
urbanization, 81–82
Basketball Association of the
Philippines, 5, 96
Basketball without Borders,
149–50, 154
battle of ballgames, 21–22
Battle of Mactan, 126, 140
Bell, Franklin, 3
Benedicto, Roberto, 97
"benevolent assimilation," 51
Bernardino, Jun, 149
Bhabha, Homi K., 23–24, 185–86
billiards, 11
Black, Norman, 164
Blatche, Andray, 4–5
"blocking foul," 8–9
bloomers, 53–54
Booth, Douglas, 10
bowling, 11
boxing, 11
Brown, Elwood, 24, 38–39, 58,
74, 180
Brown, Sean, 136
bullfighting, 66
Bureau of Education (BOE), 37;
athletic suits for girls, 54;
report about the decline of
baseball, 72; and YMCA, 58, 74
Bureau of Public Instruction, 37,
55, 81
bushido, 60

Calvo, Dionisio, 16
Canlubang Sugar Barons, 79–80

Carnival Athletic Meet, 70; girls'
basketball in, 52
Carpenter, Frank, 42
Catholic Church, 53, 57, 69, 125,
134, 209
Cebu City, 68
China: ancient Tang Dynasty
handball and basketball,
179; "basketball diplomacy,"
96–97; basketball flourished
under Communism, 101;
and contemporary popular
culture, 102; emerged as the
best team in Asia, 91, 96; first
basketball game, 178; in the
First Far Easter Games, 59; as
a football country, 90–91; the
introduction of basketball, 178;
and the NBA, 173; no longer the
team to beat in Asia, 167; in
regional tournaments, 5; sports
among the literary class, 45;
transition from empire to
republic, 59–60; use of Temple
of Heaven grounds as a sports
field, 68; women's basketball, 54
Cingiene, Vilma, 89
"civilizing mission," 29
cockfighting, 21, 66, 122–25, 139,
146
Co, Atoy, 113
Cojuangco, Eduardo, 97
Cold War, 94; and Asian
basketball, 96, 117; and Cuba,
67; and the entry of American
cultural products, 99, 181; and
Hollywood films, 99–102; and
the 1972 Olympics basketball
championships, 95; and the
politics of sports in Asia,

95–99; and the rise of mass media, 99, 181; and sports in the Philippines, 97–99
Columbia Club, *74*
"competitive advantage," 90–92
"containment," 100
Cordillera Region, 37
Crawford, Garry, 136
Crispa Redmanizers, 127–28
Cronin, Mike, 7
Cuba, 66–67
Cullinane, Michael, 8-9
"cultural literacy," 22

De La Salle University, 163
Department of Public Instruction. *See* Bureau of Public Instruction
Distrito, Rudy, 132
Dominican Republic, 187
Douhit, Marcus, 161

"ending," 125
England, Frederick, 38
encomienda, 47
Estrada, Joseph, 138, 143
"exercise," 33–36

Fajardo, Gabriel, 84
Falcous, Mark, 173
Far Eastern Championship Games (FECG): Manila 1913, 58, 59; Manila 1934, 97; Osaka, 1923; and Philippine basketball, 63, 188
Far Eastern Games. *See* Far Eastern Championship Games
Fernandez, Ramon, 106
FIBA (Fédération Internationale de Basketball), 3; and Basketball without Borders,

149; lifting of restriction against professional players, 110; 1963 suspension of the Philippines, 95
FIBA Asia, 4, 89–90, 96, 116, 117–18; 2013 Philippines, 165–66
FIBA World Championship: 1954 Rio de Janeiro, 3–4, 17, 88; 2006 Doha, 13; 2014 Spain, 4
FIBA World Cup. *See* FIBA World Championship
"Filipinization," 56, 60, 75, 78; of basketball, 181
Filipino-Americans (Fil-Ams): "Fil-Sham controversy," 159–60; marginalized local players, 160; national loyalty, 160–61; in the PBA, 158
The Filipino Athlete, 72, 76
Filipino height, 13–14
Filipino indolence, 44–45
"Fil-sham controversy," 159–62
Floro, Pablo, 97
football, 73, 135, 174, 176
Forbes, William Cameron, 59, 73
Fort McKinley, 70, 79
Fox, Jimmie, 71
Freer, William, 69, 76

Galily, Yair, 153
gambling, 124–25
Germany, 94
Games of the New Emerging Forces (GANEFO), 95
Gehrig, Lou, 71
Gems, Gerald, 2, 40, 185
Ginebra, 31; after Jaworski, 147; blue-collar image, 129; "fan anthems," 133–46; fandom as an "imagined community," 135;

Ginebra *(cont.)*
losing underdog image, 147;
rise as PBA's most popular
team, 128–29; style of play, 128,
131–32; winner of the 1997 PBA
Commissioner's Cup, 147
"Glamour Boys," 112, 115
globalization: of basketball, 9; and
Filipino players overseas, 169;
and foreign NBA players,
175–76; and the PBA, 154–56,
167–71, 183; and the rise of
collegiate basketball, 162–64;
and sports, 150–54
Glunx, Charles, 56
Gomez, Lefty, 71
Granada, Gary, 133
Groves, J. M., 45, 124
Growee, 1–2
Guha, Ranajit, 7
Guttmann, Allen, 133
gymnastics, 35

headhunting, 41–42
"hegemonic sports culture," 11,
132, 175. *See also* Hellerman,
Steven; Markovits, Andrei
Hellerman, Steven, 11, 65
Hollywood: and the entry of
American cultural products in
Asia, 99, 181; films and Cold
War, 99–102, 181
Hollywoodization of hoops, 30,
93, 115, 118, 181
"hoops hysteria," 11, 146
hybridity, 23–24, 186–87. *See also*
Bhabha, Homi K.

Ileto, Reynaldo, 133, 184
illustrado, 20, 22

India: cricket and decolonization,
20–23; cricket and *gulli-danda*,
179; football in West Bengal,
70–71
Indonesia: first PBA game
overseas, 168; participation in
the 1934 Far Eastern Games as
Netherlands East Indies, 62;
2008 SEABA winner, 12
Indonesian Basketball League,
169
indoor baseball, 54
Industrial Revolution, 34–35
Internal Revenue, 74
International Olympic
Committee, 95
Israel, 95, 153

Jackson, Frank, 56
Jackson, Steven, 107
Japan: baseball and occupation
of the Philippines, 86, 90–91;
domination of baseball in Asia,
73; in the First Far Eastern
Games, 59; muscular
Christianity and *bushido*, 60;
sports fans in, 136; "Taisho
Democracy," 60
Jaworski, Robert, 111; as a coach,
130; long basketball career
of, 145; as a player, 130; as a
senator, 129–31; 25 all-time
best player, 128
Jaworski, Robert, Jr., 145
Joaquin, Nick, 37
Jones, O. Garfield, 46–50, 53, 69

Kline, Alan, 187
Korean War, 100
Kramer, Paul, 40

La Feber, Walter, 173–74
Laos, 99
Laskiene, Skaiste, 89
"liminal period," 139
Lithuania, 88–89
Little League World Series, 79
Loyzaga, Carlos, 17
Lyon, Willard, 178

Maguire, Joseph, 173
Malaysian National Basketball
  League, 169
Mandelbaum, Michael, 78, 80, 172
Manifest Destiny, 40
Manila Baseball League, 69
Manila Bay Baseball League, 22,
  79; extended careers of its stars,
  83–84; games resumed after
  World War II, 87
Manila Carnival, 61
Manila Industrial and
  Commercial Athletic
  Association (MICAA), 104
Manila Interscholastic Athletic
  Association, 76, 85
Manila Sporting Goods, 76
Marcos, Ferdinand, 5, 94, 97–98
Maria Clara, 52
Markovits, Andrei, 11, 65
Maxwell, J. Truitt, 58
Mckinley, William, 36
Meralco Athletic Club, 76
mestizos, 158
Mills, James, 7
mimicry, 9, 23–24, 104, 164,
  186–87. See also Bhabha,
  Homi K.
Ministry of Youth and Sports
  Development, 98
Moro Province, 41–44

Moros, 42
Mountain Province, 41–44
"muscular Christianity," 28, 57, 60

Naismith, James, 8, 177
Nathanielz, Ronnie, 97
National Basketball Association
  (NBA), 24; and the decline of
  the PBA, 157, 183; the entry of
  foreign players, 158; global
  expansion, 149–50, 170–76;
  and globalization, 120, 150;
  increasing popularity in the
  Philippines, 156–57; Junior NBA
  Camp, 156; NBA Madness, 156;
  outreach programs, 149;
  promotional strategy, 149–50;
  as a transnational company,
  172–76
National Basketball
  Championship, 74
"national basketball culture," 34
National Collegiate Athletic
  Association (Philippines), 72,
  75, 76, 163
nationalism, 19–20, 34
National Open Championship
  (basketball), 75
"national sport," 152
Nike, 174
non-Christian tribes, 41–44
Nozaleda Park, 72

offensive charge, 8–9
Ohmae, Kinichi, 162
O'Holligan, Michael, 42
Olympics: baseball in 1992
  Olympics, 87; basketball
  in 1936 Olympics, 3, 15, 77,
  88–89, 131; basketball in 1948

Olympics *(cont.)*
    Olympics, 15, 84; and the global
    diffusion of sports, 152; 1972
    Munich, 95, 131; 1992 Barcelona,
    172; 2012 London, 14
Oriental Olympics. *See* Far
    Eastern Championship Games
    (FECG)
Osmeña Park, 81–82

Padilla, Ambrosio, 17, 131
Pampanga Sugar Mill, 79
Paner, Manny, 116
Parezo, Nancy, 61
patron-client relationship, 46–49
Philippine Amateur Athletic
    Federation (PAAF), 16, 59, 98
Philippine-American War, 18,
    36, 42, 44, 56, 77; and the
    introduction of basketball in
    the Philippines, 178; and the
    Manila Baseball League, 69;
    soldiers staying after the war, 78
Philippine Baseball League, 71
Philippine Basketball Association
    (PBA): All-Star Game, 167–68;
    coping with globalization,
    167–70; declined in the early
    2000s, 155; and globalization,
    150, 170–71; "imports," 103;
    increase in attendance and
    revenue, 168–69; local players
    as the main attractions, 106;
    losing fan appeal, 154–55; and
    the Marcos regime, 97;
    modeled after the NBA, 103–4;
    and multi-national companies,
    170; national team, 165; 1997
    Commissioner's Cup, 138, 147;
    overseas games, 168; PBA

Legends Tour, 168; players as
    celebrities, 111–14; and politics,
    137–38, 142; as a popular
    entertainment, 146; and the
    rise of collegiate leagues,
    162–64; and social mobility,
    113–14; as a subaltern space,
    126–29; sustained basketball's
    popularity, 93; and television,
    107–11; television ratings, 108
Philippine Independence Act, 3, 15
Philippine Interscholastic Meet.
    See Carnival Athletic Meet
Philippine National Basketball
    Team, 4, 111, 116
Philippine Patriots, 170
physical education: as
    Americanization, 2; as part of
    colonial health program, 37–38;
    for social control, 38–39. *See
    also* sports
"playing with modernity," 21, 23.
    See also Appadurai, Arjun
Plaza Washington, 69
Polumbaum, Judy, 102
popularization, 182
post-binary, 9–10
postcolonialism, 6–8, 150
Prieto, Leo, 146
professionalization, 5, 105, 107, 117
"promise of the foreign," 18–19, 23.
    See also Rafael, Vicente
Protestantism, 2, 57
"prowess," 34

Rafael, Vicente, 18–20, 22–23, 187
Ramos, Fidel, 142
Ramos, Geraldo, 169, 170
Reach Co., 74
Reeves, Joseph A., 64, 67

Reyes, Chot, 161
Rizal, Jose, 146
Rizal Memorial Stadium, 79
Ruth, Babe, 71

Salvador, Luis, 111
sambunot, 179
San Mateo High School baseball
team, 70–71, 79
San Miguel (Beermen), 134, 137
San Miguel Corporation, 136
Santa Lucia (Realtors), 134, 137
Santa Lucia Barracks, 37
Santiago, Luis, 79
Scott, James, 45
Serrano, Conrado, 81–82
Sheard, Ken, 153
Silverio, Ricardo, 97
Singson, Carlo, Jr., 157
sit mens sana en copore sano, 43
slippage, 186–88. See also Bhabha,
Homi K.
"small ball," 15–16
social Darwinism, 15, 39, 55
social engineering, 34
Southeast Asian Basketball
Association (SEABA), 12
Southeast Asian (SEA) Games, 11,
166
Southern Luzon Athletic
Association, 70
South Korea, 92, 117, 167
Soviet Union, 94, 99
Spain: as a backward colonial
power, 46, 51; basketball silver
medal in 2012 London
Olympics, 14; introduced
bullfighting in Cuba, 66
Spanish-American War, 18, 56, 67;
and sports, 19

Spanish colonial regime, 18
Spartan Co., 74
sports: and citizenship, 48–49; as
a Cold War propaganda tool,
98–102; as a colonial tool, 2, 35,
44; and gender, 51–55; and
leadership, 49; as modernity,
34; and nationalism, 3–4; and
nation-building, 49–51; in
postcolonial societies, 66; and
subalternity, 2–3; used by the
U.S. to distinguish itself from
Spain, 57
"sport space," 65
Springfield College, 177
Stephens, Nate, 103
St. Louis Exposition, 61
subaltern, 7–9; its contradictory
origin, 20; Ginebra game as a
subaltern spectacle, 133–41;
spaces in sports, 124; sport as
subaltern spectacle, 122, 184–85
subalternity, 2
Sulu, 43

"Taisho Democracy," 60
Taiwan, 91
Tatangkad din ako!, 1–2
television, 107–11
Temple of Heaven, 68
Tokyo First Higher School (Tokyo
Ichiko), 70
Toyota Super Corollas, 127–28,
170
Trinidad, Ricah, 125, 133–34, 140
Turner, E. Stanton, 56
"tutelage," 62

"unfit for self-government," 36
United Kingdom, 155, 173

United States: basketball gold medal in 2012 London Olympics, 14; and Cold War films, 99; colonial administrators against cockfighting, 123–24; colonization of the Philippines, 2; control of Cuba and the Philippines, 67; distinguishing itself from imperial Spain, 51, 57, 60; effort of "modernizing" the Philippines, 18; feminized representation of the Philippines, 51; and the global popularity of basketball, 176; as imperialist, 141; objection to height limit proposal, 16; as the "occupying power," 77; Philippine basketball team visit, 86; popularity of basketball in women's educational institutions, 52

University Athletic Association of the Philippines (UAAP), 163

University of the Philippines, 74, 76

U.S. Army, 74; 15th Infantry, 74; 60th Coast Artillery, 76; withdrawal lead to the decline of baseball, 77

U.S. Major League Baseball, players visit to the Philippines, 71

U.S. Navy: Submarine Flotilla, 74; USS Huron, 74

Uytengsu, Wilfred, 110

Vandello, Joseph, 122
Vargas, Jorge, 16
Vargas, Ricky, 168–69
vernacularization, 20–23
Villanueva, Pedro, 57
volleyball, 12, 54

Wann, Daniel, 144
Webb, Freddie, 111, 131
Whannel, Garry, 114
"the white man's burden," 40
Whitney, Vernon, 43
Winter Olympics, 94–95
Wolff, Alexander, 132, 136–37
Worcester, Dean, 41, 43, 76

Yao Ming, 102, 167
Young Men's Christian Association (YMCA), 28; American-European YMCA Branch (Manila), 74; arrival in the Philippines, 56; and basketball's introduction in the Philippines, 35–36; City YMCA as basketball champions, 74; the invention of basketball, 177–78; membership restricted to Americans and Europeans in Manila, 56; partnership with the BOE, 58; promotion of sports and athletics, 45, 73; trained U.S. soldiers to propagate sports, 37

Zamar, David, 169
Zambales, 52
Zamboanga, 42, 79